David the Dogman's A-Z Guide to

DOGS

An encyclopaedic reference book
with more than 300 headings.
Facts about dogs and their training.
More than 250 canine Internet sites.
Articles by world experts.

Editor: Ronald Elliott

SANTANA BOOKS

First edition published in September, 1999 .

Graphic design and typography by Jon Harper.

Illustrations by Diane Bartlett.

Copyright © 1999 by David Klein • E-mail: david@thedogman.net

DAVID THE DOGMAN'S A – Z GUIDE TO DOGS
is published by:
Ediciones Santana S.L., Apartado 422,
29640 Fuengirola, Malaga, Spain.
Tel: (34) 952 485 838 • Fax: (34) 952 485 367 • E-mail: santana@vnet.es

Printed by Graficas San Pancracio S.L.
Pol. Ind. San Luis, Calle Orotava 17, Malaga.

Deposito Legal: MA-1.026/1999

ISBN: 84 - 89954 - 08 - 9

DEDICATION

This book is dedicated to the 14 family pets,
past and present, of the author and editor.
In alphabetical order they are:
Chica, Goldie, Jill, Kim I, Kim II, Rebel, Rex,
Rover, Sasher, Sheba, Suki, Tanya, Tara and Tina.
They gave us, or are still giving, their love and affection.
In return we hope this book will help to ensure that dogs
everywhere have understanding, loving owners.

Contents

INTRODUCTION

A dog is truly man's best friend but man is not always a dog's best friend. This is mainly due to lack of understanding of the canine mentality and what is a dog's normal behaviour.

No other animal gives us the companionship, loyalty and devotion of a dog. The aim of this book is to give you a better understanding of your dog and knowledge about it from the serious to the frivolous (to remind you that dogs are fun) so that you can give it the loyalty and devotion it deserves.

Whether you are thinking about acquiring a puppy or have owned dogs all your life, I hope you will find plenty to learn in these pages.

I am fortunate in having many friends among the leading canine behaviourists all around the world thanks to the Internet forums I manage. These forums enable all the latest ideas, techniques and problems to be discussed immediately, whereas previously this could only be done at occasional meetings or conferences which were rarely world wide. The Internet has given me much information previously impossible to obtain.

Many of my distinguished friends and some of the world's leading authoritative sources have kindly agreed to share their expertise by contributing sections to this book. I am most grateful to them all. You can see how highly qualified they are in the section starting on page 310 entitled **Acknowledgements and Profiles.**

This book is written in the form of an A–Z reference work with more than 300 alphabetical references, some short, others long, so that you can easily find information about any behavioural problem (and a solution) as well as most facts about dogs.

Each alphabetical section is self-contained with cross-references to other relevant material so that you can quickly refer back to a section which you might want to look up at a later date.

As a people canine educator, the slogan in which I believe is "commitment, firmness and kindness".

COMMITMENT because a dog is for life. Before you acquire one you must be committed to looking after your friend for his or her life.

FIRMNESS. A dog needs to respect you as the dominant person in the household. Be firm and you will have a happier and more enjoyable life together.

KINDNESS. Physical punishment will solve no problems, indeed it may cause some. Kindness costs nothing but I promise you the rewards will be great.

Beware the person who boasts about knowing all about dogs. "I've had dogs all my life". People who have had several spouses will know each one was different.

Finally, always remember two things:

- Dogs are not small, hair-coated humans: they most probably regard humans as big, many-coated dogs.
- The person who said you can't buy happiness forgot about dogs.

Happy reading.

David the Dogman.

ACKNOWLEDGEMENTS

I am pleased to acknowledge the following friends and highly respected experts in the world of dogs for permission to reproduce their articles in this book:

Lynn Aitchson, Diana Barbara, Lou Castle, Beverley Cuddy, Ian Dunbar, Dr. Dennis Fetko, George Grayson, Ron Lawrence, Pamela Mackinnon, Kevin McNicholas, Catherine O'Driscoll, Natalie Ray, Terry Ryan, Joyce Stranger, Barbara Sykes, Grant Teebon, Ann Thibault, Sheilagh B. Wilson, Dee Woodcock

I might not agree with everything they say or advocate but I respect their right to air their opinions as much as I respect them personally. Their contributions have added much wisdom to this publication.

Brief profiles of each are on page 310-315

Some of the material, poems and lighter-hearted items have their source from Internet forums where they have been exchanged among members. Often the name of the author has been lost. I have tried to acknowledge the source wherever possible and I apologise to those whom I could not find.

SEEING IS BELIEVING.

By Ronald Elliott, editor.

You are probably not going to believe this. Our young puppy was trying our patience. She was a so-and-so. She had decided she was the leader of the pack. Apart from actually operating the remote control for the TV (which did not work too well after she had run round the room with it a few times), she dominated life in what we had regarded as our sitting-room but which, since her arrival, had become her den.

She chose where she wanted to sit or lie, where she wanted to wander, whether she wanted to come or not when called. She was the dominant dog in our house despite our protestations...we certainly barked at her a lot.

Then, one evening, David the Dogman called. Believe it or not within five minutes that uncontrollable young puppy came when called, sat when told and contentedly lay on her blanket in a corner of the room — her corner in **our** den.

AND NOT A WORD HAD BEEN SPOKEN TO THE DOG.

In only five minutes, my wife and I had become the dominant dogs. We would not have believed such a transformation was possible had we not seen it.

All it took was a few small liver tablets in an old 35 mm film can, a long leash, a water squirter*, a blanket, a bit of patience and quite a few pats and cuddles (for the dog not my wife).

First David the Dogman taught her (the dog not my wife) to come to the sound of the liver tablets being rattled in the can**. Each time she did so she was rewarded with one and briefly praised. Soon she came every time that can was rattled — and did so the next day at around 100 metres. She has come when called ever since as we gradually substituted her name for that rattle.

Then she was placed on the blanket, lead attached so that there could be no games of chasing her (the dominant dog) round the room. Each time she left that blanket she was either squirted with a fine jet of water (a plant spray with an adjustable nozzle is very effective), pulled back by the leash or grabbed by the collar. She soon learnt that it was not a good idea to leave the blanket. Back on base, she would receive a quick pat before being left in peace.

There she decided to chew the lead. That game was soon stopped by some judiciously placed Tabasco sauce...mustard would have been as good.

She caught on to her new role in our lives very rapidly and an older dog would have done so just as quickly. So, by management of the situation, not training, David the Dogman had achieved the unbelievable in just five minutes. Seeing was believing.

Now, if you can spare an hour or so to read this book and a few more hours to practice what you learn, you will achieve more with your dog than you could ever believe to be possible.

It will make you happy. And stop you having to bark.

Seeing and believing was the start of the concept and additional research required for this book. I have had dogs all my life but knew little about them and their behaviour. When you have read this book I hope that, like me, you will know a great deal more.

The Editor

* A plant spray with an adjustable nozzle to create a jet can be aimed to give a harmless but very effective shock of water on the face as a reprimand for any unwanted behaviour. It also has other uses which will become apparent in some of the following sections. It is also good for spraying plants.

** The film can is convenient to carry in a pocket but gravel or anything else which creates a rattle can be substituted for the liver tablets as long as the dog is rewarded with a biscuit or something. However the liver tablets also happen to be good for the dog. They won't do you much harm either.

A WORD ABOUT WOLVES

It might seem strange that we are starting a book on dogs with a chapter about wolves. The reason is simple. Truly to understand dogs you first need to understand the behavioural instincts they have inherited from their forebears the wolves.

Your dog's normal behaviour has its roots in the highly socialised wolf pack with its clearly defined dominance structure in which behavioural problems do not exist. The pack reflects a wolf's desire for contact and affection, the two key attributes of our pet dogs today which have helped to make them man's best friend.

Wolves live in social packs of around a dozen. When a litter is born to the dominant female the whole pack will help in its rearing. One example of how caring and protective the pack can be is the fact that one or two of the senior females will also produce milk in case, for some reason, the mother cannot do so.

The mother licks the pups to stimulate defecation and cleans up by eating the faeces. The den, with an access tunnel up to 12 feet in length, is always kept clean. As they grow older, the pups will learn to leave the den to defecate in a designated area.

The fight for dominance and a place in the strict hierarchy within the pack begins the moment the pups cluster around the mother's teats for milk. The stronger, bolder pups get the rear teats with the best supply of milk. (This does not happen with cats as each kitten claims its own teat.)

The pups will soon start playing games amongst themselves. These games, fundamental to their learning process, involve chasing (preparing them for the day they become hunters), biting or mouthing (which develops the jaws

15

for eating but in play is never hard enough to hurt), and tug-of-war (for wolves tear their prey apart and the winners gets the most meat).

The mother praises her pups when they behave well by nibbling them around the ears or neck, the places you should pat a dog. She will show annoyance by eye contact or growling or, if absolutely necessary, by a mock attack which never hurts the pups.

The whole pack, including the mother, feeds the pups once they are weaned. In the poor light of early morning or dusk when their sharp eyesight gives them the advantage, the pack goes off to hunt, headed by the pack leader with the others following in single file according to rank.

The pack can pick up the scent of a prey more than a mile away. While closing in, any of the wolves that spot the dung of the prey will roll in it to disguise their own smell, making it easier to get closer undetected. On sighting the prey, the pack splits up and circles it. Then either the lower-rank wolves drive the prey towards the leader to allow the more experienced of the pack to initiate the attack, or the whole circle closes in on the prey.

After the kill, the pack leader will be the first to eat. Then the rest will gorge themselves, also eating whatever grazing material might be in the prey's stomach. Wolves are carnivores but they supplement their diet, in the same way a dog will eat grass to supplement its food if there is a need.

Any remnants are buried, to be dug up and eaten later, a thrifty habit inherited by dogs that dig up the bones they bury in the garden. When the wolves return to the lair, the pups will jump up and lick their mouths to get them to regurgitate some food, a behaviour reflected in the way puppy dogs today jump up to lick your hand. As the wolf pups get older the mother will bring back chunks of meat for them, an instinct we are reminded of today when our dog brings back a ball or stick to us

When threatened, a wolf, just like a dog, will fight, take flight or freeze. A submissive wolf will even roll over on its back. Growling and staring precedes an attack, which is carried out silently.

The male wolves in a prowling pack will mark out a territory by urinating in short spurts or by defecating. The males can aim higher by cocking their legs and the higher up the urine is deposited on an object, the further the scent travels. Other packs of wolves and other animals will respect a marked territory. A pack hunting a prey has even been seen to give up the chase when the prey crosses over into another pack's territory.

A young male wolf, subdued by a more dominant one, might flee the pack to join other outcasts and form a new pack, in just the same way wild packs of dogs are formed today, or a fatally sick wolf might leave the pack, often at night, to die. When this happens, the ranks within the pack have to be adjusted and there can be fights to decide which one moves up or down, but they rarely result in wounds. There is no problem when the leader dies. Its place is automatically taken by the number two in the pack.

The leader of the pack picks the most dominant female to mate with when she comes into season along with all the other females. So started selective breeding. The other males accept that they cannot mate but will indulge in mounting the females when they are not on heat. All the females menstruate around the same time. The lower ranking females (the weaker ones) instinctively know they have no right to be mated, but some will have a phantom pregnancy and will produce milk as a back-up for the one selected for breeding.

Around 10,000 years ago, early man allowed wolves, attracted by the smell of food, to approach his camp fire. Puppies might have been taken from packs for children to play with but the wolf's main attraction for man was it's ability to guard by scenting danger.

So the first dogs were working dogs, guarding the camps of early man, scenting danger or prey, and retrieving.

Through breeding over the centuries, the working dog developed into different types to do specific jobs and in our own times was further refined into the special breeds seen at dog shows such as Crufts. Eventually, dogs came into our homes as pets and companions, completing the journey from Stone Age camp fire to the hearth rug.

Today, we tend to pay too much attention to pedigree and ignore or fail to understand the dog itself and the basic instincts it has inherited from the wolf. Not understanding these basic instincts causes more behavioural problems between a dog and its owner than anything else – with the possible exception of giving your dog the wrong kind of food.

For instance, dogs have inherited an instinctive urge to dominate but at the same time will respect its place in the pack. If you allow it, your dog will quite readily dominate you and be the leader of the "pack", but if you assert yourself as the dominant one, it will accept you as the leader and will also quite happily accept its position in the family pecking order once it has been firmly established. For this reason it is not cruel to dominate your dog.

The great behaviourist John Fisher, whom I am honoured to call a friend, has said our problems with dogs arise when their "normal behaviour is exhibited at the wrong place at the wrong time." The dog is behaving normally but for us the behaviour is untimely or undesirable or, far worse,we don´t understand why it is behaving in such a way. The fault is ours, not the dog´s. It is our lack of undertstanding of the dog that creates the problem.

All the instinctive behavioural actions mentioned in this chapter are elaborated on throughout the following A—Z section and there are many cross references because they are the normal behavioural actions of our dogs today and it is so important to understand them.

Make sure you do the right thing, in the right place, at the right time. And always remember, a dog is a dog. It is not a hairy human being. So don´t treat it as one.

A-Z
Guide to
Dogs

**Practically everything you will ever
want to know about your dog.
You can read it all or just browse through it.
More importantly you can easily find whatever
behavioural problem or fact you may be seeking
for yourself or a friend.
(Don't let another dog owner borrow this
book...you may not get it back).
I make no apology for the repetition which
occurs in various sections for they are written to
give self-contained material on a subject,
with a cross-reference where applicable
to other relevant sections.**

ABBREVIATIONS (See **Initials**)

ADDRESSES

Animal Care College
Open Learning Courses. Veterinary Nursing, Kennel & Cattery Management, Animal Care Canine & Feline Psychology, Judging, Breeding, Showing, Grooming,Training. Ascot House High Street, Ascot Berkshire SL5 7JG

Telephone: 01344 628269 Fax: 01344 622771

E-mail: David Cavill@compuserve.com

Net site: http://www.k9netuk.com/commercial/edu/acc/

Animal Health Trust
PO Box 5, Newmarket, Suffolk CB8 7DW.
Tel: 01638 661111

Blue Cross
Shilton Road, Burford, Oxon OX18 4PF.
Tel: 01993 822651

Battersea Dogs Home
4 Battersea Park Road, London SW8 4AA. Tel. 0171 622 3626

British Flyball Association
PO Box 39, Petersfield, GU32 3XS. Tel: 01726 861191 -Fax 01726 861079. General Information: bfa@flyball.org.uk

The British Dog Breeders Council
Jill Terry. (BABREES) 10 Eastwood End, Wimblington, Cambs. PE15 0QQ.
Tel: 01354 740547. E-mail: Babrees@compuserve.com

Centre Of Applied Pet Ethology
PO Box 18, Tisbury, Wiltshire SP3 6NQ

APBC, Association Pet Behaviour Counsellors
46,Worcester, WR8 9YS,England
Tel/Fax: + 44 (0) 1386 751151
E-mail : apbc@petbcent.demon.co.uk

Dogs for the Disabled
The Old Vicarage, London Road, Ryton-on-Dunsmore, Coventry, CV8 3ER.
Tel: 01203 302050 Fax: 01203 302055
E-mail:dfd@dial.pipex.com

Guide Dogs For The Blind Assoc.
Edmondscote Manor, Warwick New Road, Leamington Spa, Warks CV32 6AM. Tel: 01926 337244

Hearing Dogs For The Deaf The Training Centre
London Road (A40), Lewknor, Oxon OX9 5RY.
Tel: 01844 353898

Kennel Club
1-5 Clarges St., Piccadilly, London W1Y 8AB.
Tel. 0171 493 6651.

People and Pets Society
8 Bransdale Walk, Altofts, Normanton, W Yorks. WF6 1SR.
Tel: 01924 897732

Pets As Therapy (PATAT)
Rocky Bank, 4-6 New Road, Ditton, Kent ME20 6AD.
Tel: 01732 872222

Royal College of Veterinary Surgeons
Tel. (44) 171 222 2001 Fax: (44) 171 222 2004
E-mail: admin@rcvs.org.uk
Publication information -E-mail: publications@rcvs.org.uk

Wood Green Animal Shelters
London Road, Godmanchester, Huntingdon, Cambs. PE18 8LJ.
Tel. 01480 830757

AFFECTION

Pets are an important part of many families. A recent survey by the American Animal Hospital Association of 1,206 pet owners in the United States and Canada showed that more than 80% of the respondents were female and an incredible 48% of these said they rely more on their pets than on a spouse or child for affection.

"Pets can provide their owners with unlimited affection and unconditional love," says Dr. Jay Geasling, president of AAHA. "In return, many people treat them like members of the family."

Significantly 50% of dog and cat owners said they had given their pets a human name such as Molly, Sam or Max. More than 60% include news about their pets in their holiday postcards, and 36% include a photograph of their pets with correspondence. An amazing 27% said they had taken their pets to a professional photographer to be part of family photographs or to be photographed with "Santa Claus" or the "Easter Bunny."

Nearly 50% take their pets in the car on errands and 53% vacation or travel with them. 25% per cent blow-dry their pets after bathing them, 45% provide a special bed, and 75% buy special premium pet food. Nearly 60% of pet owners said they love their pets so much that when the pets die, they will bury them on family property. Although nearly 80% of the respondents were dog owners and 61% cat owners, 11% had birds, 6% own "pocket pets" such as a gerbil or hamster, and 5% own a reptile. Another 13% had other types of pets ranging from fish to horses. (See **Health benefits** and **Walkies**).

AGES

Dogs mature much faster than humans. The common belief is that seven years for a dog is equivalent to one human year, but that is incorrect as dogs age at a different rate from humans.

This is especially important during their rapid growth rate from nine to 17 months. As can be seen from the table, from around nine months to 12 they are effectively juveniles and from 12-17 months they are teenagers when their testosterone levels rise much the same as human teenagers with accompanying instability.

Below is an approximate table based on a dog of around 8-15 kg (15-30lbs). Heavier dogs will have a higher human life equivelent.

Dog	Human	Dog	Human
3 months	5 years	8 years	48 years
6	10	10	56
8	13	13	64
10	14	14	72
12	15	16	80
18	20	18	88
2 years	24	20	96
4	32	21	100

AGGRESSION

There are four basic forms of aggression:

1 To other dogs.

2 To the owners.

3 To other humans.

4 To children.

1. Some dogs are aggressive to other dogs because all pack animals (and many other species) depend on a dominance hierarchy in their community or family. Often the more dominant dog can establish its

higher ranking by growling and baring its teeth, with ears erect, tail trembling and held high, "hair on end" along the shoulders and back (to make itself look bigger) and by staring fixedly. Less dominant animals submit by lying on their backs or putting their tails between their legs. This is called the "Beta Roll".

If the more dominant animal (the Alpha) is not happy with the speed of submission or the extent of the submissive reaction, then aggressive action can follow. Normally this is limited to the minimum of damage, if any, as long as there is no human interference. If a person hits one of the dogs it may think the pain has been caused by the other dog, thus escalating the conflict. (See **Alpha dogs** and **Beta rolls.**)

The closer the status ranking, the greater is the risk of serious damage. This is particularly true of two female dogs in the same household. If there are two male dogs, one can be castrated to reduce its rank but this does not work with two females if both have been spayed, an action which should never be taken. As puppies, they may well have lived happily together but problems are likely to start once they become adolescents at around eight months. If neither have been spayed it is vital to spay the one that is challenging for dominance. Make the wrong choice, and it is easy to do so with two close ranking females, you will have problems later on. (See **Bitches fighting** and **Fighting**).

Even if a dog is submitting, the more dominant dog might decide that the "comfort distance" is not sufficient, especially if food is involved, and attack.

2. A dog can be aggressive towards a human owner for several reasons, all of which are more likely to occur if that owner has not established, in the dog's view, his or her dominance over the animal. Possession of a food or

a bone could be the trigger if the owner intrudes on what the dog regards as its comfort distance, something which less dominant dogs in the wild would respect. Establishing your dominance as the owner is vital. (See **Ten Commandments**).

3. A dog might see other humans, especially those who enter its territory or home, as a threat or there may simply be nervousness about the unfamiliar. This could result in the relatively mild reaction of mouthing the hand which is stretched to pat it or there might be a more aggressive reaction (fear, fight and bite), preceded by growling with hair erect, tail upright, baring teeth and even snarling. The dog will stare at the visitor between the eyes. The safest thing to do in these circumstances is to avoid eye contact and stand absolutely still and tall (do not bend down) until rescued by the owner.

   Sometimes there is no apparent reason for a dog´s aggression. An aggressive reaction to someone not belonging to the pack can be triggered by a sudden movement of the head, body, arms or feet. Dogs with elderly owners with slow movements can react differently to those with younger owners. (See **Biting**, **Training programmes** and **Triggers**).

4. Aggression towards children can be a very serious matter and there is a whole section on it. (See **Child attacks**).

Case history 1:

Following are some consultations I have given relating to aggressive dogs:

At two years the dog had bitten the owner badly three times and each time it happened when the owner chased the dog after it had stolen some food or something. When the owner tried to take away the object the dog had stolen, it went into a biting frenzy. Afterwards it was quiet, depressed and drained.

The owner of course should not have left food or anything else around that could be stolen. And there is no point in chasing the dog. If anyone chased me, I would also stop and bite them.

Each time the owner yelled at the dog, it cowered and rolled. This type of behaviour – the owner´s, not the dog´s — is not acceptable. Dogs should not cower. It was obvious to me that it was the owner who needed training.

Case History 2:

A dog had bitten three children. Each time the dog had felt frightened or threatened and in one instance its paw had been squeezed in the car door. Another time it became very stressed when having a pinch collar put on. It ducked its head and shoulders, pinned its ears back and tucked its tail in. The owner continued to try to put on the collar and the dog became even more stressed. The owner said that when the dog was in this state he was most likely to bite.

I told her it will bite again and not to trust it with her daughter (aged 11). She should put the dog in a room when visitors came as she had the equivalent of a loaded gun sitting on the coffee table, just waiting for someone to pull the trigger.

I found out that the dog had been abused by humans and realised that it now had an owner and children who needed to be educated. Worse still, there was a new puppy in the house, which was contributing to the problem by making it more nervous, jealous and edgy.

This family (not the dog) needed a few in-depth consultations. I showed them a 30 minute video, "The Dominant Dog" by John Rogerson. It helped to underline what I was telling them which I felt they were not absorbing due to their stressful situation. The best part of the film is the Do's and Don'ts. These people needed to learn about correct feeding and sleeping/rest areas for the dog and to give the dog space and not treat it like a naughty child.

Case History 3.

A large eight-months-old Spanish Mastiff bitch was brought to my class. It was ready to attack any human or dog that came near. The lady owner had been sent by a vet as he thought the dog was dangerous and should either be found another home or put down.

I checked the dog's collar and lead. Often the collar is either too big, too small or it is a choke collar which, in my opinion, is both unsuitable and unnecessary. The ideal collar for this kind of dog is a half check collar which is half webbed with a small piece of chain allowing the collar to tighten without choking. I combined this with a long leather lead and a muzzle.

With the dog correctly secured, the new collar and lead being fitted before the old ones were taken off, I put the lady and the dog in the centre of the class. This allowed her dog to look at the people and dogs around it and take in the new smells.

After about five minutes, the dog was a lot calmer and I was able to stand on the right hand side of the lady with the owner between me and the dog. I then held the long lead and the lady's left arm and started to walk with her, getting the dog to walk to heel. The dog thought the lead corrections were being done by the owner and its behaviour instantly improved.

I then allowed some well-behaved dogs from the class to approach one at a time, with the owners close to their dogs, so that the mastiff could smell them with the lead loose. The quiet dogs were then placed in a Down position to send a submissive signal. Rarely will another dog attack one in this situation. Soon the mastiff was quietly walking around the Down dogs on a loose lead without any sign of aggression.

Some 10 minutes later in a large field, I asked all the owners to let their dogs free, including the Mastiff which was still muzzled. There was no problem. Five minutes later, I removed the muzzle and the dog was as normal as the other dogs. I have a video showing exactly what happened.

That dog had lost all its fear. With fear we have fright and with fright we have bite. The mastiff no longer feared people or dogs after an exercise taking only around 40 minutes. The owner was delighted, the dog was happy and I was pleased. The sad part of this story is that the lady never came back for another lesson. So somewhere out there is yet another dog which could benefit from further training. (See **Child attacks, Submission,** and **Ten Commandments**).

Handling Skills - Agitation training

The following article was published in the AGGRESSION NEWSLETTER, by Captain Haggerty, who has been working professionally with aggression problems in dogs for well over forty years.

Everybody wants to know how to handle aggressive dogs. Look around and see how many people are expounding on handling aggressive dogs. One of my favourite stories is of the musician carrying a bass fiddle up the steps of New York's 57th Street subway. He turns to a New Yorker and asks, "Man, how do I get to Carnigie Hall?" The hip New Yorker answers, "Practise, man, practise!" That is all it takes. Practice! I could write a book on what it takes to develop these skills. When eighty pounds of snarling dog is coming up the leash after you it is too late to start learning. It has to be a lifelong process.

A really worthwhile tip is to learn to agitate dogs. This teaches timing, balance and reading the dog. From a theoretical point of view it teaches you how to get a dog to bite. From a practical point of view it will teach you coolness under fire. This coolness is probably the best single item you need in handling aggressive dogs.

Now if you feel it is not necessary to handle aggressive dogs and your approach is to "counsel" the owner, fine! A suggestion would be to not have the dog present when you are counselling the owner. A careless owner, a dropped leash can put your life in harm's way. How do you bail out? If you want to learn how to bail out or protect yourself, agitation is a good starting point.

Finding a place to learn how to agitate can present a problem. The opportunities are there but you may have to travel to find them. I remember years ago in New York there was a "trainer", one that everyone considered a "nut job"* who would go to the dog training schools and agitate dogs free of charge. He even carried his own equipment. Equipment is an expense in any type of attack training. I always had novices wanting to borrow equipment. I knew they were novices because I would have to explain to them that the equipment is a consumable product. It is like asking to borrow toilet paper. They return it when they are finished with it.

You may foolishly not think highly of people training dogs for this work and not want to deal with them. It is natural to be afraid of that which you know nothing about. Well, the world is made up of all sorts of people, with different outlooks on life. This type of work is:

1.   Necessary in this society and

2.   Is an enjoyable past time or hobby.

The world is not going to change to your point of view. It is your choice to work with or not to work with these people. This is not meant as a philosophical discussion on this type of training. It is giving you suggestions on how to improve your handling skills.

If you are opposed to dealing with people that put bread on the table through the training of dogs for police, military and security work, all is not lost. You will reduce your opportunities considerably but there are other ways to gain this experience. Go with the people who do it as a hobby. Find the nearest SchutzHund or Ring Sports Club. It is roughly the same type of training but the uninitiated doesn't seem to realise that.

Yes, agitation can teach you relaxation under pressure. I remember years ago the US Army was trying to find ways to put people under pressure so they would have an idea how they would stand up in combat. The two pressures that the military felt they could control and still test the troop's reaction under pressure was attacking dogs and fiery burning buildings. Developing this coolness will help you analyse every bite objectively.

Yes, a good way to learn is to get bitten. I am not advocating that you look to have dogs bite you. The safest recommendation I can make is don't handle aggressive dogs.

*What happened to that "nut job"? Where is he now? He shall remain nameless to protect the guilty. He is a very wealthy man. He didn't turn into the Uni-bomber. Did he become wealthy training dogs? No! He wasn't as dumb as some of us thought he was. His secret to wealth was choosing the right ancestors. He inherited his money.

AGILITY CLASSES

These are not only fun for the dog and the handler but they also stretch the dog's mind and increase its level of obedience, for a dog that is happy and enjoying itself is much more likely to try hard to please the owner.

Most of the equipment consists of jumps, hurdles, long jumps, weaving poles, an A-frame, tyre hoop, a tunnel and see-saw.

Big breed, heavy dogs under 18 months should not do agility work as it could trigger physical problems while the

dog is still developing. Heel, Sit, Stay, and Send-away are part of the lessons as well as walking the dog off the lead. Given the right training, the dog will be able to complete the course off the lead.

Owners should have good footwear and clothes to run in comfortably. The dog should have a leather or webbed buckle collar. Leads should be fairly long and made of leather, nylon or rope, never chain. Chain leads can get caught up in the jumps.

The A-frame has been singled out as being particularly dangerous but there are miniature A-frames which I use and which cannot damage a healthy dog.

AGORAPHOBIA

Like humans who refuse to leave their homes for fear of open spaces, some dogs suffer from agoraphobia. Often this goes back to a bad experience during the critical "fear imprint" phase of between eight to 12-weeks-old. Feeding the dog outside the home could help. So could homeopathic treatment. (See **Homeopathy.**)

ALLERGIES

An allergy is a condition in which the immune system reacts abnormally to every day substances such as pollens, animal dander, mold spores, mites, certain foods and chemicals. All of these allergic reactions are unpleasant, some are serious, and a few can be fatal. The offensive substances causing allergies are known as allergens. An allergic reaction may be caused by inhaling or ingesting the allergen or may be the result of direct contact with the allergen.

What are the signs of an allergy?

The most common signs are scratching, face rubbing and biting and chewing at the skin. Usual locations for signs of allergy are the flank, feet, face, particularly around the eyes, mouth and ears, as well as areas around the base of the tail. In dogs, allergies are often the underlying cause of persistent skin disease. However, not all scratching is due to an allergy. Thyroid disease, fleas, certain infections, and ringworm can cause similar signs.

How do dogs get allergies?

They are generally inherited. The typical allergic dog starts with a short period of biting and chewing the first year. This may be mild and hardly noticeable. With repeated exposures to the offending allergens, the dog gradually experiences longer periods of discomfort and the signs become severe.

Allergies occur whenever the offending allergens are present. The more common allergens such as house dust, mites or mould spores will produce signs of allergy year round, while allergies from plants that pollinate during warm months obviously only happen in that season.

Food allergy can happen by itself or it may be a component of an overall allergy problem. Because of the complexity of allergy diagnosis, the combination of patient history, physical examination and allergy signs in the pet are all important in helping your vet make an accurate diagnosis.

Can allergies be prevented?

Since allergies are inherited, there is no absolute way to prevent them, but allergies can be controlled. The best control is to avoid contact with the offending allergens. For instance, if your pet is allergic to fleas, it is essential to prevent flea infestation, but allergens like dust and mites are virtually impossible to avoid and some kind of treatment is needed.

How do I know if my dog has an allergy?

If your dog is persistently chewing its feet or scratching at its face, an allergy may be a possible cause. Unfortunately, there are no specific signs and you will need to consult your vet. Allergy diagnosis requires eliminating other possible causes of your dog's clinical signs. This involves taking a detailed history of your dog's signs, a complete physical examination and some preliminary laboratory tests. If it is found that an allergy is the likely cause, your vet will recommend allergy testing to confirm the diagnosis.

How are allergies treated?

There are a number of different ways to treat allergies. If it is mild, control may be achieved through avoiding contact with the offending allergens and medications to control the clinical signs.

Pets with more severe allergies or with allergies that occur year round, could need specific allergy treatments such as immunotherapy (allergy shots). This is often recommended because prolonged use of certain medications, especially steroids, can produce serious side-effects which may decrease the quality and length of your pet's life.

How successful is treatment?

The success depends on several factors including the overall health of your dog, the severity of the allergies, and a commitment to therapy. In general, the steps to successful allergy treatment involve the following:

- Try to avoid or reduce the allergens in the environment.

- Use recommended medications to control clinical signs.

- Identify the specific allergens causing clinical signs in your dog and apply allergy immunotherapy treatment.

With most pets this combination will result in success.

ALLERGIES TO DOGS

Sneezes, rashes or asthmatic reactions can be triggered by any breed of dog. Dander from the top skin and certain proteins in saliva and urine cause allergic problems in humans.

Most research on allergies caused by pets has centred on those created by cats. This is not surprising because they are twice as likely to make their owners sneeze as dogs. For example, it has been discovered that cats with long hair tend to shed less allergen and so their owners have fewer reactions. Cats with short hair give off more allergen.

Sufferers should keep their dogs outdoors at night except in those areas where leichmaniasis is prevalent. (See **Leichmaniasis).** Certainly dogs and cats that live indoors should not be allowed on beds or even in the allergic person's bedroom. Research has shown that if a cat or dog is washed once a week the airborne allergens are cut drastically.

Dander collects on the carpets and in upholstered furniture so, for those suffering allergies, it is better to be without carpets and have wooden furniture or leather. If carpets are essential they should be steam cleaned every three months to remove allergens. It is also advisable to wash walls and floors.

Animal allergens are very small and very sticky and once they are secreted they dry on the animal's fur. There they stick until becoming airborne during petting and grooming. Then, because they are so small, they can stay airborne for a long time and, because they are sticky, they adhere to walls, clothing, and heating and cooling ducts.

Some years ago I gave up smoking and noticed that I was coughing and choking when handling dogs. After a few tests I was told: "Mr. Dogman, you are an asthmatic and allergic to dogs."

Sadly I now have to take all kind of things to help control my allergic symptoms from medication to inhalers and I wash my hands more than a surgeon, change my clothes several times a day and wash my dogs every week.

But, with all my allergies, I could not live without dogs because I know that dogs enhance our quality of life and are worth having around. So, if you are allergic to dogs, don't give up on them.

ALPHA DOGS and BETA ROLL
As stated under **Aggression**, the submissive dog Beta rolls to the more dominant Alpha dog. All the activity, mental and physical, is taking place within the submissive dog. Among dogs and their ancestors, the wolf, ranking is sorted out by ritualistic display and posturing, rather than physical confrontation.

ANAL GLANDS
When dogs scoot along on their bottoms many owners think they have worms. But it is more likely that their anal glands, which secrete a strong, very unpleasant smelling liquid used to mark territory, are blocked. Take your dog to your vet who can squeeze the liquid out.

ANIMAL SHELTERS and RESCUE
(See **Rescue Centres**.)

ANTHROPOMORPHISM

The word that is used when we believe dogs have the same feelings and emotions as humans and that they understand our language. A mistaken belief, of course. Dogs are not small, fur-clad human beings. They are canines. True, they are man's best friend and companion because their natural instincts and hierarchical society blends into our own, and because they show loyalty and devotion to the hand that feeds them.

As we have seen in the chapter on wolves, this bonding between man and dog happened thousands of years ago when both man and wolf lived similar nomadic lives as hunters roaming the country to seek food.

The dog's adaptation to our way of life was assisted and accelerated by man using selective breeding to develop the most desirable features, first to work for us and then to turn them into pets.

Even so, there remain of course fundamental differences between us and our dogs. To take just one example, dogs live totally in the present moment. They do not worry about the past. They do not dream about the future.

They are not endowed with imagination or feel grief, hate, jealousy or greed or other emotions that bedevil our human society. They do have a high sensory ability which is often mistaken for a kind of sixth sense. (See **Extra-sensory perception**).

They will understand that certain words like Sit, Stay, Down require the right reaction if they are to be rewarded with a tit-bit or praise. They will understand whether your tone of voice and your facial expressions are good or bad when you are talking to them, in whatever language, but they will not understand longer phrases.

We often attribute human emotions to dogs when, in fact, they are reacting instinctively. We assume our dog is happy to see us when we return home and it looks pleased and wags it's tail. All it is doing is reacting in the same way a wolf puppy reacts when the pack returns with food from a hunt. It behaved in the same way when it was feeding from its mother along with the rest of the litter. It is true the dog is enjoying a pleasurable experience but it is not pleased in human terms.

Another example of anthropomorphism is when we believe our dog is "sulking" when it returns home from a stay in kennels (See **Kennels**), or is grieving over the death of a member of the family. In the latter case, what it will be feeling is the loss of a higher member of the "pack" and the anxiety caused by no longer knowing its position in the family hierachy. It will also be confused by the vibrations of distress it picks up from the family. Once the "pack" has settled down again, the dog will make a quick recovery, for it lives in the present and doesn't mourn the past

So please do not attribute dogs with human emotions. Try, instead, to understand their simple canine minds, which are untroubled by so many of our emotions. (See **Instinct, Intelligence** and **Present living**).

ANXIETY

If your dog barks when you go out and is destructive while you are away, it is simply showing symptoms of anxiety. It is barking for the pack to return.. Start by being cool towards the dog for 10 to 15 minutes before you go out and on your return. Also carry out all the points under **Ten Commandments**.

APARTMENTS

Whether or not a dog should be kept in an apartment depends to a large extent on the size of the dog. Obviously, smaller breeds of dogs are more suitable for apartment living than a Great Dane, but here are a number of factors to be considered, the most important being when and how often the dog can be exercised (30 minutes, twice a day is adequate), and is there a place nearby where it can be taken on foot or by car to run freely? The frequency and length of time it will be left alone are other important questions. In other words it all depends on the lifestyle of the owner and the family.

A.P.D.T

A.P.D.T. stands for; Association of Pet Dog Trainers
(See **Training Organisations**.)

AVERSIVE CORRECTIONS

An aversive correction is applied to stop the dog doing something wrong by making it an unpleasant experience. The important point is that the dog blames itself for the event, not you.

For example, there is *taste* aversion. A dog which jumps up in the kitchen to steal food can be put off by putting some Tabasco sauce or other obnoxious substance on a bit of the food. Unfortunately, some dogs will endure the nasty taste for the sake of a quick snack.

Water aversion can be used for a variety of bad habits by squirting the dog's nose with water from a plant spray.

Then there is *noise* aversion. Use an empty drink can into which some nails, screws, small coins or pebbles have been inserted and the hole sealed. Throw it beside the dog (not at it) to deter an unwanted behaviour like stealing.

Alternatively there is a commercially available aerosol which emits when pressed a loud screech called "Dog Stop" and, in extreme circumstances, explosive caps with a spring loaded detonator can be used. Before using these forms of sound aversion, professional advice should be obtained.

Whatever the method, always give praise when the unwanted behaviour has stopped.

BABY – a new arrival

Most people treat their dog like a baby and often problems will occur when a real baby is brought home. You must plan for the new baby's arrival.

1. Acquaint the dog with a friend's children. Let them feed it some of its favourite treats. Stay calm and keep the dog on a lead. If at this stage the dog is showing any signs of aggression, then professional help is needed.

2. If the dog is used to sleeping in a bedroom (which it should not be allowed to do), place the dog bed outside the room in its basket or on its blanket. If necessary, put the dog on a lead and restrict it to an area.

3. Consider walking around with a stuffed doll. Even talk to it in a baby voice as if it is a real baby. When changing the baby's nappy — both the real one and the toy one — always put your dog in the Sit Stay command. Let it sniff and watch, for this is the time to accustom it to baby sounds and praise it for being good.

4. Use different phrases and voices for the dog and the baby.

5. For safety reasons and hygiene, dogs must not be allowed on the furniture near the new baby. Start the new house rules by taking the dog by the collar and lead and taking it to its bed. Move the bed around the home to every room (except bedrooms) in the house. The dog must learn to stay where it is put. (See **Blankets, Mat training**)

6. Start getting a little more removed from the dog in three 20-minute intervals. First, go into another room for 20 minutes. Close the door behind you so that it cannot follow you. Then come out for 20 minutes before returning for another 20 minutes. Stop all tug-of-war games, wrestling and all games involving chasing.

7. Remember hygiene. Stop feeding the dog from the table or from your hand. It should eat only from its bowl. Babies have to be fed several times a day so, to prevent jealousy, give the dog four very small meals a day...the same amount split into four.

8. Toys are a big headache. You don't want a dropped toy to be licked. No more shoes, socks, slippers, and plastic or stuffed toys for the dog. Now is the time to take away all its toys from the floor. Train it to play with one at a time. Paint the others with a mouthwash which dogs do not like. If your dog goes for it, pick up the toy and shout at the toy (not the dog). Very soon the dog will keep away from anything smelling of mouthwash.

9. Babies like to grab and pull but dogs don't like it at all. Start getting the dog used to this treatment by gently pulling it and grabbing its tail and then, within three seconds, hug it and and give plenty of praise.

10. When the baby is born, ask a maternity home nurse for some bed sheets from the baby's nursery. Have these put in the new nursery at home and around the area of the home where the baby will be nursed. Let the dog sniff around the house at the new smells and praise it.

11. Plan your homecoming and let the dog welcome the baby by sniffing while on a lead.

12. Keep the lead trailing on the floor for the first week so that it can be used to correct all mouthing and jumping. Praise when the dog does not jump or mouth.

13. Many dogs are interested in the smell of a nappy. If you do not use disposable ones, keep the used nappy in a special bin and put a touch of Tabasco or Bitter-Bite around the top to keep the dog away.

14. Your dog should now accept the new house rules and the new arrival.

BACH REMEDIES (See **Homeopathy**)

BARKING

Barking, at night

The simple answer is to ignore the dog. By barking, it is training you to respond. You might have a few noisy nights but you will be showing it that barking is not productive. Certainly do not respond by shouting or scolding. If you do so the dog will only know that its barking has been productive by making you bark as well.

Barking, excessive

The reason for excessive barking in one word is FEAR, and it is frightened because it has not been socialised. It is nervous of every sound it hears and barks in a futile attempt to send the perceived threat away. Sometimes a dog which constantly whines, cries, barks, or is destructive, suffers from skin problems brought about by scratching and licking themselves because of the stress of being left.

Generally this is not a problem with dogs which have been socialised through training classes at an early age. The solution is socialisation through obedience classes and home management. (See **Ten commandments**).

Barking when the owner is out

This is a big problem caused by bad owners. The dog is a pack animal and if, as a member of the family pack, it is given the freedom of the home by being allowed to rest on the furniture and sleep in bedrooms, then it will suffer a form of stress when the pack goes off to work because it expects to go with the pack.

When people leave home they should not look, touch or talk to the dog for about 10 minutes beforehand. The same applies when coming home: ignore, no talking, no patting, no looking, nothing. This way, the dog understands that its barking has not brought the owner back. If it has been barking while you were away and is rewarded by your attention when you come back, it then thinks it was its barking that brought you back to the house.

A dog's bark is said to be worse than its bite. It certainly is for the neighbours of a constantly barking dog left alone for too long, unsocialised and with uncaring owners. Hopefully no readers of this book would permit their dogs to be such a community nuisance.

Barking at the postman

The postman or any kind of regular deliveryman is regarded by your dog as an intruder and so it barks and is immediately rewarded by the postman going away. It thinks it has frightened off the intruder and done its duty. Talk to your postman and try to get him to cooperate. Tell him you will leave a tit-bit outside the door and ask him to push it through the letter-box before the letters. The tit-bit will be a better reward for your dog than chasing the postman away.

Barking when the telephone rings

If you shout (bark) at your dog when it barks at the telephone ringing, you are encouraging it to bark more. It feels there is danger if you react.

Get a friend to phone you at several agreed times. When the phone rings do not move and do not speak. After your friend has done this a few times your dog will no longer bark when the telephone rings.

Barking from balconies

When a dog barks from a balcony at someone passing by, it is simply asserting its dominance, firstly by looking down on humans and secondly by successfully telling them to shove off. As far as the dog is concerned, it is objecting to someone invading its territory. And even more pleasing, its barking is rewarded by the passerby walking away. Answer: ban the dog from the balcony.

Barking deterrent

Abistop is a French invention resulting from chemosensory research into the dog barking problem. It is attached to the dog´s collar and automatically emits a small spray of citronella whenever the dog barks.

Brief exposure to cintronella immediately distracts dogs but does not cause them distress and even smells pleasant to humans.

It is effective but expensive at £90. A cheaper method might be a quick squirt of water from a plant spray bottle or putting a bit of food in front of the dog's nose. It cannot eat and bark at the same time.

Barking at Horses

Try a muzzle

BASKETS

If you have decided not to use a crate or pen (See **Crates** and **Puppies – eliminating**), start with a basket as soon as possible because a dog feels more secure in its own place. The problem is young dogs often make short work of wicker baskets.

The fibre glass type is preferable, as long as it is cleaned weekly and the bedding laundered. Once a dog has been trained to go to its basket, it can be put in any room in the house or taken when visiting. (See **next section**).

BASKETS and SLEEPING AREAS

Whenever I go to the U.K., I always try to visit Annette Conn and Kevin McNicholas who run the Barnet & District Training Club. Annette has an exercise called "Go to your bed", which I have used and expanded.

"Go to your bed" is a key command. Some dogs have been allowed to think they are just as important as their owners and can sleep anywhere they like in the house, even the owner's bed, a bad habit which can cause many behavioural problems.

Some owners create another sort of problem by treating a dog like a child. "Go to your bed" becomes the place to send a naughty dog. What does the dog do when put in this "sin bin"? It sneaks off as soon as possible.

So here is the way to train a dog to go to its basket or bed:

- Start with the dog on the lead and a piece of bedding for the dog to lie on.

- Take the dog to the bedding with the command "on your bed" in a pleasant tone of voice.

- Settle the dog on the bed repeating the command "on your bed" pleasantly. Do not give any other commands such as Sit, Down or Stay.

- If the dog likes tit-bits, give it one so that it regards the bed as a pleasant place to be.

- When the dog is settled, hold the end of the lead and move 2 to 3 feet away from the bed, ignoring the dog. Within a few seconds, the dog will probably come to you. Expect this to happen. Do not give any commands to prevent it. Wait until the dog has completely left the bed.

- Shorten the lead without bending over the dog. Scold it: "what a bad dog". Act very angry but do not wag your finger. Stand upright and continue scolding for about 10 seconds. Try to keep the dog still. It must understand that disobeying has displeased you. Do not give any other commands or use any other gestures to confuse it.

- Repeat the exercise until the dog becomes wary about leaving the bed. When it stays on the bed for 3 to 4 seconds and makes no attempt to follow you, praise profusely and giving it a tit-bit if you want.

- Then give the release command "off you go" so that the dog knows it is all right to leave the bed. Make it leave the bed area, even if you have to pull on the lead.

- Repeat the exercise frequently but do not increase the time the dog is left on the bed to more than 15 seconds. Do not remove the lead until the dog obeys the command "On your bed" without fail.

- Change the location of the bed regularly to the hall, lounge and kitchen and repeat the training frequently for short periods.

BEAGLES (See **Top Dogs**)

BEHAVIOURISTS

What is the difference between a behaviourist and a trainer? The difference is not always obvious but in my opinion my friend the late John Fisher has defined it better than anyone. He said "Trainers suggest ways of controlling behaviour. Behaviourists take away the cause, so there is no need to control."

Every year, unscrupulous persons calling themselves behaviourists, animal consultants, pet advisers, trainers and so on are fleecing thousands of dog owners throughout the world. There are many genuine people who provide a really good service but there are many more who do not do so.

Worse still there are still some so-called trainers who rely on punishment and other brutal methods. They are, hopefully, a dying race.Here are some simple rules to check:

1.   Make sure that you are not being charged for the initial phone inquiry and obtain details of all costs you are likely to incur.

2. Find out all you can about the organisations to which they belong before making any form of commitment (See Point 10).

3. Read advertisements carefully. Beware of behaviourists who give such gaurantees as "Immediate results for a lifetime".

4. Ask to see the person's dogs. Just because someone has a Border Collie or German Shepherd that will walk beside him or her like a zombie is no proof that they can help you with your Beardie, Terrier or Jack Russell which chases the postman or barks at next-door's cat. Someone with a fat and lazy Cavalier King Charles Spaniel will not necessarily be able to help stop your Rottweiler lunging at everything in sight.

5. Be especially wary of anyone who wants to take the dog away from you to train, even if it´s out of your sight for only for a few moments. Professional trainers do not take dogs away from you for training.

6. Beware of the person who gets very high scores in obedience trials and then claims to be able to cure all basic behaviour problems.

7. Never go to a trainer for novice/open/utility run-through who has not taken part in a dog trial in the last year or two. There are some behaviourists who are still trading on past glories of many years ago.

8. No matter what problem you have with your dog, speak to your vet first in case it is caused by a medical situation.

9. Always try to shop around for a trainer. It may take a few days longer to find someone with whom you are really happy but that could also make a big difference to the life of your dog.

10. Do not go to a trainer who uses a choke chain. The chances are he is not registered. All professional trainers who are registered with organisations such as the U.K. Association of Pet Dog Trainers (APDT), the Federation of Dog Trainers (FDTCB) and the UK Pet Dog Trainers (UKPDT) do not use choke or check chains or pinch collars. All members are required to sign an agreement not to use choke chains. (See **Breeders' organisations**).

I hope this helps you to avoid incompetent and unscrupulous money grabbers. If you find a really good trainer/behaviourist tell the world, and if you find one who is not good, do the same.

A lot of different methods can be used but I believe the best results can be obtained if the behaviourist visits the home. When people are alerted by their vet or feel they need a behaviourist, they often create a stress factor between themselves and their dogs. Far better to have a relaxed visit to the home where leading questions can be asked and a judgement can be made.

It is important that owners answer the behaviourist´s questions truthfully and that they accept the fact – even though it might come as a shock – that the fault lies with them and not the dog because they have caused the behavioural problems by incorrect management.

I have spotted many clues when visiting a home that I would not have picked up at a clinic. I start making observations the moment I arrive at the home.

Where is the dog? Does it run out of the front door, jump up, bark? How do the children behave? Is the dog nervous? Is it handled roughly? Where is its territory in the home? What are its sleeping and resting areas? Is it allowed in the bedroom or on the bed? Does it act as a pack leader? What games does it play? Is there a problem with wetting, barking or chewing? Are there hyperactive children? And so on.

Whatever the problems might be, and most of them will stem from the same triggers, I always ask about feeding. When, how and what is the dog fed? Could there be a food allergy or too high a protein level? (See **Feeding**).

My first concern are the clients and their emotions. I make an effort to explain the problems to them in a way they can easily understand but I am careful not to give them too much to absorb on my first visit.

The importance of correct feeding and the right sleeping arrangements must be stressed, and it must be explained logically why a dog barks, soils, jumps up, pulls on the lead, demands to be petted, is destructive and aggressive towards humans or other dogs or both, all of which problems are dealt with under the appropriate headings in this A—Z section.

Behavioural problems are a hands-on job. Behaviourists should be able to take the client's dog and demonstrate such things as walking on a lead without pulling. Given a correct collar and lead, this can be achieved in a few minutes. Not only is a client impressed but I have proved they have a good pet and I have gained their respect and trust. My relationship with the owner improves immediately.

Once accomplished, the rest is easy. (See **Training classes**)

BEREAVEMENT
*by Dee Woodcock (*See **Acknowledgements**).

"We know - of course we know - that the life span of our dog is much shorter than our own. Over the years we may share our home with many dogs.

Each one will be special to us in their own unique way, and we willingly have another dog knowing that in time we shall suffer again the pain of losing a treasured companion.

We may grieve for him for weeks, months, and even years. At the time each of us may feel isolated in our grief, but the feelings experienced when a dog dies are startlingly similar to those felt at the death of a human friend or relation.

That realisation may be hard to face, and we may be made to feel by those who do not share our love of dogs that we should feel less strongly. The fact is that generally we spend more time with our dog than we do with the very large majority of our human family and friends. Should it be surprising then to feel profound sorrow and to be aware of the sudden gap in our lives?

It is not unusual to be taken unawares by the strength of our reactions. Tears are a wholly natural expression of great joy or great sadness. Yet so often we are told that we must keep a stiff upper lip, be brave, anything in fact rather than show what we are feeling. Shock, grief, anger and feelings of guilt may be experienced, some more deeply and longer-lasting than others.

We may punish ourselves for having brought about the last act of love in asking for euthanasia, even though we know that our dog was terminally ill and suffering. Sometimes there is a short period in which it is impossible to accept that death has taken place. It is easy to direct anger at ourselves even when we know that everything possible was done, thinking "I should have done more". Anger may be directed at the person or object thought responsible for an accidental death, or the vet who gives our dog a gentle and peaceful ending.

Newly bereaved owners sometimes speak of a dreamlike feeling from which they struggle to escape, or speak of being in the midst of a nightmare from which we will soon wake. Some will speak of feeling the presence of the dog in the house, hearing the click of his claws or his soft breathing.

This sense of presence is one that many owners mention. When newly bereaved, we may feel incredibly lonely, even when surrounded by family and friends. There is a strong sense that no one understands how we are feeling, and this may be even stronger if friends suggest the immediate purchase of a new puppy.

This well-meaning suggestion may well cause animosity and friction. Often there is a deep need to speak of our dog, to reminisce, and to remember and the suggestion that his place can be so easily filled is painful.

There will be far reaching changes in our lives if the dog is the only one we have. If we live alone and have relied on our dog for company and protection there may be a natural feeling of anxiety.

There may be some physical signs of our distress – difficulty in sleeping, little desire for food, and sometimes headaches and stomach pains. The daily routine of feeding, grooming and exercise is lost, and for a time this space may be hard to fill. Saddest of all, perhaps, is the lack of excited greeting when we return home from even the shortest of absences.

Just how long we grieve depends a great deal of the strength of feeling we have for our dog. It is possible to feel more for one than another, and this too may engender guilt. It is a fact of life that we like, love, or care for one person more than another. It is wholly normal, therefore, to have different strengths of feeling for our dogs. Family and friends may suggest that having several dogs at the same time will make it easier to bear the loss of one. But because we value each as an individual and recognise its different qualities and appeal, we are saddened by the loss of each one. Owning several does not seem to make the emotional readjustment any shorter or less painful.

Eventually we will reach the stage of acceptance, the first step on the road to recovering from the pain and distress. Just how long it takes for any one person to reach this stage is wholly individual as is every aspect of grieving, and the path to this point will also be different for each of us.

But at some stage we will begin to recall happy memories, the comical incidents and the individual characteristics of the dog which made it important to us. In the months ahead, there will be moments still when the loss brings a fleeting sadness, but the time to grieve is passing.

This too is natural, and in the years ahead we will remember with increasing pleasure the special relationship we shared with that particular dog. (See **Euthanasia**).

BETA ROLL (See **Aggression**)

BIRDS
A bird-chasing dog is in danger of being lost. It will run and run, across roads without looking. I have known one that did this — much to the distress of the owners. It had not been taught the Recall. (See **Recall**).

BITCHES (See **Sexual Tendencies**)

BITCHES FIGHTING
The cure depends on when the fighting starts, the home environment, the state of the dog's hormones and much more. In the wolf pack only one female will probably come on heat. There is much fighting over the females and those that lose might leave the pack. In the domestic home the less dominant female cannot leave the pack, so the fighting continues, one probably fighting for dominance, the other through fear.

This fighting can cause bad injuries to both females and even death for one dog. In the wild the dominant female will decide which male dog will service her. Much competition goes on between females and this is reflected in the domestic dog.

Most fighting starts in the presence of the owner through jealousy. Unfortunately owners often get themselves injured trying to part the dogs. Unlike male dogs, where castration helps, provided the correct dog is castrated (normally the junior dog), spaying a female has no effect when there are two bitches in one household which have already started fighting. Spaying the less dominant one could be considered after seeking the opinion of a behaviourist, or one of the females could be re-homed.

BITING

Often dogs lash out when reprimanded for doing something wrong. The dog does not know what it is doing wrong. It only knows you are being aggressive. Remember a dog should not be punished for anything more than three to five seconds after the act. It just does not understand because it does not remember what it has done. Any punishment after that time can result in the dog fearing you and this can often cause aggression.

Smack a puppy which nips you and you will just teach it to nip and run. Shout "ouch" and ignore it. Teach it that nipping is not rewarding by ignoring it.

Biting by dogs is a serious problem as these statistics from America show. According to the Journal of the American Medical Association, dog bites are responsible for 4.5 million injuries every year in the U.S.A., 750,000 people requiring medical attention and 334,000 ending in a hospital emergency room.

The Insurance Information Institute reported that insurance companies paid an estimated $250 million in dog bite liability claims in 1996.

More than half of all dog bites come from familiar dogs, those of friends and neighbours and even your own dog. All dogs are potential biters, so don't be misled by size.

Some breeds may have more aggressive tendencies. The Humane Society of the United States reports that five breeds, the Pit Bull, Rottweiler, German Shepherd, Husky and the Alaskan Malamute, were responsible during the period from 1979 to 1996 for two-thirds of fatal dog attacks. In two years, 304 people died from dog attacks.

The American Veterinary Medical Association reports that dog attacks in the U.S. are the number one public health hazard for children, with more than half of all children bitten by age 12. The leading reason for dog euthanasia is aggressive tendencies. (See **Aggression** and **Child attacks**).

Case history.
I have an eight-months-old Maltese (Maltse) that bites at my feet or socks when the phone rings. She goes crazy trying to bite my feet real hard. I have scolded her and also use the fly swatter to no avail. Please tell me how to correct this.

I am always sad to read of this type of problem with an eight-month-old dog. This is not a pup and dogs at six months can walk to Heel on or off lead, obey Down, Stay, and do Recall and simple tracking. It is obvious you have not been to a training club. You only get out of a dog what you put into it. The Maltese is a lap dog and maybe you carry it and also allow it on the furniture and on the bed.

Dogs that are allowed these privileges will behave as you describe. Your dog is correcting you, he considers he is the boss. I would also guess he is not getting dried dog food: human food can make a dog hyperactive.

Not being castrated can also make him hyperactive and have high hormones, especially when you have a period. You should contact your vet and ask him to recommend a behaviourist to call at your home.

BLINDNESS

Sometimes owners can be unaware that their dogs are partially blind, particularly when they gradually lose their sight as they grow older. Blindness does not affect a dog's quality of life so much as in a human for they rely more on their sense of smell and hearing.

Don't move the furniture around in the house and don't take the dog out without putting it on a lead. And continue to enjoy your companion.

BLOAT

Larger and "barrel chested" breeds are more prone to bloat than smaller-boned breeds although any dog can bloat given the wrong circumstances. Dogs that bolt their food and those that are exercised too soon after eating usually bloat. It is best to wait 30 minutes after a meal before exercising your dog.

BODY LANGUAGE

This is important to a dog. It learns much from the posture of another dog (See **Aggression**) as well as from the posture of us humans, even though we have no tail to wag. Bending down with legs apart makes a person smaller and more welcoming. This is friendly body language. Standing upright with hands raised above the head, making yourself look bigger, is threatening to the dog and is therefore interpreted as unfriendly body language.

BONES

Another human misconception is to think bones are necessary for dogs. Apart from the risk of broken teeth, bones in a household with more than one dog can create jealousy, possessiveness and fighting. And well-fed dogs will most likely bury a bone, a habit they inherited from wolves that bury any remnants from a kill to prevent scavengers from eating the left-overs.

BOREDOM

Tail chasing and being destructive are signs that a dog is bored. (See **Destruction** and **Tail chasing**).

BOWLS

It is best to use stainless steel or thick ceramic bowls for feeding pets rather than plastic bowls that can harbour germs in any surface scratch.

BOYFRIEND PROBLEM

This can be an important issue. One lady wrote to me saying she would like to continue her relationship with her boyfriend who had moved in with her but, if the problem with the dog continued, her boyfriend would have to go!

Like a new baby in the house, the arrival of a boyfriend or a new spouse can trigger behavioural problems such as aggressive jealousy, fear or premature peeing which is a sign of fear. It could be the cause is genetic. It could be the boyfriend or spouse is too dominant. Or it could simply be the way he walks or even smells. Also, the dog could be picking up anxious vibes from the owner. Get the boyfriend to feed the dog and to be more relaxed. I recommend you get a homeopathic remedy called "Rescue". Put five drops on the dog's tongue in the morning and evening. Incidentally, "Rescue" is also excellent for humans. (See **Homeopathy**).

BREED CHARACTERISTICS

Some people want large, fierce-looking dogs simply because they think they add to their own personal stature. Others want a tiny lap dog which they can carry around. The weight can vary from 2 lbs. to 300 lbs. Between these two extremes is a tremendous range of breeds.

So which breed should you choose?

Here is a breakdown of the characteristics of the different breeds. It is not absolutely definitive because a dog´s characteristics do not depend entirely on the breed but also on the genes inherited from the parents and early socialisation as a puppy.

1. *Highly excitable and aggressive but quite obedient:*
   Chihuahua, Dachshund, Schnauzer, Terrier.

2. *Very aggressive and very obedient but not very excitable:*
   Akita, Doberman, German Shepherd, Rottweiler.

3. *Highly obedient and not very aggressive but very excitable:*
   Australian Shepherd, Brittany Spaniel, Collie, Keeshond, Labrador, Newfoundland, Retriever, Shorthaired Pointer, Vizzla.

4. *Very obedient , quite aggressive and very excitable:*
   Bichon Frise, Poodles, Sheepdog, Shin Tzu, Springer Spaniel, Welsh Corgi.

5. *Highly aggressive and not very obedient but not very excitable:*
   Afghan Hound, Alaskan Malamute, Boxer, Chow, Dalmatian, Great Dane, Saint Bernard, Samoyed, Siberian Husky.

6. *Not easy to train but not excitable or aggressive:*
   Basset Hound, Bloodhound, English Bulldog, Norwegian Elkhound, Old English Sheepdog,

7. *Very excitable, not very obedient but not very aggressive:*
   Beagle, Boston Terrier, Cocker Spaniel, Irish Setter, Lhasa Apso, Maltese Terrier, Pekingese, Pomeranian, Pug, Weimaraner, Yorkshire Terrier,

The American Kennel Club recognises 142 breeds, many of which few people have even heard about. Make a short list of those breeds that interest you you and then study books and Internet sites to help you make a choice.

(See **Mongrels, Puppy – breeding and buying** and **Rescue centres**).

BREEDERS - British Dog Breeders Council

Formed in February 1997, the objectives of the British Dog Breeders Council are to promote the interest and welfare of members and encourage good breeding practices through education and exchange of information

All responsible breeders wish to see an end to puppy farming and irresponsible breeding practices and the B.D.B.C. provides them with an informed "voice" to represent them in dealing with proposed new laws.

The B.D.B.C. have been instrumental in forming a Working Party, along with several other reputable canine organisations, to formulate a Parliamentary Bill in order to bring about well constructed laws to protect dogs from bad breeding practices and to help eradicate poorly managed puppy farms.

Applications for Membership of the BDBC are checked before being approved.

Further details can be obtained from the Secretary: Jill Terry, 10 Eastwood End, Wimblington, Cambs. PE15 0QQ. Tel: 01354 740547.
E-mail: Babrees@compuserve.com
Web site: http://www.k9netuk.com/bdbc

BREEDING

Case history 1:
When out at a restaurant one evening, I met a delightful couple who regularly listened to my radio broadcasts and read my newspaper articles. They proudly told me how they have taken their Labrador bitch to a kennels to be mated as they believed every bitch should have one set of pups.

"Did you get a blood test and hip displacement x-rays for both dogs", I asked? "No", was the bemused answer.

So they did not know what problem dogs they might be breeding. "What will you do with the pups", I asked?

"We're going to keep two so that they can be company for each other".

Now they will have two siblings and a mother in the same household, a recipe for disaster. Further conversation revealed their knowledge of dogs was pretty limited to put it mildly.

"Do you realise that people buying the pups will regard you, the breeder, as God? They'll believe every piece of advice you give them."

Another recipe for disaster for the buyers. The moral from this sad story? Ignorance is not bliss. I hope I did not spoil their meal.

It certainly spoilt mine to have yet another example of a bad breeder and an ignorant owner.

Case History 2:

A lady rang me up to ask if I would train her two eight-month-old Rottweiler bitches that were fighting to establish dominance.

"No", I said. "Why?" she asked.

I explained that the combination was lethal. They would eventually fight to the death to establish dominance.

"But the breeder said it would be better to have them both and that training should be left until they were one year old".

"Then the breeder was wrong on both counts", I said.

Worse still the breeder sold them when they were only four-weeks-old instead of from seven to 12 weeks. That was far too young for them to leave their mother. She paid the equivalent of around £650 for the pair. No wonder he wanted to sell them both!

She asked what she should do. I told her to re-home one of them and have the one she kept spayed. She asked her vet to do this and, against all accepted practice, he advised her to leave the spaying until after the dog's first season. What a sorry tale: a so-called breeder selling two sibling bitches, far too young, to the same buyer, advising against training until they were a year old and a vet not wanting to spay until after the first season. Buyer beware!

An open letter to a breeder:

Dear Breeder,

I brought your puppy home today. He's tan and he's fuzzy and he smells good, like a puppy. The boys loved him and pestered him so much I had to make them let him rest. They've named him Rover, even though I told them his long, fancy, pedigree name.

We stopped by the vet on the way home, just like you said we should, and then by the pet shop to get that food you said he should eat. We've got Rover's basket next to Michael's bed, he's the oldest and so Rover will be his responsibility, with my help, of course.

We puppy proofed the house, again, this afternoon. Rover has toys to chew, a new collar, a new lead and special food bowls. I signed up for that social class you recommended, with David the Dogman - all positive reinforcement!

We love Rover very much and he seems to like us too. We're following all your instructions and promise to take good care of your baby. I'll send you the pictures as soon as we get them processed.

Just a few quick questions (you know how new "Mums" worry) :

- When Rover grows up and his hips hurt him, will you explain to my boys why they can't take him for walks?

- If his elbows hurt when he goes up the stairs, will you comfort him when he can't sleep next to Michael anymore?

- If he goes blind, will you teach the boys to play carefully with him so no one gets hurt?

- If he pees on the floor every time we get home, will you convince my husband that he still has to be an inside dog?

- If he growls at other children, will you help us when we try to take Rover to school for Pet Day?

- If his heart should skip one beat too many when he's only three years old and we lose him before his time, can you bring him back?

I know how hard you've worked to produce "sound" dogs but did you do all you could? Was there some little thing that you decided just wasn't necessary to check? You see our future happiness depends on how carefully you did this breeding because Rover is not just a dog, he's part of our family now.

Respectfully,

Rover's New Mummy.

(See **Hereditary Diseases** and **Puppy** – buying).

BURYING FOOD
This could be a sign of the dog being overfed. Many dogs do it instinctively for survival. They are keeping food for later.

BUYING A DOG
(See **Breed characteristics, Hereditary Diseases, Mongrels, Puppies,** and **Rescue centres**).

"To his dog, every man is Napoleon;
hence the constant popularity of dogs." — Aldous Huxley

"If there are no dogs in Heaven,
then when I die I want to go where they went." — Unknown

Burying a dog

There are various places in which a dog may be buried.

I am thinking now of a Setter, whose coat was flame in the sunshine, and who, so far as I am aware, never entertained a mean or an unworthy thought. This Setter is buried beneath a cherry tree, under four feet of garden loam. And at its proper season, the cherry tree strews petals on the green lawn of his grave.

Beneath a cherry tree, or an apple, or any flowering shrub is an excellent place to bury a dog. Beneath such trees, such shrubs, he slept in the drowsy summer, or gnawed at a tasty bone, or lifted his head to challenge some strange intruder. These are good places in life or in death.

Yet, it is a small matter, for if the dog be well remembered, if sometimes he leaps through your dreams, eyes kindling, laughing, begging, it matters not at all where that dog sleeps.

On a hill where the wind is unrebuked, and the trees are roaring, or beside a stream he knew in puppy hood, or somewhere in the flatness of a pasture lane where most exhilarating cattle grazed, is all one to the dog, and all one to you. And nothing is gained, nothing is lost if memory lives.

But, there is one place to bury a dog... If you bury him in this spot, he will come to you when you call - come to you over the grim, dim frontiers of death and down the well-remembered path, and to your side again.

And though you call a dozen living dogs to heel, they shall not growl at him nor resent his coming, for he belongs there. People may laugh at you who see no lightest blade of grass bent by his footfall...who hear no whimper, people who never really had a dog. Smile at them, for you shall know something that is hidden from them, and which is well worth the knowing.

The one best place to bury a dog is in the heart of his master.

CALCIUM

Calcium aids bone growth but an excess if it in early life can create rapid growth and cause hip dysplasia later on in life.

CARS

It is not kind or safe to allow a dog freedom in a car. Both the dog and you will feel much safer if it is either secured in a travel kennel or is restrained on the floor of the car with a dog guard between you and it. An unrestrained dog could fly through the air, go through the windscreen or break your neck in an accident. The National Canine Defence League urges dog owners to give their dog the same attention they would give a small child when they travel. So always make sure that the dog is properly restrained in the rear of the car. In many parts of Europe it is an offence to allow dogs to be loose□or unsecured in carsA costly fine can result if stopped by the police.

Part of the problem is caused when the puppy is brought home from the breeder on the lap and, while it is still small, continues to travel in that way. When it gets bigger it is put in the back of the car and, not surprisingly, does not like the idea. This can result in barking and jumping about. The owner turns round to shout and an accident can happen. Whose fault? The dog or the owner?

Stupid owners let dogs hang their heads out of the window. This can cause severe eye and nose problems and many a dog has been killed having jumped out of a travelling car through the window. Far better for the dog to be on the floor without even being able to see out of a window. They will feel much more secure this way.

Never leave a dog in a car during hot weather for longer than a few minutes. Park in the shade and never forget that the sun moves round in the sky. Even if the windows are left open, the temperature can reach 35° C. in a few minutes and dogs can suffer from heatstroke within 10 minutes or less. If you see a dog suffering from the heat in a car, do not hesitate to call the police. You may save its life.

Train your dog to sit before allowing it into the car. Train it to stay when opening a car door so that there is no chance of it jumping out onto a road and causing an accident or being killed. Better still to have it on a secure lead.

If your dog gets over-excited because it knows it is being taken somewhere in the car to walk or run freely, take it around the block or to the shops and back again sometimes, without allowing it the excitement of a walk.

In many countries, your private car becomes a public vehicle when it is on a public highway. The same rule applies to your dog in your car. Dogs loose in cars and barking are causing a nuisance in a public place, and if someone is bitten by your dog through an open window of your car, you are liable.

CAR CHASING

This is a dangerous pastime, enjoyed by some dogs with an excessive zeal when protecting their territory. Some just chase the back of the car which is a herding instinct often found in Border Collies used for herding sheep. Others might run into the vehicle to head off the intruder in what the dog regards as its road. Ask a friend, armed with a plant spray loaded with water, to drive slowly past and squirt the dog.

CAR RESTRAINT

Restriction prevents excitement which is demonstrated through barking or jumping around. Tether the dog to a chain (it might bite through a leather lead) which is short enough to prevent it looking out the window. Use a guard rail between the luggage area in hatchbacks and estate cars. (See **Crates**).

"Some dogs chase the back of the car which is a herding instinct ..."

CAR SICKNESS

In 95% of cases, car sickness is stress related, not motion related. One of the most powerful memories imprinted on any dog's brain is probably the car ride when it was taken away from all it ever knew to be safe and secure, the litter mates and mother. This most traumatic of memories is associated with car travel, so it is not surprising that subsequent rides in a car should evoke very strong mental and physical trauma.

The first thing you should do is clean the inside of the car thoroughly to make sure there is no remaining smell to remind the dog of that first traumatic ride. Then put the dog in the car for a short while each day without the engine running or moving the vehicle.

After a week, put him in the car and start the engine but do not move it. After another week of doing this every day take him 100 yards then stop and take him for a walk.

There is another simple solution. Work out how long the dog was in the car before being sick. If, say, it was in the car 20 minutes, drive him to a park or exercise spot about 5 to 10 minutes from home, preferably one he has been to before. Ideally you should have someone else in the car to soothe the dog and distract him from the ride. Keep him happy all the way to the park.

Once there, do all the enjoyable things that the dog likes, such as fetching the ball and chasing the Frisbee. The visit needs to be as enjoyable as possible. Then drive the dog home, soothing him all the way. Once home, make just as much fuss of the dog as you did at the park. Finish the session with his meal or a treat if time and conditions permit.

Repeat several times a day, or daily if time is limited. Once the dog is enthusiastic to go in the car, lengthen the trip from 10 to 15 minutes.

When you can drive with the dog for 30 minutes with no signs of stress or anxiety, you have the problem pretty much solved. Some dogs may take a little longer than others.

The idea is for as many happy repetitions as possible to wipe out the initial mental trauma the dog had on its first ride.

Rarely, a dog may suffer from a kind of balance problem, in which case a trip to the vet may be necessary.

CASTRATION

Some owners don´t have their male dogs castrated because they believe it will cause them to get fat. It is not castration but over feeding that puts weight on dogs. A castrated dog has an increased appetite and, if owners give them more food, then they will get fat. Keep to the same feeding levels as before castration and, if the dogs get normal exercise, there will be no problem.

You must keep in mind, however, that castration can eliminate some of the dog´s motives to exercise. For instance, a castrated dog's desire to chase a female on heat is greatly reduced or eliminated totally.

American research has shown that there is a 70% improvement in behaviour after castration. Castration reduces testosterone levels, so the dog is less likely to be attracted to other male dogs. Aggressive and dominance tendencies will also be reduced or eliminated. Neutered males still lift their legs but are less inclined to mark their territory. They are also less prone to certain cancers and prostate problems.

Many owners think it is cruel to castrate a male dog and not let it satisfy its natural urges. This macho attitude is the reason why many Mediterranean countries have so many wild packs of dogs roaming the countryside. (See **Excuses**.)

CATARACTS

Expensive and specialised equipment is now available to eliminate cataracts through micro-surgery. Because it costs so much, not all vets can afford to install it or spend the time to train to the necessary standards, but they can certainly refer a client to a surgery with this equipment. The high cost can be covered by insurance.

Operations on older dogs have less chance of success and there is a greater danger of a secondary infection. One of the problems is that an older dog will need a special anaesthetic to ensure there is absolutely no movement of the eye while micro-surgery is performed. (See **Glaucoma**).

CATERPILLARS (See **Processionary caterpillar**).

CATS

Dogs chase cats because they run away. It starts in the garden where the cat is regarded as an intruder. More often than not, if the cat is cornered and stands its ground, the dog does not know what to do. The cat could lash out with its claws and cause a severe injury to the dog's eyes.

Dogs can also be great friends with cats who do not run away, especially those that share the dog's home. The relationship, good or bad, usually depends on the cat's behaviour.

CHAINS

Rather than leave a dog in the house when you go out, why not chain it up in the garden where it has a greater freedom to move around and relieve itself?

Buy a thick chain so that it cannot get tangled (ropes and leather leads can be bitten through) and put a swivel at each end. Put a hook into a wall or several hooks if you want to change the location from time to time.

Alternatively, a short chain can be attached to a running line of wire. The dog will be much happier outside than indoors.

Always ensure that there is an adequate supply of water, within reach of the dog, but not where the dog can entangle the bowl in the chain, over-turning the water.

CHASING

Dogs which chase joggers, cars and birds should have been taught the Recall and Down commands. The alternative is to keep them on a long lead and teach them that answering to the Recall is rewarding by giving a treat.

CHEWING

When a dog chews it is a sign that it lacks fibre or is feeling anxious or simply bored.

CHILD ATTACKS

When a child is badly mauled by a dog, it is nearly always the dog that is blamed, but I never blame the dog. I blame owners, the parents, the breeders, the public and the vets. Why?

I blame the owners because they should never allow children to be left unsupervised with their dog. The owner will defend the dog with remarks such as "He didn't mean it" or "He´s not dangerous" or "He has never done anything like that before" or "He is wonderful with our children". But this is no excuse.

The dog should have been confined, trained and castrated. Male dogs which are not castrated are more likely to escape seeking a partner and roam the streets. If approached they can be dangerous. And all large dogs should be muzzled.

I blame the parents because they should teach children to respect dogs and not antagonise them by pinching them, pulling their ears and tail and poking them in the eyes. And they never should be allowed to play with dogs without supervision.

Any large breeds like the Rottweiller, German Shepherd and Doberman are not suitable for homes where there are children. The dog may be wonderful with the owner's children because they are part of the family pack. But the children of visitors can be regarded as intruders and if the children start playing rough with the dog, it can attack.

I blame the breeders because they as professionals are under an obligation to meet the highest possible standards (See Puppy - breeding). Sadly, some of them know little about canine behaviour. They carry out no tests to ensure the bitch and the mate are genetically sound. Not surprisingly, the advice about rearing they give to the buyer, who usually takes their word as gospel, is unsound.

I blame members of the public because they should be better educated. So many still believe a dog should not be trained until six months old and so many do not even bother to attend training classes. They could eventually be the owner of an aggressive, dangerous and uncontrollable dog.

I blame the vets because they should see when owners bring their dogs to be treated whether or not the dogs are trained or out of control. They should be directing these dogs and owners to local training clubs. If I was involved in an investigation into the mauling or death of a child, I would want to know the name of the vet and why he did not recommend the dog to be trained. They should be advocating the early neutering of dogs if they are not to be used for breeding by a responsible breeder.

There must be thousands of attacks by dogs on children around the world every day. In Australia alone, 100 dog attacks occur on average every day, mostly on children. If only those responsible – owners, parents, the public, breeders and vets — took their share of the blame and acted accordingly, many of these attacks could be avoided. (See **Biting**).

CHILDREN AND DOGS

*This article is written by my very good friend Terry Ryan (See **Acknowledgements**), who is a lady working out of Washington University and who has formed an organisation called Prevent-a-Bite.*

"The most frequently bitten people are children. By the age of 14, about half of all children have been bitten by a dog. The overwhelming majority of bites occur in children under nine years of age, sometimes resulting in both physical and emotional damage.

Through an understanding of canine behaviour and preparation for what to do in the event of a canine confrontation, many such bites can be avoided.

Most dogs are fun and safe to be with, but certain dogs, and it's hard to tell which ones, have their own set of 'rules' regarding children. Whether or not we humans feel the rules of this minority appropriate, we must help our children become aware of situations to avoid.

This article is not meant to blame children if they are bitten. There is rarely a good excuse for a dog biting a person, but knowing the reasons a dog might bite, from the dog's point of view, may be helpful in avoiding bites.

Here are some statistics from Chicago and Dallas University which were based over a three-year period of reported dog bites. Many are not reported.

Of all dog bites of children age four to 16, most were bitten in early July. 18% were bitten on the head, neck and face, 38% were bitten in their own home, 18% were bitten by their own dog and 50% of the dogs had no previous history of biting.

Further studies showed that 51% of the infants bitten were bitten in their cots and most were bitten by their own pets. None of the reported bites were by strays, and most were not witnessed by the parents.

This posed questions:

1. Why were the dogs allowed in children's sleeping area's ?

2. Where were the parents?

Many of these potential bite situations can be avoided by providing the proper training and environment for our pet dogs. It is not, however, the intent of this article to give information on how to bite-proof dogs, but rather how to bite-proof children.

You can tell if a dog is upset. Any dog can bite, but most won't if you act the way you should around them. The signs are: tail up, hairs on its back raised, baring teeth and growling. If a child keeps on doing what makes the dog angry, it might get angrier and perhaps bite. If the dog's ears are laid back with the tail between the legs, it is scared. It might run, but it might also bite if it cannot get away. Do not go closer if it looks like that.

If a child is bitten, it should try to remember what the dog looked like and in which direction it went. It should tell an adult who can wash the wound with soap and water. If a doctor has to be seen ask for a report to take to the police.

The warning body language of aggressive dogs is:

- Ears erect, body stiff, tail high, hackles up.

A fearful posture is:

- Ears back, body crouched, head low, tail tucked in.

Other signs to watch for are:

- Growling and barking, lips lifting, teeth bared

Dogs that have assumed either a defensive or offensive threat posture frequently have a "critical zone". A child is safe around this zone until entering the imaginary circle the dog has projected. The problem is that this zone varies between dogs and can even be different for the same dog if the situation changes. So it's impossible for humans to accurately determine the critical zone.

A defensive threat posture is adopted by the shy or fearful dog. It is hesitant, easily frightened, timid, tends to avoid certain persons or things. Frequently, these traits are not noticed until the dog encounters a new situation. The dog might assume elements of the defensive threat posture when frightened.

Shy dogs can be gentle, loving, obedient pets, but may try to bite when frightened. The dog's motive is to chase that person away. The problem is, we cannot always tell which people or actions frighten the dog.

The fearful dog may fool you by appearing brave. The dog growls and raises the hair along the neck and back like a brave/aggressive dog, but ears may be pinned back, body lowered, tail between the legs. The tail may even be wagging, but a wagging tail doesn't always mean a friendly dog.

The dog might bark and stare, but then turn away, only to turn toward you again and start all over. This dog would really rather not deal with you and hopes to frighten you away but, if pushed, it might bite.

An offensive threat posture is when a dog is hostile, assertive, ready for combat, dominant and self-confident. It does so when provoked.

The dog can be a loving and loyal pet to his immediate family if given proper training, but this type of dog can bite if challenged. The motive is to hurt the challenging person. The problem is, we do not always know what the dog may regard as a challenge.

The brave/aggressive dog's offensive threat posture, may include growling deeply, raised hackles, staring, a show of fangs, standing tall with ears and tail erect and leaning toward the opponent. If the situation is not handled carefully, this dog might bite.

So how does a child avoid getting bitten?

- Never touch a dog when it is feeding

- Do not tease a dog, its ears are not hankies.

- If chased by a dog while cycling, get off. Place the bike between you and the dog. LOOK AWAY.

- Avoid packs of dogs, if confronted, do not run away or scream.

- Do not disturb a sleeping dog.

- If meeting a new dog, pat him on the side of the face, under the chin or on the chest. Never place your head above a dog's head. Crouch down, and approach on his level.

- Ask an owner if it is permissible to pat their dog. If it is, let the dog sniff your knuckles to show you are a friend.

- Do not pat dogs in cars, it is a space they consider worth defending.

- Do not try to separate dogs fighting, go for help if necessary.

- Never approach a dog when it is chained up.

- If a strange dog comes up to you, stand still, like a statue.

Children and dogs can live happily together as long as they follow the rules we have just been through. The presence of an adult is a deterrent. Never leave dogs and children alone.

CHOCOLATE

Chocolate made for human consumption can kill dogs. They are sensitive to a class of chemicals called methylxanthines. Caffeine and theobromin are members of that family. Dogs cannot metabolise and excrete methylxanthines as efficiently as humans. The existence of the harmful ingredients in the human body is only two to three hours, in the dog it is more like 18 hours.

During this time the compounds are absorbed by the liver and transmitted via the bile into the intestine. They are then converted back into the original methylxanthines for another circuit through the animal. The circuit is repeated so, instead of getting rid of the substances, the dog poisons itself again and again.

The lethal dose of sweet milk chocolate for a dog is 2 oz (around 60 grams) per kilo of bodyweight, which is around 10 oz or 300 grams, a large bar, for a five kilo dog and around 1.4 kilos for a 25 kilo dog. Dark chocolate is at least 10 times as lethal. A 25 kilo dog could die from the methylxanthines in 5 ounces or 140 grams of dark chocolate, a relatively small bar.

Symptoms include vomiting, hyperactivity, restlessness, high sensitivity to touch (it might jump when touched), very rapid heartbeat and a rapid breathing rate. This can be followed by a loss of control of the leg muscles, muscle tremor seizures, general weakness, coma and finally death. So never encourage a dog to develop a taste for chocolate.

The alternative is something like Good Boy chocolate, which does not contain theobromin

CHOKING (See **First aid**)

CHOW

This word is the Chinese slang for food. The same word is used for an edible dog. So be careful which chow you eat. Seriously, the Chinese were among the first to realise that dogs could be trained to guard property, the alternative being to breed them for food. There are travellers' tales today of puppies being kept in cages in restaurants in some areas of China so that diners can select the one they wish to have cooked, much as we can pick fish from a restaurant tank. (See **Eating dogs**).

CHRISTMAS

A dog is not just for Christmas. It is for life. A dependent, living puppy is not in the same category as a Christmas toy. A puppy that makes its first appearance as a gift at Christmas time is more likely to be thought of by young children as a toy, rather than a member of the family.

Do not ever be tempted to take a dog home from Christmas bazaars and markets. If you see a particular dog that you like at a rescue centre, arrange with the charity for you to collect the pet a few days after Christmas when everything has settled down. Make a deposit donation and go to the shelter by appointment to collect your new dog or cat. Never give a friend a pet for Christmas. Buying a pet is a serious undertaking and should not be taken lightly. (See **Puppy – buying**).

If you already have a dog, check to see if your vet provides an emergency service out of hours over the Christmas period and keep the telephone numbers handy. (Vet fees are double for out of hour's emergencies). If your dog is going into kennels, make sure that it has up-to-date vaccinations and, if your dog needs it, check you have enough medication for the holiday period.

Christmas is a time for celebrations and humans and children can make a lot of noise and there may be visitors who are strangers to your pets around the home. This can be a distressing time for dogs and cats. Do try to keep to your routine and please do not forget those essential walks. Christmas crackers can be terrifying to a nervous dog and you should consider buying a homeopathic remedy called "Rescue." Five drops on the tongue really calms pets as well as humans. (See **Homeopathy**).

Christmas trees are pretty and your pet might be attracted to the decorations. Your dog could take a fancy to one of the decorative glass balls (don't put them too low down on the tree) and bite it off, or one might fall off and break and the dog swallow some of the shattered glass. You need not panic if you have taken the precaution of buying some cotton balls beforehand.

Dip them in some tasty beef or chicken stock and feed the dog small pieces. The cotton should wrap itself round the glass bits and help them to pass harmlessly through the system. If it doesn't work and there is blood in the dog's stools, get it to the vet quickly. Obviously it is a good idea to keep the tree off the floor and put a hook in the ceiling to which the top of the tree can be tied. Also make sure that any electric wires are out of reach. Tree lights should only be on when pets can be supervised.

Watch out for those fruit bowls, which might contain walnuts, peanuts and Brazil nuts. Remember human chocolates are dangerous to pets. "Choc Drops" made for dogs are not dangerous as they do not contain theobromine. (See **Chocolate**.) At Christmas time, we feast and drink and tend to over eat. Dogs, too, often suffer from over eating.

No pets should ever be given any form of alcohol and certainly no bones from the turkey. You can of course, give your dog a small Christmas treat but avoid anything fatty. Never leave tempting treats lying around the floor and remind the children not to feed sweets to dogs.

The following are Christmas gifts to avoid:

Poinsettia: This is poisonous. A small part of the plant can cause stomach or mouth irritation. Bigger portions could require a rapid visit to the vet as tolerance to poinsettia can vary from animal to animal.

Mistletoe: This plant is even more toxic than the poinsettia (particularly the berries).

Other plants that you might have around your house during the holidays that are also dangerous to animals are *Christmas rose, English holly, Jerusalem cherry and Amaryllis*.

Tinsel: Particularly dangerous for cats. Ingested tinsel can get tangled in the cat's intestines and surgery will be needed to save their lives.Finally there is that traditional turkey – for you, not your pets. Animals cannot digest turkey as well as humans and the bones should not be offered to your pet either. They can splinter easily and become lodged in the pet's throat or perforate it's intestinal tract.Having said all that, only two words remain: Merry Christmas!

CIRCLING BEFORE LYING

When a dog circles before lying down it is instinctively looking for a position it regards as downwind so that it can scent danger, or it will lie with its back against a wall so that it faces outwards, also to scent danger.

CLASSES

Every trainer has different views on how a class should be held. There is no one method which is necessarily better than any other, although it must be admitted that some arrogant trainers believe they are right and everybody else is wrong. The truth is that some trainers get better results with their methods than they would do so using the methods of others. This is not the same as saying they are right and everybody else is wrong, a claim I most certainly do not make.

A dog training friend from Scotland, Lynn Aitchison (The Dog Lady), a member of the Association of Pet Dog Trainers, describes below what she saw at one of my social training classes.

"We started off in a car park – well, a Spanish car park, so really just a bit of rough ground. The owners were shown how to get their dogs to Sit – this only took a couple of minutes. Then they did a Stay – to hand signals only, no voice. At the second Stay, David told everyone to drop their leads. There were some horrified looks, but they all did this and all the dogs stayed.

Then we all set off for a walk. There were about 20 dogs of all shapes and sizes. The owners were only allowed to use the words "Let's go" to their dogs each time we started walking. Every so often, David told everyone to about-turn and walk the other way – nothing being said to the dogs. After a few about-turns, all the dogs were released. The "pack" of humans continued their walk, still doing about-turns every so often.

I have to admit there were some anxious looks from certain owners at this "release your dogs" command, but they all did let their dogs go. Dogs that had been pulling on the lead immediately stopped trying to get to other dogs. The human pack walked on together in a tight pack, rather like those shoals of fish you see in coral reef TV programmes that all move as one.

The dogs all stayed. Although they were free to run for miles if they wanted, few went any distance from the "pack".

David then asked everyone to crouch down and stretch out their arms. Nearly every dog ran to its owner and was loved. Because the humans were in a tight pack, some dogs took a while to actually find their owners. This was where the assistants helped out a bit, directing some dogs back to their owners. There were happy smiling faces all around. This walking as a pack, about turning and occasional stopping, went on for about half-an-hour.

At some about-turns, a few dogs had gone charging ahead of the "pack" and did not immediately realise the pack was now leaving them behind. After a few seconds, these dogs would come belting back as fast as their legs could carry them, tails wagging.

We then did some work on Stays. At this point a stray horse wandered through the class (remember we are on a piece of Spanish scrub-land). The opportunity was taken to walk the dogs past the horse – a great opportunity that I do not get in my local hall.

I have to say I was gob-smacked by the whole experience. Since then, I have introduced some of David's methods into my own classes. Being indoors is a disadvantage, but I have not been able to find a suitable open location to duplicate this type of class locally and the climate is not suitable anyway. It is freezing cold outdoors. That´s the big advantage of Southern Spain.

In a hall, you have really to work to persuade people to walk around the perimeter in a tight pack, but that is what we do. I use the method for about 10 to 15 minutes of Weeks 1 and 2 of my beginners' classes.

What do I gain from this? I now have very few problems with multiple commands, as folk know from Week 1 that their dog is able to Sit, Stay and Come without verbal commands.

Any dogs that walked through the door, straining to get at the others, settle much faster as they are all part of the same "pack" – with the humans in control. (I am not totally stupid here and do muzzle any dogs that appear iffy.)

If dogs start to eye each other up, the "pack" walking away from them (which includes the owners) defuses the situation. Getting the owners not to look at their dogs further assists the defusing.

Being in a hall means I am not able to get the full advantage of what David is doing, but even this limited use of his methods has paid off. Getting people to drop their leads on a short Stay within five minutes of entering the hall is a major way of letting people appreciate that the "umbilical cord" can be broken, and this reinforces the notion of the loose lead being used purely as a safety chain.

And all this is from a Yank and Stomp trainer of 15 years, prior to converting to motivation. Yes, I have done a good bit of hauling dogs around on check chains. I have used prong collars. I have "hung" aggressive dogs. I freely admit to this, as we thought at the time that this was how to train dogs.

Having been sceptical of motivation, if not downright scathing, for many years, I perhaps appreciated the change more. I am now a clicker trainer, using Touches, homeopathic remedies and food treats (I previously totally banned food from the hall).

I now consider David's overall ethos as possibly the next step beyond motivation, making optimum use of body and pack signals." (See **Training**).

CLAWS (See **Dew claws** and **Grooming**)

CLICKER TRAINING

The primary means of controlling dog behaviour has been with a collar, lead and the strength of the trainer's hand, even though most pet dog owners do not have the strength and skill required for proper control.

Over the past 12 years, a new form of dog training has developed based on the system used by Karen Proyer, pioneer marine mammal trainer who developed the "Clicker" for dolphin and whales. The training of dolphins is based on positive reinforcement – a reward for doing what is required, usually a bucket of fish.

Pryor's experiences planted seeds in the minds of many dog trainers and behaviourists. They figured out if marine mammal trainers can control 600-pound sea lions without shouting and force, then why couldn´t they adopt a similar technique for dog training?

Marine mammal trainers use whistles and clickers because before they can even say the word "Good" the mammal has disappeared under the water or jumped 30 feet into the air. As soon as a mammal reaches the highest part of a jump, it knows that unless it hears a click it will get no fish. The mammal has learnt that if it obeys a command, it hears a click and gets a food reward. No click, no reward.

I believe that the more we talk to our pets in training the less they understand. It is important to try and shorten praise words to one word like "Good" rather than "Now that's a clever boy". With a clicker, there are no words. Good behaviour is rewarded with a click, then a treat. If any dog knows you have a treat it will sit. When it does so, click and treat. When the dog is getting up, say "Up", click and treat. If the dog lies down, just as it does so, say "Down", then click and treat. When the dog comes to you, then say "Come", click and treat.

You will be amazed at how quickly the dog will understand simple one-word commands that are followed by the click and treat. Remember the dog only gets the click after it has carried out the required command.

There is an excellent booklet called "Click and Treat" by Sarah Whitehead about teaching fun tricks using clickers. It costs £3 from Alpha, PO Box 372, Windsor, Berks, SL4 4WH.

"Click For Success" by Lana Mitchell is also a good clicker guide.

There is a web site worth visiting at: http://www.click-l.com, which has Frequently Asked Questions.

Here is some further advice on clicker training by Sheilagh B Wilson. (See **Acknowledgements**).

"My training method uses a conditioned reinforcer or bridge (usually a click) which marks the desired behaviour and tells the dog that it will be rewarded for it.

The American behaviourists Karen Pryor and Gary Wilkes have popularised this method with dog trainers over the past few years using a small box clicker as a bridge. The click is always followed by a reward. The reward can be anything the dog desires although it is usually food, a treat or toy.

Enthusiasts of the method say its benefit over other methods are that the dog understands clearly what is wanted, as the click is far more distinct than any verbal marker, and it can be used on behaviours at a distance from the handler such as sendaways and retrieves. The clicker is only a training tool. Once a behaviour has been thoroughly learned and randomly rewarded, the clicker is no longer required.

You can get the behaviour you want by using one of the following three methods.

a) *Luring*. Take a treat and, by moving it influence where the dog is and what it is doing.

b) *Shaping*. Have a vision of your goal. Click and give a treat for any movement towards this goal, asking for a little more each time until you achieve the goal. You may have to back up a few steps if the dog gets confused.

c) *Wait for it to happen*. There are many behaviours that the dog will do naturally. When it does, click and treat them.

When you are sure the dog will do what you want, start giving the CUE as the dog does it. Try using a word to cue it. If this fails, go back to saying it as it happens.

Once the response is on cue, start varying how often you ask the dog to do it before clicking and rewarding. Click sometimes twice sometimes once, sometimes three times and so on until eventually you can fade out the click altogether.

Stop rewarding the dog if what you require is done without a cue so that it only happens when you ask for it."

Sheilagh B Wilson, UK APDT 00441, Sheilagh's K9 Centre, Central Scotland

---

COCKER SPANIEL (See **Top Dogs**)

COLLARS

There are a whole variety of collars available, from the conventional plain leather or nylon ones to the controversial choke chain, banned by several organisations of trainers, and the often frowned-upon pinch collar.

There are also head collars which give a greater degree of control. The four basic head collars available in the U. K. are the Halti, the Gentle Leader, the Dogalter and the Kombi. The Halti is a U.K. registered design made in five sizes of very fine nylon and is loose fitting. The Gentle Leader is a design first patented in the United States and then Europe. It is made in three, snug-fitting sizes of 19mm nylon.

The Dogalter is also in three snug-fitting sizes and is made from 15 and 19mm polypropylene but with a padded nose band. It can be left on the dog and used for behavioural problems where it is necessary to correct the dog, i.e. when it whines, chews, or gets excited, etc. The calming effect on some excitable dogs can be remarkable.

Personally I use the half-check Kombi designed by the highly respected George Grayson, though the Halti is also very good. The Halti was designed by the famous Dr.Roger Mugford, Britain's first animal behaviourist. He based it on a halter used 100 years ago in America to control weaning calves.

The advantage of head collars is that they control the dog by the head, like a horse, and using one increases the handler's control. They also have a calming effect on some dogs, putting pressure on the shoulder and neck. Not all dogs like them.

They are a training aid, assisting control in many cases. If the dog is anti-social or too strong for the handler, they are vital as long as the owner is taught how to use them properly.

Many people do not like them because they look like muzzles, but most find that their use has enabled them to walk happily with their dog when before it was a struggle.

Pinch collars:

These are not to be confused with the generally frowned-upon choke collar with prongs turned inwards. Initially these were used the other way round with the prongs pointing outwards as a neck protection for the dog.

When people are in a formal training situation at a class, the dog tends to behave quite well. As long as a trainer is there telling them what to do, and when, they gain control.

But when some slow learners are away from the class, they do not have the same control at all. It must be admitted that some trainers believe the use of a pinch collar in these circumstances can be most effective, but I do not recommend it.

The respected dog trainer Lou Castle of Los Angeles Police Department believes that they are a far better tool for aversive work than a choke chain. He says: "No damage to the neck is possible with that tool. A top trainer I know goes so far as to say that it is the only completely humane training collar that exists." (See **Electric collars** and **Pulling on a lead**).

Collars with bells

Most pet shops sell little bells to attach to cat collars. They can also be put on the collar of very small breeds of dogs to avoid them being stepped on.

COLOUR BLINDNESS (See **Sight**)

CONCRETE PROBLEM

Many breeders and some pet shops have pens with concrete floors upon which the dogs eliminate. Consequently, when you buy a dog it would never have used or known grass. If you have an area of concrete at home, your dog will continue to use it. A cure is to collect some stools and place them on some grass. The dog will go where it can smell the stools. At the same time, make certain that you hose, wash down and disinfect the concrete area properly to remove all smell and odour.

CONFORMITY

This is an important issue. As the leading animal behaviourist Dr. Roger Mugford states in his excellent book "Dr. Mugford's Casebook", dogs have an intelligence and keenness to conform to their master's wishes which makes complicated and aversive methods unnecessary.

He adds: "We never begin to utilise the full extent of a dog's intelligence in our training. Since consistent repetition of any procedure tends to produce a change in the dog's behaviour, it is not surprising that each of the methods of training described here (in his book), and many more, have attracted their disciples.

"But I and many of the pet owners we see do not really wish our animals to conform to strict universal rules. We want them to retain their personality, their joie de vivre, their trust in us based upon a sense of security and affection rather than fear."

Wise words, indeed. Each dog is an individual and they should no more be made to conform to every rule in this book than I would expect every trainer and behaviourist in the world to conform to the same methods.

Dr. Mugford goes on to state in his book that:

"the greatest misunderstanding afflicting the world of dogs is the notion of dominance...the owner and his family are supposed to fit within such a pack structure, exerting a regulatory hand over all aspects of the dog's life. I have always been uneasy about this concept because it has been used to justify excessive punishment and force in training."

I have highlighted these words because they are so important for an owner to understand. I advocate the theory of dominance in this book but it should never be taken as justification for trying to control everything a dog does and never as an excuse for unkindness.

No dog should ever be made to conform to all our human requirements. (See **Ten commandments**).

CONTROL

An owner reported that his dog was out of control after having been sent away to a "trainer" for three months, but when the lead was taken over by somebody running a training class the dog responded to Heel, Sit and Down. The problem was not the dog but the owner. This is a good example for not sending dogs away for training.

I can have most dogs under my complete control in a few minutes without a choke chain. That is no big deal. I should be able to do so after more than 40 years during which I have tackled most forms of training except with sheep.

It is easy to get any dog, irrespective of breed or age, to walk to Heel, Sit, Down and Stay in a few minutes (the Stay can be a dropped lead only, with a short step back) and there is no need even to know the dog's name or give a verbal command So I cannot understand why it takes some trainers weeks to achieve this.

The problem is to educate owners. The more frequently they repeat the words "Heel, heel, heeeeeel" and say "Sit, sit, siiiiit, the more the dog waits for repeat orders.

I ask the owner to stand on the right side of the dog and I stand on the right of the owner with the lead. Any correction or adjustment made to the dog via the lead will come from me because the owner does not handle the lead at this stage, but the dog thinks the owner is in control.

I ask the owner to start walking with the left foot. As soon as the dog goes forward, I correct it with the lead. Most dogs are surprised because this is coming (as far as the dog is concerned) from the owner.

Then when we do go forward, I teach the owner to nudge the dog with the left leg and turn left into the dog. At the same time, I nudge the owner to the left with my body forcing a left turn.

Within minutes, and without speaking, the dog is walking to heel. I then hand the lead to the owner, asking him to hold it lightly so it is not tight on the dog. I stay alongside, keeping pressure on with the left nudge, before allowing the owner to walk forward on his own,being ready within a second to get back in control and take the lead.

The dog has learned a lot in a few minutes. Now it is up to the owner to gain confidence. If I see the dog and owner are doing well, I send them off on their own to practice, watching from behind to give them verbal instructions to turn left. I also frequently change the walking pace.

Depending on the dog and owner, a Sit and Stay can be achieved within the first few minutes. Obviously the Stay is raw but when the owner holds his hand above the dog's head as a stop signal it will work from one pace immediately.

CORRECTIONS

These need to be applied immediately the dog has done wrong to get the dog's attention. One excellent way is to use an old drink can. Insert a few small coins or pebbles then tape up the hole. Just by rattling it you can get the dog's attention. Having achieved that, always praise.

Alternatively, if the dog has stolen something and run away, don't chase it because that is the reaction it wants from you. Throw the can to land alongside it. That should get its attention, resulting in the release of the stolen object. Then immediately give praise or "positive reinforcement".

> *"If dogs could talk it would take a lot of the fun out of owning one."* — *Andy Rooney*

CRATES

Crates or pens, which dogs can regard as their den, are very popular in the United States. They are now being widely accepted in the UK and are ideal to confine a young, potentially destructive dog.

Most are collapsible so that they can be folded into the boot of the car, which is useful when visiting friends. They are also excellent for dogs that have had surgery and must rest. Most good pet shops sell them or can obtain them for you. You can also buy special water bowls that fit on the inside wall of a crate. (See **Puppy – eliminating**).

Creation

On the first day of creation, God created the dog.

On the second day, God created man to serve the dog.

On the third day, God created all the animals of the Earth to serve as potential food for the dog.

On the fourth day, God created honest toil so that man could labour for the good of the dog.

On the fifth day, God created the tennis ball so that the dog might or might not retrieve it.

On the sixth day, God created veterinary science to keep the dog healthy and the man broke.

On the seventh day, God tried to rest, but He had to walk the dog.

DACHSHUND (See **Top Dogs**)

DEAFNESS

As long as you have had a dog before and the consequences have been thought through, there is no reason why you should not give a home to a deaf dog. You will have to be more patient and persevering with the training, which will take longer than with a normal dog, and you will need the full support of any family members. Deaf dogs can lead a perfectly happy life and, given the right training, can be taught all the commands of a normal dog using sign language.

Breeders are alert to certain tell-tale signs of deafness in puppies. For instance, when they notice a puppy is sleeping or playing while the rest of the litter is at the "milk bar", they will isolate the puppy and make a loud noise behind it to see if it responds to sound. The definitive test is called the Brainstem Auditory Evoked Reaction (BAER) test, which requires a specialist who can perform it when the puppy is only six or seven weeks old.

Three small electrodes are put under the skin around the puppy's head. These electrodes are then connected to a computer. Various levels of sound are played into headphones over the puppy's ears. The brain's response to the sound is measured on the computer to ascertain whether the puppy is totally deaf or has partial hearing in one or both ears.

Deafness can creep up on older dogs, around 45% being deaf by 10 years. When this happens, a relationship can be established whereby the dog always looks to its owner for guidance. Leashes are an obvious guide, but so are highly scented foods and flashlights. Hand signals are easy to teach and you can also stamp your feet to vibrate the ground. Rewards are, as always, important. Use food, toys or pats.

Deaf dogs have the advantage sometimes of not being able to hear their owner ranting and raving at them. They can, however, detect when their owners are speaking kindly to them. So it is not so stupid to talk to a deaf dog as some might think.

An excellent book on this subject is called "Hear, Hear!" written by my friend Barry Eaton (There are details at www.dogsworldwide.com/deafdogtraining.htm). In the UK, it costs £5.45 incl. p.& p. direct from Barry Eaton, Pine Cottage, Station Road, Chilbolton, Hampshire, SO20 6AL. Cheques should be made payable to B. Eaton. In the US, the book is available from Direct Book Services. E-mail: barry.eaton@virgin.net

Making a vibrating collar:
I am grateful to Miranda Spindel, an Internet friend, for the following story about her deaf dog Emma, and how she and her father overcame the problem.

(spindel@holly.ColoState.EDU)

"Emma is a four-year-old Australian Shepherd who is deaf and partially blind as the result of a birth defect. I adopted her from the humane society at which I worked when she was six-months-old. She went through regular obedience training and learned basic commands using touch signals (Sit is a touch on her butt, Down a touch on the back, Stay a touch between the shoulder blades.

The only command I couldn't teach her was Come. So my father, an electrical engineer, and I designed a collar based on the principle of the shock collar, though instead of a shock our collar gave her a signal through a gentle vibration because Emma has always known positive, loving training, and I didn't want this to be different. I taught Emma that this vibration meant she should come to me. And it worked. It was also a way to tell her to come to me to work with her off the lead. It was a great breakthrough for us. Since putting the directions on the web, many owners of deaf dogs have written to tell me the collar has helped them as well.

Emma is an inspiration to me. She is a joyful, loving dog and lives a very normal life despite her disabilities. We hike, run, play in the park, and live life to the fullest. I would be very happy if her story helps deaf dogs to become well trained and better companions".

Her electrical engineer father, Bob, wrote:

"The basic idea is to use the guts of a radio remote controlled toy car as a means to turn on and off a vibrator fixed to the dog's collar. The car has everything you need - hand held radio transmitter/actuator, small radio receiver with antenna, and a small motor that forms the basis of the vibrator. Buy the simplest and cheapest.

Ideally the battery, receiver electronics and on–off switch should be next to each other in a plastic assembly which can be extracted. I broke the car apart until this was all that was left. You want these components to occupy as little space as possible because they will be hanging on your dog's collar.

I also extracted the motor, and glued a small piece of metal to the side of its shaft. The idea is to fix something to the shaft that will cause the motor to be out of balance so that when it runs it will vibrate. Anything will work, even a pebble. Heavier things will cause greater vibrations.

I put the motor in a plastic 35mm film canister (you can get them free at any photo store) and stuffed some paper in to hold it in place.

The battery/receiver/on-off switch assembly, and the vibrator, are sewn onto a collar. It's probably best to sew the antenna in too, and not have it stick up where it might get in the dog's way. If the remote controlled car you started with only runs when activated, then you're finished.

In mine the motor ran all the time, only changing direction. Thus, it vibrated all the time, whether the actuator was pressed or not. To stop this I put a diode in series with one of the leads to the motor. Try the diode in each lead to the motor, and in each direction in each lead, until you hit upon the right lead and direction to do what you want.

If this seems complicated, find a car that is normally stopped and only runs when activated (either backwards or forwards, it doesn't matter).

That's it. I'm happy to try to answer any questions, or to clarify the above.

Bob spindels@aol.com (See **Hearing** and **Hearing dogs**).

DEAF – Dogs for the (See Hearing and Hearing dogs).

Hearing Dogs For The Deaf The Training Centre
London Road (A40), Lewknor, Oxon OX9 5RY. England.

Tel: 01844 353898

Dogs for the deaf

10175 Wheeler Rd., Central Point OR 97502. USA.

(541) 826-9220 – E-mail: info@dogsforthedeaf.org

Web site: http//www.dogsforthedeaf.org

DEATH

Old or sick wolves will leave the pack to die and often a sick domestic dog will find a quiet corner in the garden or house to do so. There are many stories of dogs having said "farewell" to their owner by licking or some other sign of affection before dying from a natural cause. It is said that wolves stretch in the morning to ascertain their position in the pack when a member has left to die during the night

DESTRUCTION

Here's a common scenario…

A dog is left at home alone. It feels insecure and wants something to do. It starts to play with something and destroys it. The owner comes home. The dog is delighted to see the owner. The owner pats the dog. Then he sees the destruction which has taken place and grabs hold of the dog to take it to the scene of the crime. The dog is given verbal and sometimes physical abuse. This is a mistake. A dog should be corrected within five seconds of any wrong-doing, otherwise it will have forgotten what it had done and will not know why it is being punished.

Next time the owner goes out, the dog destroys again and sets in motion the same cycle of events. Consequently, the dog never knows whether its owner will be in a good or bad mood when he returns and therefore acts submissively out of fear, which can be mistaken for guilt. It knows that it has done wrong but doesn't know exactly what it has done wrong.

One solution to this problem is to stuff a Kong – or a bone from which the marrow had been eaten – with liver pills, cheese or biscuits soaked in water and leave this for the dog when you go out. This should keep the dog occupied.

If on your return you discover the dog has destroyed something, you ignore the destruction and instead show the dog the bone or Kong and praise it. If it gets rewarded for chewing the bone or Kong instead of being punished for destroying something, it will eventually stop destroying things while you are away.

DEW CLAWS

Some breeders remove dew claws, though there is now believed to be no good reason for doing so. They are the remnants of the fifth (big) toe which nature removed to give a higher running speed. We humans, with only two legs, need our big toes to help us to balance. (See **Grooming**.)

DIET (See **Food**)

"In order to keep a true perspective of one's importance, everyone should have a dog that will worship him and a cat that will ignore him."
Dereke Bruce.

DIGGING

Dogs that insist on digging up the garden are bored. Try getting a repellent at your local pet store and spray the area. You can also fix a hose with a sprinkler in the area and when the dog digging starts, you turn the tap on.

DISABLED, DOGS FOR THE

The charity Dogs for the Disabled trains dogs to undertake dozens of everyday tasks for the disabled such as:

- Help them get up off the floor if they fall, or raise the alarm.

- Open and close doors, particularly in narrow hallways.

- Help them maintain balance when walking.

- Perform tasks which involve bending and reaching, like emptying a washing machine.

- Retrieve items from around the house.

In short, they provide their owners with greater independence and an increased sense of security and dignity as well as companionship.

The charity was founded in 1986 by Frances Hay, a dog lover, who was herself disabled through bone cancer. Frances trained her own dog, Kim, to carry out tasks that she found increasingly difficult to do. Following her death at the early age of 41, friends and family continued with her work, realising the value of a dog trained to help disabled people. Dogs for the Disabled became a registered charity in 1988.

You can contact Dogs for the Disabled at :
The Old Vicarage, London Rd, Ryton-on-Dunsmore, Coventry CV8 3ER. Publicity and Fundraising: Tel. 01203 302050, Fax 302055. Training Dept: Tel. 01203 302057. E-mail: dfd@dial.pipex.com

---

DISTEMPER

Also called Hardpad Disease, the main danger period of Distemper is eight to 12 weeks. Immunity given to a puppy by its mother quickly wears off, hence injections at 3 to 4 weeks and another at 6 to 16 weeks, thereafter once a year. (See **Symptoms**).

DIVORCE – and your dog

Divorce is a sad fact of life. These human problems can cause stress to dogs. A dog is a social animal bonded to a family routine and a way of life. It relies on us for its mental, physical and emotional welfare.

When it comes to difficulties in relationships, the family pet is often the last to be considered. Couples shouting and arguing with each other will affect the dog (and also the cat). Our blacker moods and tantrums can create nervous behaviour in dogs.

If I am called to a home where there is a dog howling, barking, being destructive, digging, house soiling or showing any signs of anxiety-related behaviour, where it is apparent that the dog has an inability to cope with life, I always ask if there has been a death, separation or a divorce. Any of these could have triggered the problems which are a typical expression of canine anxiety.

Another extreme behaviour pattern is for a dog to go to the bottom of the garden, as far away from the home as possible. It could stay close to walls. This often happens when a dog's instinct tells it that it is dying. In the wild, dogs leave their packs and go away to die. If there is no known medical problem and a separation has taken place, then these behaviour patterns can also be considered an expression of extreme canine anxiety.

Dogs are creatures of habit, functioning to our timetable of wake-up, meals, play, bed, etc. When faced with the upheaval that accompanies divorce, some dogs find it harder to accept a change of routine than others. This is especially so for the older dog, which more often than not may go rapidly downhill.

We have made the dog into a social animal. It is also a sensitve and silent watcher, able to pick up our vibes, react to changes in its schedule or environment or changes in atmosphere caused by arguments within the family.

Marching out in anger and slamming doors will cause stress in a dog. The dog hears the shouting and feels the aggression and this can be frightening. Some owners aware of this will put their dog outside the room when they argue. This can be another form of punishment for the dog,

Sometimes, a dog can have a positive influence. Divorce can cause behavioural changes in a child, from bursts of angry rebellion to periods of deep brooding silence. Dogs play a beneficial role, since a child can make the dog his best friend to be hugged, to be cried with, and to be told any secret, knowing his best friend will neither pass judgement nor tell anyone.

When a couple separate or divorce, my advice is to keep the children and dog (or dogs) together. Sharing a dog between two households rarely works, as this causes stress to the couple, the child and the dog. It is the couple´s responsibility to decide what is best for it now.

Case histories:

I was once called to the home of a very nice lady who told me that her German Shepherd dog Rex had started howling and pacing. I asked the usual questions and found that she had recently separated from her husband. They had agreed he could visit their dog every Sunday to take him to his regular agility class.

I decided it would be in the interest of Rex to arrange to meet both the lady and her ex-husband together. The meeting was not only a strain for them but also for me. They both loved the dog and they both wanted him. As we could not ask the dog with whom it would rather live, I could see that a battle was about to develop. It took me some time to explain the "pack" had split and that Rex could not cope with the separation.

In this particular case, I managed to convince the lady, who was at work all day, that the dog would be more settled with her ex-husband, since he worked from his new home, and maybe she should consider another pet, possibly a cat.

When couples split and the one that the dog regards as "Alpha" goes, then the consequences can be serious.

In another of my cases, the husband left his wife and within a week their dog, a Doberman, had attacked the wife so severely that she had to spend three days in hospital to recover from bites to her leg and arm, which she received when trying to send the dog to bed. The dog is now with the husband and is perfectly well behaved.

A different situation existed at another house to which I was called. There the lady explained that she had recently "lost" one of her dogs and since then her three-year-old Jack Russell was house soiling.

It turned out that when she and her bushand had split up and they had decided to take one dog each. After some further questions I learned that her ex-husband's dog was also soiling and being destructive. So now we had two dogs which were brought up together, very attached, trained and fed together, being suddenly separated and both being unable to cope.

After some discussion, the pair agreed that the dogs should be kept together. All the soiling and howling ceased. Although this ended up in the favour of the dogs, I have also known couples that have separated and would not give up their pet. In these cases one can only advise them that they can expect the related behavioural problems associated with separation.

So if your human relationship is going through a shaky patch, or worse, remember that our pet dogs are unable to ask questions or understand what is going on and that our personal problems can be a direct cause of behavioural problems.

DOG

The word "dog" is derived from the Old English word "docga", of unknown origin. The word has no common derivation among the major European languages (Latin – canis, French – chien, German – hund, Spanish – perro, and Italian – cani). The fact that each European tribe or nationality made up its own name for "dog" seems to indicate the close bondage that developed between each of them and their dogs.

DOG EATING

What a horrible subject, but the fact is in some parts of the world such as China, the Philippines, Vietnam and Korea, dogs are eaten when still young. Perhaps the worst culprits are the Koreans, where it became an accepted practise due to the existence of severe poverty and the fact that there was no dog-human relationship. Greater affluence has raised dog eating to a delicacy but, gradually, what we regard as a disgusting habit is dying out as more households take dogs to their hearts and there now exist organisations trying to eradicate it

DOMINANCE

Nearly everyone can train a submissive dog but a dominant one, general speaking, can only be trained by a dominant person.

Most dogs are not naturally dominant. They become so because they have not been trained correctly or understood properly. In other words, if they are dominant it is the owner's fault. The first steps should be taken when the animal is a puppy (See **Puppy - training**). If an older dog is dominant, remember that the hierarchy of the canine is not created by aggression. It is developed in a pack by submission, one wolf becoming the leader. So you must become the dominant one in your household.

In the wild, the Alpha wolf will sleep with the Alpha bitch possibly a little way away from the rest of the pack. It may also be on higher ground to allow the Alpha to keep keep an eye on the pack. Therefore the "top dogs" of the pack have an exclusive sleeping area.

As the "top dog" in your pack, you should have an exclusive sleeping area. Allowing your dog to share the privileged position of your raised bed could be interpreted by a dominant dog as a sign of weakness.

Sometime in the future, the dog could attempt to become the Alpha and prevent you from getting into your bed.

Dominant dogs will lie in the hall when the rest of the family are in the living room. This enables the dog to see what is going on in all the rooms of the house.

A dominant dog will also sit at the top of the stairs, which gives him status, especially if a human looks down when ascending the stairs. A dominant dog would regard this as submissive behaviour. (See **Ten Commandments**).

DOWN

This is one of the most important exercises which must be taught when the dog is young.

In my social classes, I often blow my whistle and shout: 'The owner of the last dog Down buys a round of drinks". This is called positive reinforcement for humans.

The Down is achieved by putting a little pressure on the back of the dog's neck, never by pulling the legs. It can be assisted by putting the lead on the ground with one foot on the lead beside the dog's neck. Once Down, reward the dog with a pat.

The Down is an excellent way of applying the brakes. It is a submissive posture and tells other dogs " I don't want to fight, I'm friendly." When Down, a dog can't run into traffic, chase or bite a jogger or jump up on guests. (See **Training programmes**).

DREAMING

Do dogs dream? Nobody really knows. There is the argument that being "present living" creatures, they have no memories of the past (except the recall of a bad event triggered by some present action, scent or sound) or thoughts about the future. Twitching legs are believed to be a natural thing for dogs to do. Medical sources say this is more pronounced in dogs that have had distemper. But could they be dreaming they are walking or running?

Imagination, forming mental images of external objects and events not present to the senses, is a requirement for dreaming. Whether dogs can form a mental image of something like a bone has not yet been proved or disproved.

I asked the question about whether or not dogs dream on my Internet forums and these are some of the answers I got. They also serve as a sample of the interesting exchanges among my international friends which can take place on all sorts of dog-related subjects.

- I believe very strongly that dogs dream. I own an almost one-year-old deaf Dalmatian. In his sleep he whines and moves. He also wakes up frightened as if he has had a nightmare. When he sees a hamster or other small animal he will run around the house looking for more. Plenty of times he has woken up and started looking all over the house for a hamster. I believe that he has dreamed of hamsters. Maybe there is no scientific or logical explanation but I believe that he dreams. *Crissy Puppyluv17@aol.com*

- Our "old boy" (BC) certainly seems to. He makes motions with his paws as if running and makes very soft yipping sounds as if chasing something. These both become more pronounced and appear to be accompanied by eye movement. Sometimes the barking builds up to a really loud bark, which wakes him up with a start. The whole picture is certainly what I would interpret as dreaming in a human being. *Steve Napier NZ*

- I am sure my Labrador Vanessa sometimes dreams about a particular person. When she wakes up and sees the person, she goes wild. Lacey, my GSD, has nose twitchy, leg moving, rabbit chasing dreams. *Julie JULIEBOT@aol.com*

- Yes, I think dogs dream. My dogs will frequently be in a deep sleep and then suddenly come to life, eyes still tight-closed, but bodies twitching (especially the feet) and they let out a series of whines/yelps, which I put down to a subconscious reaction to whatever it is they're dreaming about. *Joanne*

- I'm sure dogs dream, but I'm not sure what they dream. How many times have you watched your sleeping dog paddle his legs, wag his tail, and even let out a "woof" whilst sleeping? I try not to interrupt these dream times, but occasionally the dog seems to be upset whilst dreaming and I will touch and talk to him to calm him. Then he will settle down again in a peaceful sleep. I suspect that dogs see images, much like the images we see in our dreams. *Bobbi*

- As I write this one of my dogs is lying asleep on the floor at my feet. His feet are flapping, toes are twitching, breathing is irregular, nose and eyebrows are twitching, and his tail is thumping on the floor. Also his snores are not regular. Snores? So far everyone has mentioned that their dogs yip during their sleep. Am I the only one whose dogs growl? Oh dear, he's just farted. Time to leave the room I think. Most of my dogs dream about chasing things but Barney dreams about guarding everything and anything.
Barbara beejacks@email.msn.com

- Those twitchy paws and legs certainly look like something exciting is going on in the dog's brain! Or is that just me anthropomorphising? *Lynn, "The Dog Lady", dreamily in Bonnie Scotland.*

- I think dogs dream. How else can you explain the twitching nose, the running feet, the growling and barking in sleep? I cannot ask my dogs what they dream about, but I am certain that they dream. Even their eyes move. *Janet Skulina wuwudog@email.msn.com*

Notice: nobody said dogs did **NOT** dream.

DRINKING WATER

A plentiful supply of drinking water should always be available and if you take your dog to another part of the country, take the water it is used to drinking with you.

In the UK, there is a special squad of 12 prison department dog handlers, each with their own vehicle. They are on a 24-hour call to go to any prison in the UK where there is a riot and are required to carry one week's clothing for themselves, one week's supply of food for the dog and one week's supply of water.

This is because it has been established that when given water from another area the dogs did not perform as well as expected. Some were either hyperactive or under active.

Owners entering their dogs in competitions or dog shows should always take their own water. The same rule applies when you have a caravan and go away for a few weeks. If you are away for more than a few weeks, mix the local water with your own water on a 50:50 basis, so that your dog can be weaned with minimal side effects.

DROWNING (See **First aid**.)

DRUG AND EXPLOSIVE DETECTION

It is generally believed that a dog must be trained to seek out specific drugs or explosives. However, recent research shows that dogs can detect multiple odours. It is claimed that a dog trained on a new single-odour product from the Max Plank Institute in Germany can locate any of the 19,000 available explosive compounds. The product is called Sokks Octogen and is a combination of the explosive odours from the 20 different categories of explosives.

EATING SLOWLY

A dog that is a slow eater is inclined to be dominant. Most dogs are scavengers and it is not natural for them to be picky with food and walk away from a bowl leaving uneaten food. The dog is assuming that no member of the human pack would dare touch its food.

A dog should never be fed from the table or hand, for then we are being submissive by offering the food, with the implication that the dog is more important.

All food should be picked up after five minutes. By picking up the food and not offering it until the next meal time, we teach the dog to eat quickly. There is also the hygienic bonus of the food not attracting flies or other insects. (See also **Food**).

EGGS

Research has shown that the enzyme avidin, which is found in egg whites, destroys biotin, a B complex vitamin. Bioten deficiencies can occur in humans and animals that eat raw egg whites.

However, some experts say a dog would have to be fed six to 12 raw eggs a day to have a bad effect, but better be safe than sorry.

Despite what your friends may tell you, feeding your dog on a high quality canine diet is a much more healthy way of ensuring a shiny coat. Cooked eggs do not pose such a danger as the avidin is destroyed and they can be given as an occasional treat for dogs that are not obese.

ELECTRIC COLLARS

By Lou Castle, Los Angeles, CA

There is an excellent videotape produced by Tri-Tronics, one of the major E-collar makers. It discusses maintenance, battery charging and shows how to teach the Recall, Down and

Stay with the collar. If you can teach those, you can teach just about everything.

Here's the right way to start with an E-collar. Put the collar on the dog and give a stimulation at the lowest level. Most dogs will not show any indication that anything is happening. I know I can't feel those levels.

Change the power level (the control on some is on the collar, others on the sending unit) and go up one notch. Continue until the dog reacts, usually something like an ear flick. Some dogs will turn around, as if a piece of paper unexpectedly had hit them on the side. Some will scratch, as if a flea had just bitten them. This is the training level for that dog.

For aversive training a high prey drive dog, you should go up two levels from this, because the dog's drive will be invoked by the prey animal or object. The most modern of collars have three levels of stimulation. If you press button one, the dog gets the "base" level of stimulation. If you press button two, the dog gets a slightly higher level. If you press one and two together, the dog gets a still higher level of stimulation.

When the dog starts to show interest in the prey animal or object give the dog a short "low" correction. If it persists, immediately step up to the high level. As soon as it turns away, stop the stimulation. They seem to think at first that the ground directly in front of them is hot, or it's as if the dog ran into a sharp object in the ground.

Far too many trainers either wait too long to deliver the stimulation and the dog is deep in Drive and unreachable with any known aversive, or just throw the highest level plug in the collar and off they go.

One doesn't have to be an expert or a genius to use an E-collar. But one does have to understand the basics. Some common sense helps, too.

Personally, I still think reward based training is best.

(David the Dogman).

ELIZABETHAN COLLAR

A large, winged collar similar to an Elizabethan ruff used by vets after a dog has had an operation or if a dog is licking an area under treatment. Many owners are upset because their dogs dislike them but after 24 hours most dogs will accept them.

It is now being replaced in many countries by a new style which is clamped around the dog's neck with Velcro. It has no wings so the dog is able to move around normally and not knock into doors, which can happen with an Elizabethan collar.

EPILEPSY

A dog suffering from epileptic fits can be given medication by the vet and it has been proved that the number or frequency of attacks can be reduced by lowering the dominance of the dog. (See **Ten Commandments**).

ESCAPING

Even if fenced in securely with the bottom of the fence dug into the ground, a dog which has not been castrated will attempt to escape (and probably succeed) if it scents a bitch on heat up to a mile away. The answer? Have it castrated. (See **Castration, Excuses**).

EUTHANASIA

Your relationship with your dog is special. You are responsible for its care and welfare. Eventually there comes a most difficult life or death decision for the welfare of the animal and for you and your family.

The decision is a personal one but it need not be a solitary one. Your vet and your family and friends can assist and support you. Consider not only what is best for your dog but also what is best for you and your family. Quality of life is important for pets and people alike.

If your dog can no longer enjoy the things which once gave it pleasure, or if there is more pain than quality in its life, if your dog is terminally ill or critically injured, or if the financial or emotional cost of treatment is beyond your means, euthanasia may be the only option.

It also might be necessary if a dog has become vicious, dangerous, or unmanageable, but remember some undesirable and abnormal behaviour can be changed with a qualified behaviourist.

Economic and emotional problems together with changes in lifestyle may also force an owner to consider euthanasia of a dog. Obviously it is better to find another solution or an alternative home for these pets.

Your vet understands attachment to pets and can examine and evaluate your dog's condition, estimate your dog's chances for recovery, discuss potential disabilities and long-term problems, explain the medical options and possible outcomes. But he cannot make the euthanasia decision for you.

It is very important that you fully understand your dog's condition. If there is any part of the diagnosis or the implications for your dog's future that you don't understand, ask to have it explained again. Rarely will the situation require an immediate decision. Usually, there will be time to review the facts.

Eventually you may wish to discuss the disposal of your dog's body with your family and vet. You have several options and your vet can provide information about burial, cremation or other alternatives.

Discuss with the family what the vet has said.. Long-term medical care could be a burden, either emotionally or financially. Encourage family members to express their thoughts and feelings. Even if you have reached a decision, family members, especially children, should have their feelings considered.

Children have special relationships with their pets. Excluding or protecting children from this decision-making process, because they are thought to be too young to understand, may only complicate their grieving. Children respect straightforward, truthful, and simple answers. If they are prepared adequately, they are usually able to accept a dog's death.

Euthanasia is almost always accomplished by injection of a death-inducing drug. Your vet may administer a tranquilliser first to relax your dog. Following the death-inducing injection, your dog will immediately go into a quiet and irreversible deep unconsciousness. Death will come quickly and painlessly.

The act of saying goodbye is an important step in managing the natural and healthy feelings of grief, sorrow, and sense of loss. Your dog is an important part of your life and it is natural to feel you are losing a friend..

Once the decision for euthanasia has been made, you and other family members may want to say goodbye to your dog. A last evening with your dog at home or a visit to the dog at the hospital may be appropriate. Family members who want to be alone with the animal should be allowed to do so. Farewells are always difficult.

After your dog has died, it is natural and normal to feel grief and sorrow. The grieving process includes accepting the reality of your loss, accepting that the loss and accompanying feelings are painful, and adjusting to your new life that no longer includes your dog. (See **Bereavement**).

"Did you ever walk into a room
and forget why you walked in?
I think that is how dogs spend their lives."
Sue Murphy

Rainbow Bridge

Just this side of Heaven is a place called Rainbow Bridge. When an animal dies that has been especially close to someone here, that pet goes to Rainbow Bridge. There are meadows and hills for all of our special friends so they can run and play together.

There is plenty of food, water and sunshine and our friends are warm and comfortable.

All the animals who had been ill and old are restored to health and vigour; those who were hurt or maimed are made whole and strong again, just as we remember them in our dreams of days and times gone by.

The animals are happy and content, except for one small thing: they each miss someone very special, someone who was left behind.

They all run and play together, but the day comes when one suddenly stops and looks into the distance. His bright eyes are intent; his eager body begins to quiver. Suddenly, he breaks from the group, flying over the green grass, faster and faster.

You have been spotted, and when you and your special friend finally meet, you cling together in joyous reunion, never to be parted again.

The happy kisses rain upon your face; your hands again caress the beloved head, and you look once more into those trusting eyes, so long gone from life, but never absent from your heart.

Then you cross the Rainbow Bridge together...

Internet author unknown.

EXCUSES for not castrating or neutering

1. Just one litter and then we'll have her spayed. (Studies show that virtually the entire pet overpopulation stems from the "just one litter" mentality.)

2. My dog doesn't run loose, so he doesn't need to be fixed. (Murphy's Law says otherwise.)

3. We can always find homes for the puppies. (And that means that an equal number of puppies at the animal shelter or pound will be killed instead of being given a home.)

4. I want the children to witness the miracle of birth. (Rent a video.)

5. My dog is so cute and unique, there should be more of her. (The shelters and pounds are full of cute and unique dogs, most with only a few days to live.)

6. It's not natural. (There hasn't been anything "natural" about dogs since we began to develop breeds thousands of years ago.)

7. I just couldn't look my dog in the eye if I had him castrated. (That's anthropomorphising.)

8. A female dog or cat should have at least one litter for health reasons. (Medically, factually and ethically indefensible.)

9. Neutering my dog will make him fat and lazy. (Too much food and not enough exercise make a dog fat and lazy.)

10. Fixing my pet will change its personality. (The main influences on an animal's personality are the kindness and care with which it is raised.)

EXERCISE

Don't exercise a dog strenuously straight after feeding. Always wait for a minimum of one hour, otherwise it can be extremely dangerous and result in stomach torsion, a twisting which prevents gasses from escaping. Unless prompt veterinary attention is sought, this condition can be fatal. Likewise, do not feed your dog directly after exercise as stomach torsion can also result.

However, gentle exercise after eating burns up more calories by raising the body's rate of metabolism. It is better than allowing the dog to lie down to digest its food, for while sleeping a pet will burn up a only a few calories, just enough to keep its heart and lungs going. This can result in weight gain.

It makes sense to take your dog for a walk of not more than a half-hour after the two meals of the day. This very gentle exercise will also stimulate its digestion. Then, after a few hours have passed, you can let the dog enjoy more strenuous exercise..

For smaller breeds, simply taking a dog outdoors to relieve itself gives a certain amount of exercise. This assists but does not cause defecation, for a dog does not need exercise to loosen his bowels unless it is ill.

Taking a dog on a daily run is not necessarily in its best interest. Dogs should never be run on hard surfaces such as pavements or paved roads but on earth, and certainly should not be made to run behind your car. If you insist on having your dog jog with you, then make the pace a fast walk or trot rather than a run, but don't do this in hot weather and always check the dog's feet after a run for cuts and rawness.

Medium and large breeds should not be allowed excessive exercise, or do agility work, until at least 18-months-old, and even then with caution. Often a weakness will remain dormant in young bones if they are subjected to extreme exercise. Throwing a ball in a park for an hour could bring on a problem. Dogs do not need as much exercise as many think.

A dog should never be allowed out alone even if it has a name tag on its collar. It is an offence in most European countries for it to be roaming on public streets or highways where it can still be classified as a stray dog and impounded by the police or a dog warden.

Dog owners are legally responsible for any damage caused by their dog. If your dog's actions result in a traffic accident you may well have to pay compensation for damaged vehicles or injured persons and this could be substantial. (See **Insurance**).

No dog can ever be 100 per cent reliable when walking along a road off its lead. A sudden noise, a car back-firing, or the sight of a cat could cause the dog to bolt. Only luck will determine if the dog runs out in front of a car. So don't show off by walking your dog without a lead besides a busy road. A live dog on a lead is better than a dead one off it. (See **Walkies**).

EXTRA SENSORY PERCEPTION

ESP is a sixth sense which cannot be verified. However some dogs do have unexplainable abilities.

There are many tales of dogs returning to their owner's home from great distances. One dog, left behind by its owners in New York when they moved to California, turned up at their new home 11 months later.

Tales of dogs waiting outside hospitals where their owners are having treatment and staying by graves are fairly common.

The most famous was "Greyfriars Bobby" who visited the Edinburgh grave of his owner for years. Bobby died on January 14, 1872, and there is a headstone on his grave which reads:

"LET HIS LOYALTY AND DEVOTION BE A LESSON TO US ALL".

My Internet friend Roy Brackenbury, a former police dog handler and instructor, tells of two incidents:

In the first, he and his dog, King, were patrolling at night a graveyard where there had been robberies. King suddenly froze beside a grave, like a pointer with one front leg raised and tail parallel to ground. He grumble-growled. Roy could see nothing yet the dog would not move or be dragged along. When Roy picked King up in his arms to walk past the grave, the dog became a dervish and could not be held.

In the second incident, he and King were patrolling an art gallery from which a painting had been stolen, when the dog clearly signalled that there was a man up a chimney. Roy looked and saw nothing. Then King suddenly flew across the room and hurled himself at a door. At the same time, Roy heard a child's high pitched voice say seven or eight words. He could not understand what was said, but it was definitely a child's voice behind a locked door.

So what do you think? Those stories come from an experienced policeman with a highly trained dog. I believe him. There must have been some supernatural force at work and that dog had ESP. *(roybrackenbury@dogging.demon.co.uk)*

No doubt you have heard of similar weird events. Maybe some dogs have a heightened ESP, like some humans claim to have supernatural abilities.

EYE CONTACT

A dog about to attack will stare you or another dog in the eyes. This eye contact is also used by a bitch to rebuke a puppy. If you want to ignore a dog, do not make eye contact.

EYES (See **Sight**)

FAECES EATING

Coprophagia, to give the proper name, is a natural form of behaviour which most dogs learn from puppyhood when their mother will clean up after them. It happens more in puppies which come from rescue kennels and pet shops.

It can also be started by poor house-training where owners do not clean up after the pup.

Boredom is another cause. Dogs that spend long periods alone in the garden or in kennels can develop this habit. In kennels, dogs will copy other dogs doing it.

Don't rub a dog's nose in its excrement This only teaches dogs to eat the evidence to avoid punishment. Don't shout or chase the dog away. It will only learn to eat faster.

Do remove the faeces, for they encourage flys and mosquitoes. Also treat faeces with Tabasco or peppers. The dog will not find that taste very rewarding.

It could be the dog is just hungry. Split the daily food ration into several portions and feed the dog three or four times a day with a higher fibre content.

Alternatively, the dog could have a health problem. There is a condition called exocrine pancreatic insufficiency, where a lack of enzymes in the pancreas will result in dogs being ravenously hungry. Dogs suffering from this will eat anything.

Although the eating of faeces is absolutely repellent to humans, the smell and texture is attractive to dogs. They have a different palate to our own. (see **Taste**). If all else fails, only allow the dog off lead with a muzzle. (See **Muzzles**).

FASHION ACCESSORIES

A lot of people make a lot of money selling them to humans. Sensible dogs would not waste their money on them.

FEAR

A timid dog can react aggressively when frightened and there are a whole variety of things which can induce fear in any dog. The main antidote is not to react by trying to soothe the dog as that reinforces its belief that there really is something to be fearful about. Drown fear with confidence and authority. (See **Shyness** and **Strangers**).

FEAR IMPRINT PERIOD

This is a critical period in a puppy's life from around eight to 12 weeks when a bad experience can have a lasting effect, and memories of these past bad experiences can be triggered in later life by sounds, sights and smells associated with those experiences.

FEDERATION of DOG TRAINERS and CANINE BEHAVIOURISTS.

(See **Trainers' organisations**).

FENCES

If you are a DIY enthusiast and decide to build a fence to keep a dog in a garden, beware of using pressure treated wood which can contain dangerous carcinogenic toxins, including arsenic.

FIGHTING

A dog which fights another has nearly always lacked early socialisation. Normally, as long as there is no human interference, dogs will quickly sort out which is the dominant one without causing much damage to each other as long as they are off the lead.

Putting a lead on a dog, when you see another dog approaching, teaches it that it must get to that other dog quickly to escape the punishment of being put on the lead. Take the dog to a training class where it can socialise.

"One dog is a pet, two are a problem and three are a disaster waiting to happen". Two male dogs will fight over status or because of jealousy over you. A behaviourist can analyse who is the Alpha. Once this has been established, and there must be no error, then the junior should be castrated to reduce his status. This normally stops the fighting.

Two female dogs that fight are another matter altogether. It is no good having one of them spayed and the only real answer is to find one of them another home.

An older dog and a newly acquired puppy can work out how to live together if you allow nature to take its course. Simply walk away when the older one gets vocal. Feed and pet the older dog first. If they start fighting, always walk away because your presence causes jealousy. Similarly, when you touch the young pup you put your scent on it and the older one gets jealous. (See **Aggression** and **Bitches fighting**).

Film fan

I went to the cinema the other day and in the front row was an old man and his dog. The film was both sad and funny in parts. The dog cried its eyes out during the sad bits and laughed at the funny parts. After the film, I said to the man: "That's the most amazing thing I've ever seen. Your dog really seemed to enjoy the film." He said: "Yes, it is amazing. He hated the book."

FIRST AID

When a dog is involved in an accident of any kind, it is important to keep calm. If you get agitated, upset or panic, the dog will also be affected. It may come to you for help or it may bite if you are seen as the source of its pain or because you make the pain worse.

Traffic accidents

These are the major cause of injury and are most likely to result in aggressiveness. If you have to move the dog, do so on something solid or a blanket if nothing else is available. Stop any bleeding by holding a handkerchief or pad over the wound and apply a tourniquet if possible, but not for more than 10 minutes. Get the dog to a vet quickly.

Burns

There are a whole variety of things that can cause burns from scalding water, chemicals to electric wires. Run cool water in a steady stream over the affected part before taking the dog to a vet.

Choking

If you can get your fingers around the object choking the dog, you may be able to pull it out but there is a danger you will push it further down the throat. You can try putting both hands on its stomach just in front of the hind legs and lifting the dog's back up into the air several times. Pumping the chest as for Drowning may also help.

Drowning

Not all dogs can swim. After rescuing the dog from the water, try to empty its lungs of water as soon as possible. Place the dog's head lower than its body, open its mouth and begin to pump the chest by pressing down on the ribs and releasing the pressure immediately. Repeat at five-second intervals.

Heat stroke (See **Heat danger**)

Poisoning

Signs of poisoning may include collapse, muscular twitching, vomiting, bleeding or convulsion. If you see your dog pick up a poisonous object, don't panic because the dog could swallow it quickly to prevent you from taking it away. Calmly try

119

to distract it with a tit-bit or toy. If you're too late but know the poison has been swallowed recently, try to make the dog sick with salt and mustard in water. Take whatever the cause of poisoning was with you to the vet. (See **Poisons**).

Stings and bites

Dogs will shrug off most insect bites and stings more easily than a human. But there are dogs, like humans, who can have a severe allergic reaction. If there is severe swelling, vomiting, a high temperature or obvious pain, get to a vet.

Snakes rarely attack unless cornered and most of them are harmless anyway if they are the same colour all over or have stripes running down the body. The dangerous ones are thin vipers and those with stripes around the body, diamond backs, or with a blotchy pattern, or with fangs for injecting poison. Get the dog to a vet quickly and, if possible, take the snake (better dead) with you.

FLEAS

Fleas live everywhere. They attach themselves to dogs only to feed. They do not live on dogs. A preventative is Program, a monthly tablet which stop the fleas feeding. You can give your dog a small amount of garlic. Too much can cause enterogastritis. If you see fleas on your dog, use a spray (there are many products on the market) and groom regularly. Use a "Zoom Groom" which has rubber "fingers" to pull out all the dirt and dead hairs. Put some of this in a few drops of water. If it turns pinkish red, your dog has a flea problem. The colour is caused by flea excrement. Vacuuming carpets will help to get rid of the larvae. Chemical treatment may be the only answer if the infestation is general.

The latest research through a U.K. Canine Health Census has shown that some chemical flea treatments are dangerous. They include shampoos with chemicals which can cause cancer, sprays which attack the central nervous system, and flea collars that children must not touch but which pets can have around their necks for up to four months.

For dogs with a flea problem, Catherine O'Driscoll of the Canine Health Census recommends that you first give your pet a complete vitamin and mineral supplement. Fleas do not like certain vitamins and minerals, which act as an effective natural repellent. If fleas are causing a big problem, a homeopathic vet should be consulted. The problem be an indication of hypersensitivity caused by vaccines.

For more information contact Catherine O'Driscoll Canine Health Census, PO Box, 1 Longnor, Derbyshire, SK17 0JD U.K. E-mail: CODriscoll@aol.com

FLOPPY EARS

Like those on a wolf, a dog's natural ears are upright and can be turned to focus on a sound. Dogs with upright ears are good at hearing. Man's breeding has created dogs with floppy ears to reduce the distraction of sounds, thus allowing the dog to concentrate on the scent. Some people also think they look prettier.

FLYBALL RACING

By Kevin McNicholas., member of the Federation of Dog Trainers and Canine Behaviourists. (See **Acknowledgements**).

This is a relay race in which two teams of four dogs, in separate 51 foot lanes, race over four low hurdles adjusted in height depending on the smallest dogs in the teams.

At the end of each lane is a Flyball box with a pedal which the dog has to push to release a tennis ball into the air. The dog has to catch the ball and race back across the hurdles to the owner at the start. Then the next member of the team continues the race until four dogs and four balls are over the line.

121

I believe Flyball is the most exciting and enjoyable dog sport that has been invented. There is no more electrifying and exciting competition to be found than watching two teams of Flyball dogs racing neck and neck against each other.

Flyball is the only dog sport that is the same all over the world, comparisons can be made between dogs and teams and it is the only dog sport with meaningful world and national record holders.

It was invented in California in the late 70's when Herbert Wagner showed the first Flyball box on the Johnny Carson Show to millions of Americans. Soon afterwards, dog trainers and dog clubs were making and using Flyball boxes.

Growing rapidly in the USA and Canada, it is also becoming one of the most popular dog sports in Europe, where there are now over 100 Flyball teams. It is easy to see the reason why. All dogs love playing it.

Watching a Flyball race you may mistakenly think that the dogs are out of control. Nothing is further from the truth. Flyball dogs are some of the best-trained dogs in the world. They have to be because they are competing in a very distracting environment with dogs running past them and balls all around. Only the fittest dogs with superb Recalls and accurate Retrieves will succeed in fast and competitive 30 race tournaments.

The benefits of Flyball are:

- Excellent Recalls even in a very distracting environment.

- Keeps you and your dog fit and improves its stamina.

- Teaches dogs to work in close proximity to other dogs and people.

- Aids good social skills.

- Exercises the minds of dogs because when things go wrong the dog has to work out the solution on it's own, the handler being 20 yards away.

- Improves general dog training skills: Heel, Sit, Stay and Down are essential qualities of a Flyball dog,
- Teaches positive attitudes and motivation,
- Provides fun for both dog and handler.

For more information about Flyball training, competitions, and instructor training in the UK or Europe contact: Kevin McNicholas, 50 Tudor Road, Barnet, Herts, England, UK EN5 5NP. Tel 0181 449 7539.

FLYING

Check with the airline about the crate which should be used. The way dogs cope depends on breed, size and temperament. Tranquilisers can be given if you have a nervous dog but are not generally necessary. Double check that the dog has been loaded. The hold is air-conditioned and usually lit in the part occupied by animals. After landing, try to make sure the dog is taken to the baggage claim area by truck, not put on the conveyor belt from which the crate can fall.

Like flying with children, you have to take extra bits and pieces as well as food and water. One advantage: dogs do not complain.

FOOD

At least 30 per cent of my clients who have behavioural problems with their dogs find that a change of food alters some, if not all, of the unwanted behaviour. If your dog has been fed incorrectly and you wish to switch to a dry food, remember that dogs are influenced by smell, not taste. So, instead of simply offering the dry food, try mixing some powdered liver treats or a meat extract gravy in it for a few days until the dog accepts the change in diet.

I recommend that a dog is fed on meal from one of the leading dog food manufacturers and not tinned meat, which has a high percentage of water (See **Food - tinned**), or specially cooked chicken, vegetables or anything else. A good dog meal will provide all the proteins and vitamins a dog needs. The recommended portion might look small but it can swell up to three or four times in the dog's stomach. Even though a "dry" meal actually contains up to 10% of water, a plentiful supply of water should always be available.

Dogs generally eat enough food to meet their energy needs. If the food is high in nutrients, providing a large number of kilo-calories per cup, the dog needs to eat less of the food to meet its energy requirement.

The main problem is that most feeding directions are based on an average size dog or puppy. The formula used to calculate the energy requirement of this theoretical dog depends on the number of kilo-calories of metabolised energy per kilogram of body weight with allowances for growth.

Since these are average figures, and since no two dogs are the same, these feeding directions can be misleading because many dogs are unlikely to fit the average.Another unfortunate fact is that some marketing departments use feeding directions as a sales tool, stating that less food is required because of the alleged high quality of the product.

Determine the correct amount for your dog by starting with the recommended level on the bag. Increase or decrease the amount according to the dog's appearance. For example, if you have a 20lb dog eating one-and-a-half cups per day and it starts gaining weight, decrease to one cup or, if the dog begins to lose weight, increase the daily intake to two cups. Split the amount into two or three portions depending on how often a day the dog is fed.

All puppies and young dogs up to the age of 12 months should be fed three meals a day. Adult dogs from 12 months to eight years should be fed two meals a day. When the dog gets older, after around eight years, it should again be fed three meals a day.

Care should be taken not to over feed any dog, either puppies, adults or older dogs. Overweight animals usually have more health problems than those at their proper weight. If you do not know what your dog's ideal weight should be, ask your vet. (See **Obesity**).

The problem of quality.

Dog foods vary in quality. So does the quality and competence of some of the companies that make the food. Ultimately, the quality of a dog food is best measured by your dog. How it performs, how it looks, feels and acts are the best measures of the quality of any food. No matter what a food company claims, unless your dog has bright eyes, silky hair and supple skin and is not overweight, the food is not right for it.

Not all dogs do well on a particular brand of food. Some dogs simply do better than others. Most foods are classified as Economy, Regular, Premium, Super Premium and Performance with different formulas.

Don't buy the cheapest. It can lack all the necessary ingredients for a balanced diet. I know of one Labrador whose owners bought a cheap meal and the dog's coat became dull. As soon as they switched to a better, well-known brand, the dogís coat became shiny again.

Dogs have simple stomachs and short digestive tracts for digesting meat. They also lack the saliva enzyme amylase, which is necessary for pre-digesting starch. Pet dogs have adapted to foods with high vegetable protein levels, but they perform better when fed foods high in meat protein and animal fats.

When you check the label of a Super Premium or Performance food, an animal protein will be listed as the first or second major ingredient. These should include either chicken, or turkey meat, or poultry by-products, pork or other animal by-products. Fat or oil should be included for adequate energy and essential fatty acids.

Fat in food is the dog's source of energy. Animal fat contains essential and non-essential fatty acids as well as providing a highly digestible and easily metabolised energy source. Generally, poultry fat is better because it has more unsaturated fatty acids and is more digestible than animal tallow.

Vegetable oils, such as soybean oil, corn oil, wheat germ oil, sesame seed oil or linseed oil all contain high levels of linoleic acid, an essential fatty acid for dogs. These should be combined with animal fats for the best long-term results by producing a glossy hair coat and soft pliable skin.

Carbohydrates are the third most important nutrient and ingredient class in modern Super Premium and Performance foods. Simple carbohydrates in dog food come from quality cereal sources like rice, oatmeal, corn or wheat. These are easily digested when properly prepared.

Fibre, a complex carbohydrate, is essential for proper digestion and stool formation. Sources of fibre include rice, soya hulls, oat hulls, wheat bran and peanut hulls. All these come from the external portion of the seed coat. These sources, except peanut hulls, have microscopic sharp edges, which can cause small cuts in the intestine. This reduces the intestine's effectiveness in nutrient digestion. Peanut hulls, on the other hand, have the potential of being contaminated with aflatoxins and should never be used in a quality dog or cat food.

Vitamin and mineral fortification is an absolute necessity in nutritionally balancing any food for dogs. While the vitamins and minerals generally make up less than 2% of the total food by weight, they provide some of the most crucial nutrients. Often the list of these micro-nutrients is much longer than the list of major ingredients. Expect to see this list on the label of all dog foods. Super Premium usually feature more than one source for each vitamin and mineral. Don't add anything by way of food supplement or vitamin to Super Premium Foods.

Some meal is made to look more attractive to humans by including red, yellow and green dyes. The implication is the colours represent meat, cereal and vegetables The result may look attractive to a human (not to a dog that will only see the colours as faint pastel shades), but there is evidence that these dyes can produce hyperactivity and cause destructive behaviour. Too much salt and sugar can also be detrimental.

Never give your dog any snacks and certainly no sugar, sweets or chocolates. Neither should they have raw fruit or vegetables, raw cereals, nuts (not processed or roasted), avocados, olives, carrots, apples or milk.

After your dog has eaten, wipe under the chin where it cannot lick. Any food left sticking to the dog's fur in that area can attract insects or mosquitoes, including the so-called sand-fly which in hot climates can carry the incurable leichmaniasis disease. (See **Leichmaniasis**).

Final fact: A dog can survive up to three weeks without food but it would die in days without water.

Case history:

Question: "I am giving my dog a good quality dried food recommended by our vet, but I always add some meat or chicken because it looks so boring. Can this do any harm?"

Answer: Most vets recommend a complete dried food diet. It is really detrimental to add any supplement to dry food. This will create an imbalance in the balanced food and most behavioural problems stem from incorrect feeding. Red meat or any high protein can cause aggressiveness or nervousness. High protein can also increase the scale of aggression, moods, and jumpiness.

FOOD ALLERGIES.

Food allergies can cause dermatological discomfort. It has been estimated that at least 1% of all skin problems in cats and dogs are caused by dietary allergies. These can be triggered in minutes, hours or days. Sensitivity to an allergy caused by a protein can often be life-long.

Some dogs can digest the lactose in cow's milk while the undigested lactose quickly produces an upset stomach with others. This is not a true allergy but demonstrates how sensitive to certain food pets can be. Stop the milk.

Most dogs react in some way to incorrect feeding and, apart from allergic reactions, flatulence and inconsistent stool quality and large smelly motions can result. If the balance of the food is incorrect, hyperactivity or indeed low activity can be the consequence.

High values of soya and/or wheat could result in a low oil level - on average about 2.3% - and a dog needs three times that amount. Protein used up for energy can produce a loss of coat and skin vitality. Many owners give far too many vitamins. A well balanced diet should not have to be supplemented.

Scratching and licking could be an indication of an allergic reaction to food and the eating of grass, twigs and roots sometimes is an indication that the food is not being digested properly. The destruction of fibre-based material could be another sign that there is a craving for fibre to help the digestive process in some way.

Many pet shops and vets are now selling artificial bones. Beware of anything coloured since this must have an additive. I would only buy one which had a label stating what chemicals had been added. These toys have been known to cause hyperactivity and low activity. If your dog needs something to chew, try a rope or Kong stuffed with goodies which can occupy your pet for hours. (See **Kong**).

Food – tinned.

The profits to be made from selling tinned pet foods are highlighted by the immense sums spent by some manufacturers on advertising their products. When the water or moisture content can be as high as 80%, this makes a tin of dog food the most expensive way of buying water in the world. The one advantage tinned food has over meal is that there is no need for the dog to drink so much water

The manufacturers rely a great deal on anthropomorphism with their advertising, persuading humans that dogs are going to like the taste of the many varieties available better than a good meal which has all the necessary ingredients to keep the dog healthy. They ignore the fact that a dog's taste buds are five times lower than those of a human.

Empty a tin of dog food. Doesn't that meat jelly look good? But has it been produced by mixing an indigestible gelling agent with water plus a bit of colouring thrown in? Sometimes that is all it is and not so good as it looks.

A change in diet is often the cure for many behavioural problems. Buy a bag of meal, not a tin of water. (See **Food**, **Overweight dogs** and **Taste**).

FOOT ON A DOG'S BACK

Ever noticed that when one dog meets another that one sometimes rests its head on the other's neck or back? They do this as a sign of being the dominant dog. So when watching television place a foot lightly on the dog's back if it is sitting near you. This is a subtle way to indicate to the dog that you are the dominant one.

FURNITURE

Suggestion: put silver tinsel paper on the furniture to frighten the dog off. Easier still: keep it out of the room.

GAMES

A dog invites another dog or its owner to play a chasing game by putting its head and chest on the ground with paws straight ahead and its bottom up in the air on stretched back legs. This is called the "play bow" Whatever games you play with your dog you must ALWAYS WIN. (See **Balls for play**, **Tricks** and **fun**).

GARLIC

Many dog owners, including myself, swear that garlic is effective for natural flea control, even though there is no scientific evidence to support this claim and it is thought too much garlic can cause gastro-enteritis. Even so, we still believe small quantities can deter fleas and ticks. (See **Ticks**).

Scientists from the Weizmann Institute of Science in Israel have claimed that garlic may ward off infections from the common cold to E Coli disease. Researchers have found that fresh garlic disarms many poisons found in bacteria, viruses and fungi, which supports claims that garlic keeps cholesterol levels down and acts as an anti-oxidant.

So, while you are preparing garlic for your cat or dog's dinner, have some yourself. Some claim it is an effective way of stopping a cold.

GERMAN SHEPHERD (See **Top Dogs**).

GLAUCOMA

There are two types of glaucoma, one Primary and genetic, the other Secondary. Often, failing sight due to glaucoma occurs as the dog reaches old age. Several new techniques to manage it are now being developed and, when they have been tried and tested, there may well be a solution in a few year's time. Until then, drops in the eye can be an effective palliative measure to maintain sight for as long as possible. This gradual loss of sight is compensated by an improvement in the dog's ability to scent and hear (See **Cataracts** and **Sight**.)

GOLDEN RETRIEVER (See **Top Dogs**)

GOOD CITIZEN TEST

If your dog does not pass all these tests, you need the help of a good dog trainer.

1. **Appearance and grooming**. Your dog should be well groomed and allow someone else to groom it.

2. **Accepting strangers**. Dogs should not jump up, be resentful or shy when you meet somebody during a walk or when visitors come to your home.

3. **Walking on the lead**. The owner should always be in control.

4. **Walking through a crowd**. Dogs might show curiosity, but shouldn't strain on the lead.

5. **In town**. Dogs should be happy for strangers to approach and pet them.

6. **Sit and Down**. The dog should respond to these instructions.

7. **Stay**. Dogs should Stay in the Sit or Down position while the handler moves away and only come when the handler instructs them to do so.

8. **Meeting other dogs**. Although they may show interest, dogs should not leave their handlers to meet other dogs.

9. **Reacting to distractions**. Dogs should not panic, try to run away, show aggressiveness, or bark, although they may show natural interest and curiosity.

10. **Left alone**. Dogs should not bark, whine, howl or pace unnecessarily when left alone.

I am indebted to behaviourist Sheilagh B. Wilson, UK APDT 00441, Sheilagh's K9 Centre in Central Scotland (See **Acknowledgements**) for permission to reproduce her canine good citizen tests:

"There are three parts which must be passed to be awarded a collar tag. Parts I and II, for which a certificate is awarded, can normally be obtained after an eight-week course. Sections with a bracketed number after them are the same as the Kennel Club CGC test.

Part I.

1) Dog allows owner to groom and handle ears, eyes, mouth and paws. (7 + 8)

2) Owner can use the lead as a temporary collar while they remove the collar and show the examiner the dog's ID tags. (2)

3) The dog Sits and Downs on command.

4) Dog and handler can walk for 10 paces on a loose lead.

5) The dog will return to the handler when called with no distractions. (9)

6) Owner can produce a plastic bag (poop bag) and describe its use. (1)

Part II

1) Dog allows petting from a stranger.

2) Dog greets a stranger without jumping up.

3) The dog stays in a Sit or Down for 30 seconds next to handler.

4) Dog and handler can walk on a loose lead including about turn and halt. (3)

5) The dog will return to the handler and Sit in front when called with no distractions.

6) The dog will ignore an offered treat if told by handler to "leave it".

Part III

1) Dog allows stranger to handle ears, eyes, mouth and paws.

2) Dog and owner can pass through a door or gateway in a controlled manner. (4)

3) The dog stays in a Sit or Down on lead while the owner goes a distance of five metres for one minute.

4) Dog and handler can walk on a loose lead with distractions, including joggers and other dogs passing by.

5) The dog returns to the handler to Sit in front despite distractions.

6) Dog remains calm while owner holds a conversation with another handler and their dog for one minute (5).

Road safety test beginners' section

1) Basic heel work pattern including three Sits when handler halts and two about turns.

2) A novice recall with present (front) and a finish to Heel.

3) A one minute Sit Stay

4) A two minute Down Stay both with handler five metres away.

Intermediate section.

1) Heel work both on and off lead, including four Sits at Heel and about turns. An "A recall" where the dog is called while the handler walks away and joins the handler in the Heel position, sitting when the handler stops. Dog and handler finish by about turning.

2) A two minute Sit Stay in sight with the handler 10 metres away.

3) A three minute Down Stay with handler out of dog's sight.

Advanced section.

1) Heel work both on and off the lead at a fast and slow pace with two Downs on the move. The handler Downs the dog without stopping, about turns passing the dog, about turns again and picks up the dog into Heel position when passing.

2) A stop on recall. A novice recall where the dog is stopped at a set position and then recalled as normal. The dog may be stopped in either the Sit, Stand or Down as chosen by the handler.

3) A two minute Sit Stay with the handler out of dog's sight.

4) A four minute Down Stay with the handler out of dog's sight.

Senior advanced section.

1) Heel work both on and off the lead at normal, fast and slow pace with Sit, Stand and Down on the move, including two left about turns.

2) Novice recall

3) Advanced recall with handler changing of direction.

4) Drop on Recall.

5) Distance control

6) A three minute Sit Stay with handler out of dog's sight.

7) A four minute Down Stay with handler out of dog's sight.

The dogs remain in each section one year before sitting the next test. There are two test nights a year, one in the spring and one in the autumn. Certificates are awarded to the dogs that pass. Dogs may only compete in a section for one year.

The road safety tests were something I brought from the club I originally trained at. I am not totally happy with them but they will do at present. The CGC is my own with bits taken from everywhere.

Want to know something daft? My own dog has his American CGC (judged by Terry Ryan) and his Anglo-American CGC (Roy Hunter), but does not have his UK Kennel Club CGC because I have never attended a Kennel Club Registered Club and I have no intention of registering my own as you then need committees and other yukky things like that.

GRASS

Dogs do not necessarily eat grass because they are sick or have worms. It is normal for dogs to eat grass in very small amounts, possibly to aid digestion. Their ancestors ate grass.

Grass foliage contains folic acid and it has been proved that cats eat it because of a lack of a vitamin supplement in a mainly meat diet. Maybe the same applies to dogs that could also be seeking roughage. Some dogs may eat too much fresh grass and cannot digest it. Because the small barbs on blades of grass or eating large quantities act as an irritant, the dog throws up. This leads owners erroneously to think the dog ate the grass to induce vomiting. (See **Food allergies**).

The scorch marks on lawns as a result of a female urinating are due to the fact that she deposits a greater amount of urine in a concentrated area, whereas a male dog will squirt less urine, more frequently in different places, generally against a vertical object.

GREYHOUNDS and LURCHERS

Greyhounds and the hounds used in fox hunting packs are two prime examples of man's inhumanity to dogs. Far too often, having been used for man's pleasure, they are destroyed when they are retired from racing anytime before four years old. Fortunately, there are Greyhound rescue organisations seeking to get retired dogs re-homed. They make excellent pets, being loving, calm and obedient.

Lurchers look like Greyhounds except that they have rough coats and have the face of a Foxhound. They are bred for hunting, poaching and unofficial racing They, too, often suffer the same fate.

There are three main greyhound rescue organisations.

N.G.R.C. Retired Greyhound Trust: Tel: 0181 3353016

Greyhound Rescue West of England: Tel. 07000 785092

Lexus Greyhound Rescue: 01204 668589 daytime, 01706 366853 evenings.

Internet sites: http://www.greyhoundrescue.co.uk

http://www.thedogs.co.uk/ This is the NGRC web page.

Once here choose adoption.

http://members.aol.com/busher9518/greyhnd.htm

http://www.rigolo.force9.co.uk/

GROOMING

Grooming is a pleasurable social activity among wild dogs, carried out by mutual licking. Primates engage in intense bouts of hair care and flea picking and horses love to nibble each other's manes and backs. Grooming is, therefore, an important behavioural interaction between man and dog. It also establishes us as the dominant one. The dog recognises this dominance when it "grooms" us by licking our hands and exposed skin, if we allow it.

The Zoom Groom, sold in most pet shops provides the ultimate massage and grooming experience for your dog. It has rubber "fingers" that reach through thick or matted hair to the underlying skin and gently pluck out dead hair and dirt.

Start grooming as early as possible. Check and handle the ears, eyes, teeth, and nails. All dogs need grooming, some more than others. Generally, the longer the hair, the more frequently the grooming will be required.

Introduce the brush and comb as a pleasant experience for short but frequent periods while the dog is still a puppy. Even though not a lot of grooming will be required, this will result in a young adolescent dog not regarding the brush and comb as unpleasant and making grooming a struggle for you.

Do not wait until your dog becomes knotted and tangled or its fur is clogged with dried mud before you think of grooming it. This is the surest way to make your dog hate grooming, Badly knotted fur should only be dealt with by experts. Consult your vet or a grooming specialist

Some breeds such as Cocker Spaniels, Yorkshire Terriers, Scotties, Schnauzers and Poodles need to have their fur trimmed regularly. Inquire if you are in any doubt.

Bathing regularly is not a good idea as a rule. Even dog shampoo removes natural oils from the coat and dogs do not have pores through which to produce more oil quickly. Over-bathing can cause skin irritations and a dull coat.

Have you noticed whenever you bath your dog, it goes straight out and rolls in the garden and makes itself all dirty again, or when you take it for a walk after rain, it finds a muddy puddle and rolls in it? Washing a dog washes away its identity, its smell. This can result in stress. The dog does not feel good or natural. So it rolls in dirt to try to get its identity back.

A similar thing applies when it rolls in dung. By nature dogs are hunters and instinct tells it that to get close to a herd to kill for food, it should smell like the herd.

Nail cutting.

When nails are very long, cutting should be carried out by a vet because it is easy to cut into a vein in the nail, which causes bleeding as well as being painful. A vet will be able to cauterise it at once should this happen. The best way to keep your dog's nails in trim is to take lots of walks on hard surfaces. If you do buy a special cutter from a vet or pet shop, only cut the very end of the nail. If the dog is nervous, handle its paws daily until it gets used to this, and then cut the claws on one foot a day. (See **Dew claws**).

GROWLING

When dogs growl, they should never be corrected, whatever the circumstances. Instead, you should walk away. The animal will learn very quickly that this verbal display will cause owners to walk away and ignore them. Any verbal correction on the part of owners can cause more problems. Our voices can actually encourage more aggression.

Properly socialised dogs should not growl at any human. It is a sad fact that I get many e-mails from people from all over the world worried about their dogs growling. If the dog does so as soon as people enter the house, the answer is simple: put it away somewhere secure.

Some dogs will tolerate children, whom they see as being no threat, but will not allow adults to handle or go near them. In nearly every case, it is the owner's fault for not having taken the dog as a puppy to dog training classes where it can socialise with other dogs and people.

The answer with an older, unsocialised dog that growls is to find a behaviourist to come to the house to deal with the problem. There is no substitute for 'hands on' work by a specialist.

There are, however, a few things which should be done to reduce the dog's dominant attitude. (See **Dominance** and **Ten Commandments**).

Case history 1:
Somebody e-mailed me about his dominant dog that growled whenever any adult came into the house, though it did tolerate children. Two baby grandchildren were to visit during the summer and he did not want them scared by the dog's growling. "Please help", he begged.

I told him his dog would regard the babies as little dogs entering his territory – dogs that would receive more attention than him. The result would inevitably create jealousy and could be potentially dangerous.

The answer was simple: "Put the dog into kennels while the babies are with you" Better a dog in kennels than a baby in hospital.

"If there are no dogs in Heaven, then when I die I want to go where they went." — Unknown

Case history 2:
Question: Whenever I go near my Poodle when he eats, he growls at me. Why is he doing this, and should I smack him?

Answer: When dogs growl over food, never be aggressive or challenge them. Simply give it a spoonful of food when you put his bowl on the ground. As soon as it is finished, give another spoonful. Within a few minutes it will understand that you are giving and not taking. The dog will stand back when you next go near his food bowl and wait to be fed.

GUARD DOGS

Most pet dogs will guard their territory by barking at intruders. Problems arise when large, aggressive dogs are kept in a fenced area to protect commercial property. Often this happens without the owner or dog having had any sort of training. In fact, no responsible trainer would undertake to train a guard dog unless absolutely sure that the handler was also a responsible person, if not a member of the Services who, of course, have their own trainers. The reason is that aggression, once roused, is most difficult to reverse.

Be wary of putting up such signs as "Beware of the Dog" because this is an admission that you have an aggressive or dangerous dog. The sign "Guard Dog" is also an indication that you have a dog trained to guard and, possibly, to injure. It's best to put up a sign that says simply "Dog". Nobody can complain about that. The chances are a burglar will come in through the back entrance anyway and won't even see the sign, but he will probably hear the dog barking.

GUIDE DOGS

The Guide Dogs for the Blind Association, which is the largest dog training organisation in the world, has for more than 60 years been committed to providing the highest quality and most professional service to blind and partially sighted people, and to ensuring the very best in care and training for their dogs. They rely entirely on public funding to provide independence and freedom for thousands of blind and partially sighted people, aged 16 and over and resident in the U.K., who may apply for training. There is no upper age limit, and people with some hearing loss and other physical disabilities can be trained

Careful person-to-person training is given, usually during a three to four week residential course at a training centre, or at home if appropriate. An aftercare programme supports the guide dog owner with regular home visits to check that all is well, and there is an emergency service. There are seven regional training centres and eight small centres.

All this is at virtually no cost to the guide dog owner: 50p for the dog, plus £1 per week board and lodging during training. GDBA offers a feeding allowance for the dog, meets vet's bills and can help with any other costs associated with owning a guide dog

The association is the largest breeder of working dogs in the world, producing nearly 1,000 puppies per year, with a negligible mortality rate. Having had more than 30 years experience with minimal health problems, the bloodlines are in demand from overseas guide dog organisations because the temperament of the breed is now ideally suited for guide dog work. Through selective breeding of temperament and health characteristics more than 75% are successfully trained as guide dogs.

The G.D.B.A. is at the forefront of veterinary technology with progress in artificial insemination, ultrasound scanning and cytology. It has strong links with other dog organisations, including H.M. Forces, Customs and Excise, civilian police and the prison service.

It was a pioneer of early socialisation, rearing in a family home from the age of six weeks to provide a firm foundation for training. Immunisation from six weeks allows puppies to leave the litter and begin their experience of the outside world much earlier than the average pet dog

This is supported by close monitoring and individual care with professional supervision of the pups and support and advice for the voluntary puppy walkers. Adapting to the changing environment, puppies are brought up to cope with increasingly busy and noisy conditions

The association is responsible for more than 7,000 dogs: breeding stock, puppies, dogs in training, at work and retired. It has close links with the veterinary profession, including free check-ups twice a year for guide dogs, and collaborates with the Royal Veterinary College and Animal Health Trust on guide dog health issues which may also be of benefit to all dogs.

The kennel staff is qualified to City and Guilds and/or Veterinary Nurse standards and there are scrupulous health, hygiene and training routines to enable guide dogs to be given access to most places from which pet dogs are excluded

There is supervised re-homing of "rejects", with carefully selected volunteer families or other working dog organisations

Consistent professional handling produces a constant supply of dogs ready to be matched with owners. The dogs are individually trained to meet each blind and partially sighted person's needs and character.

There is a constant review of dog training methods in collaboration with other working dog organisations, in the U.K and abroad. Exchange visits and staff secondments are arranged between countries with international breeding programmes to increase the gene pool of suitable dogs.

It also supports work on the prevention, treatment and causes of blindness and encourages around 2,000 members (guide dog owners, blind and partially sighted people and sighted helpers) to take part in activities outside their everyday experience through a Holidays Group.

Hotels for Guide Dogs Owners was created especially for guide dogs owners, their families and friends. G.D.B.A.'s first hotel in Devon was so successful that another was opened in the Lake District.

It has also created a technical aid service to help guide dog owners and other blind and partially sighted people negotiate routes.There is also a bereavement study to research the effects of the ending of a partnership between guide dog and owner and the best ways of coping

As a mobility aid for blind and partially sighted people, the guide dog cannot be matched. It brings new freedom and independence, and a strong bond of friendship grows between the dog and its user. They work as a partnership and the confidence this gives a blind or partially sighted person brings about a whole new way of life.

The International Federation of Guide Dogs Schools for the Blind has a Member School in Spain: Fundacion ONCE del Perro-Guia, Camino del Obispo 7, 28935 Mostoles, Madrid, Spain

Snr. Pedro P Martin Lopesino, Tel: 34 1 613 2220: Fax: 34 1 614 5213

The Guide Dogs for the Blind Association, Hillfields, Burghfield Common, Reading RG7 3YG. Tel: (0118) 983 5555 Fax: (0118) 983 5433 - http://msn.co.uk/default.asp

---

GUN DOGS

Does your dog sometimes twitch its nose, stop, hold one front paw up in the air with its tail stiff and horizontal? That's what a Pointer does when it scents game. The problem is that the dog cannot know from how far away the smell is coming. Put two Pointers a distance apart and a human can see the junction at which the dogs are pointing.

HATRED OF DOGS

Respect those that do not like dogs. Take away some of their animosity by using a poop scoop and stop your dog barking to the annoyance of neighbours.

HEAD SHAKING

Many dominant dogs shake their heads when they first start training classes. They do not like being corrected by a short pull and release of the lead and the head shaking is an attempt to throw off authority. The next phase could be to correct the owner by biting, or as some owners kindly refer to it, play biting.

Head shaking, or holding the head to one side, could also be a sign of ear infection. Go to a vet.

HEALTH (See **Symptoms**)

HEALTH BENEFITS

"Companionship" is what most dog or cat owners would say if asked what is the single most important benefit from owning a pet. But research indicates that pet ownership may provide another important benefit: improved health.

One of the first studies demonstrating that pets could be beneficial to their owners health was conducted in 1980 by Dr. Aaron H. Katcher and his associates. They found that among heart attack patients, 94% of those who owned pets lived one year longer than 72% of those who did not have a pet.

Dr. Alan M. Beck, director of the Center for Applied Ethology and Human-Animal Interaction, Purdue University, says that a closer analysis of the findings show that only a small proportion of the difference in mortality can be attributed to pet ownership. "Nevertheless, while 2-3% may seem small, the impact, considering the frequency of heart disease, is significant and cost effective," Dr. Beck and a colleague wrote recently in the Annual Review of Public Health.

Dr. Lynette A. Hart, of the Center for Animals in Society, University of California, Davis, points to three other studies. One took place in Australia at the Baker Medical Research Institute.

The researchers, Warwick Anderson and colleagues, looked at blood pressure, cholesterol and triglyceride levels, high levels of which are all risk factors for heart disease. Of nearly 5,750 men and women, the 784 who owned pets, especially the men, had significantly lower blood pressure, triglyceride and cholesterol levels compared with those who were not pet owners.

In fact, the researchers concluded that owning a pet was as effective in lowering blood pressure as switching to a low-salt diet or reducing alcohol consumption.

Another 1990's study indicates that besides reducing the risk of heart disease, pets might also help reduce some minor health problems. In this study, conducted by James Serpell at Cambridge University, U.K., researchers began with people who did not own pets.

The participants were asked to complete questionnaires about the frequency of minor health complaints such as headaches, indigestion and problems sleeping. There were no major differences among the study participants based on their responses to the health questionnaire.

The researchers then gave some of the people dogs, some of the people cats, and left one group without pets. Ten months later, the researchers looked again at the health of the men and women and found that the group with dogs had suffered fewer minor complaints.

A third study cited by Dr. Hart was conducted at the University of California, Los Angeles, where researcher

Judith Siegel looked at the number of medical visits made by nearly 1,000 Medicare recipients. During a one-year period, the seniors who owned pets paid fewer visits to the doctor than those without pets.

Pet owners in this study spent an average of 1.4 hours each day outdoors with their dogs. This activity strengthens the heart muscle, improves blood circulation, and slows the loss of bone tissue that commonly accompanies aging. There is also evidence that stroking a dog slows the heart beat and reduces blood pressure..

Furthermore, it is a fact that dogs taken to homes for the elderly and hospices have had a beneficial effect. So your dog is not just a companion. It makes an important contribution to your health. (See **Affection** and **Walkies**).

HEALTH SIGNS (See **Symptoms**).

HEARING

A dog hears ordinary, low-pitched sounds, much the same as a human. It is a very different matter with high-pitched or ultrasonic sounds. The human range is from 20,000 cycles per second when young to 13,000 when old. A dog can hear at 300,000 cycles a second, around 15 times that of an average human. So it can hear the high-pitched squeaking of, for example, mice and rats when we hear nothing.

Their ability to move their ears independently also enables them to identify the direction of the source of the sound better than humans. (See **Deafness**).

HEARING DOGS

Hearing Dogs for the Deaf was created in 1982 by Anthony Blunt, who is now the chief executive. As a Police Dog Trainer/Instructor for 30 years, he first trained his own dog,

"Favour", which he selected from the National Canine Defence League. He travelled with Favour throughout the United Kingdom giving talks, demonstrating the work of a hearing dog and raising funds to enable him to train more dogs to help deaf people. During the following four years, he was solely responsible for the training of all hearing dogs and, in 1986, Hearing Dogs for Deaf People became a charity in its own right. To date it has placed around 400 hearing dogs with deaf people. (See **Deaf, dogs for**).

HEART PROBLEMS

Small dogs are more prone to heart problems than large dogs. They have to take many more steps when going for a walk and their hearts beat faster than larger dogs.

HEARTWORM DISEASE

Caused by a roundworm called *Dirofilaria immitis*. Heart worms are most commonly found in dogs, although they can infect a wide variety of mammals including cats , ferrets, sea lions, bears, foxes, wolves, coyotes, cats and even humans.

Adult heart worms live in the heart and major arteries of the lungs where they can be fatal. They are only transmitted from one animal to another by mosquitoes. Adult worms living in the heart and arteries of the lungs produce microfilariae (small immature heartworms) which are found circulating in the blood of the infected animal, usually a dog.

If a mosquito feeds on an infected dog with microfilariae in the blood, the mosquito will ingest some of these immature heartworms along with the blood meal. Inside the mosquito, the immature heartworms develop to a stage called the infective larval stage. When the mosquito feeds on another dog or a cat, some of these infective larvae will escape from the mosquito during the blood meal. The larvae pass through the animal's skin through the bite wound left by the mosquito. Once the infected larvae have entered an animal, they will begin migrating through the tissues. They eventually make their way to the heart and lungs where they will mature and begin producing microfilariae.

Check with your vet whether the disease is prevalent in your area and, if so, it is well worth the investment to treat your pet with heartworm tablets. (See **Symptoms**).

HEAT DANGERS

Take special care of your dog in the hot summer months. Dogs have inefficient cooling systems compared to humans. The sweat glands are in the tongue and paw pads, the primary method of sweating being the obvious one of panting

If a muzzle or a respiratory blockage interferes with this ability to pant, a dog may overheat quickly. Obese dogs suffer most.

Never exercise a dog in the heat of the day and keep its weight under control. Make sure there is plenty of shade and water.

Temperatures of more than 104° F. (40° c.) can result in rapid panting, bright red gums, tongue and other mucus membranes, vomiting, watery and bloody diarrhoea and staggering. Thick saliva is also a sign of an impending heat stroke. If a dog is not treated immediately, coma, respiratory collapse and death can result.

If there are signs of heat stroke, cool the dog off by submerging or washing it in tepid water before taking it to a vet. Flap a towel to fan the dog and allow gradual cooling.

Cooling a dog that is in shock too fast with cold water can cause further problems, even hypothermia. Do not use ice-cold water for this could produce a narrowing of the arteries to the skin, meaning the dog will retain the heat longer.

Do not leave dogs in cars even with the windows down (and do not allow them to travel with their heads out of the

car windows). If you see a dog in an unattended car in hot weather for more than five minutes, call the police. Keep water in the boot of the car and out of the sun. Dogs do not like warm or hot water. Hot pavements, tarmac and sand on a beach can burn paws. Jogging with your dog or making it run behind your car is unwise.

Remember young or small dogs take 10 steps to our one and young dogs need most of their energy for growing.

Do not clip long-haired dogs too short, otherwise there is the danger of the skin being sun burnt. Their coats are for protection against cold weather and the sun.

It is not natural for dogs that have been bred for cold climates, such as Huskies and Akitas, to be taken to warm climates. Behavioural and health problems are bound to occur.

HEEL – WALKING TO

I hope that all trainers can demonstrate walking to Heel and Sit in a few minutes. They can then point out to owners that, if the dog does it for them, it surely will do it for the owner it loves.

After my demonstration of how to do it, the owner is not allowed to speak or touch the lead. I hold it and the owner holds my left hand with the dog on the left of both of us. I ask the owner to walk, putting the left leg forward first. As soon as the dog's head moves forward I tug the lead and instantly let it loose.

Then I tell the owner to turn left and push with my body. The dog has to get out of the way so it steps back and turns its head to watch the owner. We then stop and, as soon as we do so, I tug the lead sharply and allow it to go loose. This makes the dog Sit.

I repeat the exercise again and again, turning left, stopping and making the dog sit without speaking. During this time, I will be holding the lead with only one finger and tell the owner to do the same.

Within five minutes, I will drop the lead to the ground when the dog is sitting and ask the owner to stand on the lead and put their hands on their hips. The dog knows then that the owner is confident. There is no verbal praise, a slight stroke is reward enough. The owner is, however, rewarded with lots of praise and, perhaps, a round of applause from the rest of the class.

Why do we teach the dog to walk on the left side?

Some say it goes way back to the days of the cavalry when horses were led on the left side, leaving the right-hand free for weapons. Nearer our times when dogs were first trained for the military and police services, most handlers were right-handed and, therefore, held their guns or had their batons on that side. Gamekeepers keep dogs to their left carrying their rifles in the crook of the right arm.

Today a dog owner finds that lead corrections are easier using mainly the right-hand pulling across the body. Another advantage of having the dog on the left is that it leaves the left hand free to reposition it when in the Sit position and to pat it as a reward. But if you are left-handed don't worry – do what suits you best.

HEPATITIS

This contagious disease is transmitted in the urine, faeces or saliva of infected animals and even those that have recovered from the disease because it can be passed in the urine for up to six months.

It is most dangerous for very young dogs. The incubation period is from four to nine days, followed by a high temperature. The same programme of injections is followed as with distemper. (See **Distemper** and **Symptoms**).

HEREDITARY DISEASES

Buying a pedigree puppy or dog is for most people like navigating blindfolded through a minefield with a pogo stick. Believe it or not, pedigree dogs are subject to more than 300 genetically transmitted abnormalities, according to The Association of Veterinarians for Animal Rights.

Most of the abnormalities are unpronounceable by the general public and undisclosed by the average seller, who is often not even aware of the genetic abnormalities. Selling pups with a pedigree certificate is no mark of health or behavioural quality.

The more popular the breed the greater the risk of genetic diseases, the less popular the breed the lesser the risk.

Here is listed the number of registered diseases against each breed as outlined in the Canine Consumer Report that was revised in December 1996.

Scottie	1	English Springer Spaniel	63
German Shepherd	68	Antartic Husky	2
Great Dane	45	Labrador	46
Havanese	2	Minature Poodle	48
Rottweiler	29	Dalmatian	26
Standard Dachshund	47	Toy Poodle	48

Anyone considering a pedigree dog should ask the seller if any of that dog's ancestors have ever had any of the afflictions listed for their breed.

A good breeder will be able to show you the breeding pair and full blood reports and x-rays to show that there are no defaults in the parents' joints etc. He or she will not object to you speaking to their vet. It is worth paying more for a genetically sound puppy between seven to 12 weeks than having to pay for vets' bills. (See **Puppy - buying, Hip Dysplasia and Mongrels**).

HIP DYSPLASIA

This is a terrible and complex disease, so I am especially grateful to Cornell University, Colorado, for permission to reproduce this authoritative article by probably the world's leading expert.

"Canine hip dysplasia is one of the most baffling diseases afflicting dogs today," states George Lust, Ph.D., the Cornell professor of physiological chemistry who has studied the disorder for more than 25 years.

"We know this is an inherited disease, but identifying the so-called "hip dysplasia gene" is proving difficult because this seems to be a polygenic disorder, with several different genes responsible.

Furthermore, these may be "masked" or hidden genes that are not expressed in several generations until the disease turns up again in the progeny. That's why there is such a low level of confidence when breeders say: 'There is no background of hip dysplasia in my dogs' lines.'

Conscientious dog breeders are anxious for a genetic screening procedure that would help eliminate hip dysplasia in future generations, and that is one of the topics set for discussion at an international symposium. Among other topics are improved radiographic techniques to diagnose hip dysplasia earlier in a dog's life; nutrition, including evidence that hip dysplasia can be delayed or prevented altogether when the growth rate of susceptible puppies is restricted; and the effect of maternal hormones, such as estrogen and relaxin.

Here are five misconceptions about canine hip dysplasia from the John M. Olin Laboratory for the Study of Canine Bone and Joint Diseases, James A. Baker Institute for Animal Health, College of Veterinary Medicine, Cornell University

Only hip joints and surrounding tissues are affected.
Evidence now indicates that the shoulder and knee joints and some intervertebral joints may show similar changes: the loss of cartilage, inflammation of the joint capsule, bone damage and the growth of spurs at the bone-cartilage interface. Hip dysplasia is simply the most conspicuous - and most painful - manifestation of this form of osteo-arthritis.

Only dogs suffer hip dysplasia.
While 50 percent of some of the larger dog breeds are affected, the disease is not unknown in humans. About 1% of the general human population suffers hip dysplasia, and the rate for the inherited disease is higher in some populations of American Indians.

153

Many Navajos in New Mexico went through life with hip dysplasia until mothers stopped the traditional practice of strapping infants, straight-legged, to cradle boards and allowed babies to assume the more relaxed, bent-legged position. Replacement of diseased hip joints with artificial joints is one treatment, both for canine and human patients.

The absence of hip dysplasia in canine parents guarantees dysplasia-free pups.

Unfortunately, out of 100 matings of "normal" dogs in breeds affected by hip dysplasia, 75 percent of puppies will be "normal" but 25 percent, on average, will have hip dysplasia. Genes for hip dysplasia are believed to be "masked" or hidden in some generations, making the elimination of the disease from breeding stock even more difficult. Canine hip dysplasia was first diagnosed in the 1930s, but probably has troubled domestic and wild canines for centuries.

All large-sized breeds of pure-bred dogs are candidates for hip dysplasia.

Although the disease is particularly common among certain large breeds (from Bernese Mountain Dogs, Bloodhounds and Boxers to Rottweilers, St. Bernards and Welsh Corgis), mixed breeds of all sizes also are subject to hip dysplasia and not even the toy breeds are spared. However, the incidence is lower in small dogs.

Large-sized breeds with a relatively low incidence of hip dysplasia include the Borzoi, Doberman Pinscher, Great Dane, Greyhound, Irish Wolfhound and Siberian Husky.

A hearty diet helps avert hip dysplasia.

To the contrary, dogs that are genetically predisposed to hip dysplasia seem to benefit from a lean diet during their first two years. In one study beginning at eight-weeks-old, pups that were restricted to a 24% smaller ration had a 46% lower occurrence of hip dysplasia than pups that could eat freely.

Slowing the growth rate during the early months of life, some veterinary nutritionists now believe, can lessen the severity of hip dysplasia and even prevent it."

H. Roger Segelken – Senior Science Writer Cornell News Service
E-mail: hrs2@cornell.edu

Internet site: http://www.news.cornell.edu

An interesting article can be found at:

http://www.k9netuk.com/breed/jaa/health2.html

Case History:

I have a young 18-month-old Rottweiler called Sukie. I inherited her from a client who was unable to control her when she was five months old. She has a long pedigree but I now know that the "breeder" had never bred before and only bred because she thought it was good for her bitch to have puppies.

By six months, Sukie was not walking too well. My vet told me not to be concerned because she would grow out of it. I went back a month later. This time he gave her antibiotics and assured me again that she would grow out of it. The next few months, still assuring me not to worry, he gave me some anti-inflammatory tablets.

When Sukie was 18 months old, I decided to get a second opinion. This time the vet took many x-rays and found that Sukie has Hip Dysplasia in her two back hips and Elbow Dysplasia in both front legs. The front right leg has a degenerative joint disease, which is not curable.

This vet kindly referred me to another with a fully equipped animal hospital including immaculate operating rooms. But those kind of facilities and that kind of skill costs money and trying to give Sukie a better quality of life is costing me a fortune. All of Sukie's brothers and sisters have similar problems. Guess what? Yes, two of her sisters have had puppies, and I would bet my last dollar they will all have Hip Dysplasia.

I was told by the new vet that the operation on the two front paws would take four hours, after which Sukie would need rest for four weeks, so I put a pen in the family room beside my desk to accustom her to it before the operation.

As she had never been in a pen before, I fed her at the entrance of the crate and then put the bowl just inside it. Within a few hours she went in and out on her own. I then closed the door so that she would be happy in it, either open or shut. Whenever she was in the crate, which we renamed her " den," we gave her a chewy as a reward.

I covered the den with a sheet so that all sides were enclosed except the entrance. This gave her the same security as her ancestors achieved by burrowing underground.

The vet who performed the operation said her elbows were much worse than had been thought from the x-rays and that she would need medication for the rest of her life. If she had been treated when she was six months old, the situation would have been more hopeful. If only I had sought a second opinion at that stage.

If this sad story can happen to me, then be assured it can happen to anyone.

HISTORY OF DOGS

The chapter on Wolves at the beginning of this book tells how, around 10,000 years ago, man began the domestication of wolves for his own benefit as an assistant when hunting and as a guard against intruders approaching the camp fire at night.

Indeed, an Israeli grave has been found in which were laid the bones of a human and a puppy, the hands of the human lovingly on the puppy's shoulder. Those bones have been dated as 12,000 years old.

More evidence of the development of the relationship between man and dog has been found in Ancient Egyptian wall drawings of hunting dogs dated 6,000 years ago. The Romans also kept dogs as pets and to fight with their Legions.

Nearer our own times, dogs were kept for sport by the rich from the 15th to the 19th centuries. As explorers sailed around the world, they brought back specimens of the wide variety of breeds which had been developed through the ages by various civilisations in Asia, Australia and the Americas.

Breeders have done the rest, developing and refining what they have considered to be the most desirable characteristics of dogs into the 160 to180 breeds recognised today.

HOMEOPATHY

In the early 1930's, the noted British physician and scientist, Dr. Edward Bach, discovered that preparations from 38 flowering plants and trees alleviated many emotional and psychological difficulties in both animals and humans.

He also developed a highly effective combination for the relief of stress. Called "Rescue Remedy", it can calm nervous and aggressive dogs as well as dogs that have been traumatised by injury or abuse.

The Bach Remedies can be given directly from the stock bottle or from a bottle of diluted Remedy by placing 2 to 4 drops in your animal's feed or water, directly into the mouth or rubbing on the body. It is not necessary to be precise in counting the number of drops in any of the dilution methods. You cannot overdose because the Remedies are non-toxic.

Rescue Remedy

This, the most commonly used, is a combination of five Remedies to create an individual essence.

1. *Clematis*. Increases attention span and helps an animal to regain consciousness after surgery.

2. *Impatiens*. Assists nervous animals and relieves pain..

3. ***Rock Rose***. Soothes terror and panic after an accident, injury, fire or any terrifying event. This is especially useful for dogs used in police work.

4. ***Cherry Plum***. Helps highly strung animals that lose control and are stressed by strange people, noises, other animals or gun fire.

5. ***Star of Bethlehem***. Deals with all forms of trauma - emotional, physical, birthing and trauma from extreme cold or heat.

Note: Rescue Remedy is not meant to replace emergency veterinary treatment. Further reading:

"Practical Uses and Applications of the Back Flower Emotional Remedies" by Jessica Bear, N.D.

"Bach Flower Therapy Theory and Practice" by Mechthild Scheffer . Also by the same author is "Mastering Bach Flower, "Therapies: A Guide to Diagnosis & Treatment"

HOWLING

An extreme form of barking when the owner is out, indicating an extreme form of attachment to the owner. (See **Barking**).

HUNTING DOGS

The first recorded use of dogs for hunting was made 6,000 years ago by the Ancient Egyptians in their wall drawings. The breed they used for its speed looks much the same today as it does in those drawings all that time ago. We call it the Greyhound.

Dogs, like their ancestors, wolves, are born pack hunters. Breeds with acute senses of smell and hearing such as Pointers, Setters, Retrievers and Spaniels have been used by man since guns were invented. They are trained to scent out game, but not to chase or catch the quarry, and to stop in their tracks when commanded to do so.

When these working dogs are kept as pets and their hunting skills are not used, they can become excitable if not properly trained. The same can happen to the Border Collie when its herding skills are not used.

HYPERACTIVITY

In children, it has been proved that certain food additives are to blame. The same applies to dogs. (See **Food**)

IDEOPATHIC

Your vet may use this term if he cannot identify the cause of a problem such as scratching when there is no medical reason for doing so.

If I like it, it's mine.

If it's in my mouth, it's mine.

If I can take it from you, it's mine.

If I had it a little while ago, it's mine.

If it's mine, it must never appear to be yours in any way.

If I'm chewing something up, all the pieces are mine.

If it just looks like mine, it's mine.

If I saw it first, it's mine.

If you are playing with something and you put it down, it automatically becomes mine.

If it's broken, it's yours.

INCONTINENCE

Some dogs, mostly females, have this problem. It is difficult to eradicate but medication can be prescribed.

INITIALS

The following initials are used as abbreviations in the dog world:

C.D.	-	Companion Dog
Ch.	-	Champion
Ex.	-	Excellent
G.S.D.	-	German Shepherd Dog
P.D.	-	Police Dog
Sch.	-	Schutzhund (Guard or Defence Dog)
T.D.	-	Tracker Dog
U.D.	-	Utility Dog
W.D.	-	Working Dog
W.T.	-	Working Trials

INJURIES (See **First-aid**)

INSECURITY

This occurs when a dog does not know its place in the human pack. It can be confused by the owner not being consistent in applying the rules by which total dominance by the owner is established (see **Ten commandments**).

If some rules have been enforced but the dog is allowed to get way with others, it will be confused about its stature in the household. This confusion can result in it attempting to be dominant in a variety of ways, such as attention-seeking barking, pulling on the lead, chasing, and even urinating in the house

The behaviour can be changed by not allowing it to succeed in any of these trials of strength and by going to a training club to learn how to make the dog walk to Heel, and obey Sit and Down.

In short, make the dog feel secure by making it respect your dominance.

INSURANCE

There are more than 20 U.K. companies offering a wide variety of insurance schemes.

Always study the small print to be sure what you are getting.

Obviously, the insurance should cover veterinary fees (but watch out for the "excess" which will mean you have to pay the first £10 or whatever), death from illness, death from accident, theft or straying, third party liability, accidental damage, boarding kennel fees in the event that you have to go into hospital, etc.

A useful cover could be holiday cancellation costs. If your pet requires emergency surgery within seven days before your departure, the insurance company will reimburse holiday cancellation costs up to £2,000, or whatever.

Many companies also offer cover while you are away from home, with a help line to find a vet.

Cost ranges from £90/125 a year or around £2 a week. Most allow monthly or annual payment or direct debit.

If you have more that one pet, be it a cat or dog, ask for a discount, most companies will do this if you request it.

> *"If a dog will not come to you*
> *after having looked you in the face,*
> *you should go home and examine your conscience."*
> *Woodrow Wilson*

INSURANCE COMPANIES:

Dog Breeders Insurance
Tel: 0800 - 373218. Web site: www.dbi-insurance.co.uk

National Canine Defence League
Tel. 0800 072 6677.

Pet Shield Insurance
Web site: http://www.petproducts.co.uk

Pedigree Chum Healthcare Plan
Tel: 01372 - 748889.

Pet Plan
Tel: 0800 - 282 009.

Pet Protect
Tel: 0800 - 650056.

Equine & Livestock Insurance Co.Ltd
Tel: 01423 - 330711. E-mail: remember@compuserve.com

INSTINCT

Dogs are telepathic and are able to sense your emotions and frame of mind instantly. This is one reason why a dog that has misbehaved while you have been away knows that you are reacting angrily and comes to you saying "sorry" or cowers away. It does not remember the past misdemeanour, but it can sense your present reaction.

Canine instincts vary in strength between breeds and individuals of the same breed. They are either there or not. They cannot be put there and cannot be taken away. They might lie dormant but, once developed, they can rarely be weakened.

A dog with an obsession for chasing balls can be controlled by training and by providing other outlets for its energy. If a young dog is corrected the first time it chases a car, it might give up the idea. But if it is allowed to chase cars, the hunting instinct becomes stronger and in no time it will be very difficult, even impossible, to stop it. The dog has the instinct of the hunt, which means a chase and a kill. Sadly, often the dog is killed by a car.

Instincts cover such areas as maternal, survival, hunting, guarding, the pack, and self-preservation. Self-preservation makes wild dogs furtive and afraid of the unfamiliar, which is no use to man. This type of nervousness in the domestic dog is one of the common causes of problems in present day dogs. Nearly all cases where children have been attacked by dogs and owners have been bitten by their own dog, arise from nervousness. The dog is afraid it is going to be hurt and attacks first...fear, fright and bite.

The instinct of self-preservation has been weakened by breeding from bold dogs rather than nervous ones, but has never been entirely removed.

Often some dog owners confuse instinct and intelligence. Instinct is an urge from within. It makes a dog act in certain ways and has no connection with intelligence.

Dog's first instinct is to survive. When a pup is born, it squirms about until it finds a teat and then sucks it. No intelligence or learning by any association plays a part in the process. The maternal instinct tells the female to clean up the foetal membrane etc. and stir the puppy into action by licking it. The female is not taught, she has not seen another female do this.

Most instincts provide pleasure to the dog, and because it associates the action with pleasure, the instinct grows stronger with use. (See **Anthropomorphism, Extra-sensory perception** and **Intelligence**).

INTELLIGENCE

A dog's brain is much smaller than man's, especially the cerebrum - the portion of the brain associated with intellectual function, emotion and personality. Dogs cannot understand human language or emotions. It is far more important to use sound patterns, intonation, facial and body language as a form of communication. A dog wants to please, so all learning should be based on positive reinforcement by giving a reward. A large part of a dog's brain is taken up with sensory activity, the interpretation of scent. (See **Anthropomorphism** and **Instinct**).

INTERNET SITES
(See **K9netuk** and appendix at end of book).

JEALOUSY
Jealousy between dogs or between dogs and cats can be triggered by the presence of the owner. Simply to stroke or touch a dog or cat is sufficient to put enough of your scent onto that pet to make the other animal jealous and to cause a fight.

JUMPING UP
A dog jumping up at a visitor is the worst possible introduction anybody can have to your home and to your dog. Indeed, for those who do not even like dogs, it could be the end of a beautiful friendship.

Somebody wrote to me: "I have been doing the off command as a dog trainer told me since he was small and kneed him in the chest, all to no avail. I have put him on his lead with a choke collar and he is still tugging away. I use the Sit command and eventually he calms down enough but that initial greeting is a horror story every time. It has become very frustrating and obviously not pleasant for others. I'll just keep trying"

My reply was "give it up, it will not work". The knee in the chest is outdated and is bad advice.

The sound of the doorbell or knocking on the door can be a trigger for excitement. It heralds the arrival of another potential member of the pack. The dog must jump to show it is the host. So remove excitable triggers. The front door bell rings but before opening the door put away the dog. You are the host, not the dog, this raises your status and reduces that of the dog.

By putting the dog away it cannot demonstrate dominance by going to the front door. Keep it away for around 10 minutes until its initial excitement has dwindled. Then allow it in with a bone or Kong filled with a tit-bit to keep it occupied for a while. Peace.

Alternatively, some recommend that it should be put on a lead and made to Sit

You can help matters by removing the triggers for excitability when you enter your own home. Try walking in without looking, touching or talking to the dog for five minutes. Then talk and love your dog.

Dogs jump up at other times because the act is rewarded by attracting attention. If it were not rewarding the dog would not do it. It is as simple as that. Often it interprets the act of bending down to pat it as a signal of submission, a reward for jumping up.

So when a dog jumps up, do not be aggressive and knee it in the chest. Simply hold it up by its front paws and calmly tell the dog you love it. The dog has jumped up, so you react by holding him up. Do not let it down, keep it up as long as you can.

By keeping the dog up, I mean stretching it up and making it walk on two legs. The dog will then start to mouth your hands. When that happens, and only then, drop it down. Do not place the dog down, drop it on the floor.

When it is on all four legs, love it, cuddle and talk. Then encourage the dog to jump again. As soon as it does, grab the paws and repeat the whole exercise.

It is important to get the timing right and that the whole family learns to do this. Your dog will quickly learn that to jump up will make you react and your reaction is not very rewarding. The cure is easy, simple and kind.

Another answer is to explain the problem to a dog-loving friend. They could also give the dog a lesson when they enter the house by holding up the front paws when it jumps up.

Alternatively answer the door with a spray bottle filled with water and squirt the dog in the face when it jumps up at the visitor. The surprise may teach it a lesson. This may not work at first with every dog but it can be repeated by keeping the spray bottle near the door.

Children can be a problem because they want to pet the dog. Tell them to stand still and look up to the sky to see if it is raining and keep their hands beside them.

Case History:
A client took my advice by having a spray bottle handy. Problem was the dog jumped up, knocked my friend's hand and he squirted water over the visitor's face. I know this is true because I was the visitor.

K9netuk
This was the first all-round U.K. web site covering the British dog scene and it attracts visitors from around the world. Now the leading web site of its kind, it was started in 1996 by Sue James and is run by a team of dog people experienced in showing, breeding and working dogs and know what site visitors and advertisers want to see.

Categories include a shopping mall, a breeder's and exhibitor's showcase featuring some of the top British breeders and kennels, canine societies, quarantine and boarding kennels, training articles, news items, features from some of the U.K.'s specialist publications, book reviews, reports and photographs from the UK's major championship shows, a show diary and problem pages.

The K9netuk team covers some of the major annual UK canine events, including Cruft's, with news of group winners and show photographs being uploaded each evening during the show. For information: Tel. 01664 444310. Web site: http://www.k9netuk.com E-mail: info@k9netuk.com

---

KENNELS

Don't book until you look. If a kennel will not allow you to look around, then go somewhere else because they may have something to hide. If the kennels smell doggy, they're not clean. Try another place.

Tell the kennels what food you are feeding your dog and if they do not have it, supply it. If the kennel will not use your own food, try another kennel.

All good kennels will ask to see your vaccination book, which must of course be kept up to date. They should also require details of any medication your dog is taking, together with the name and phone number of your vet.

Provide the kennel with a list of your commands and pet phrases but do not take along the dog's favourite toys. Familiar smells makes the transition take longer.

Owners worry that their pets will pine and be miserable, but dogs are "present living" creatures and quickly adjust to a new environment, within two days in most cases.

Before you go away, be a bit cooler in your relationship towards the dog and, whatever you do, don't let the dog see you are upset at leaving it in the kennel. It will pick up your reaction immediately. Finally, never let a friend go to visit it.

I strongly recommend that all young dogs should be put into kennels as soon as possible, even if it is only for a day. If dogs are not trained at a young age for kennels they could well suffer stress. This could result in a dull coat. When this happens, kennels are often incorrectly blamed for not looking after dogs properly.

Finally, do not be fooled into thinking that your dog is sulking when it comes home from the kennels. It could be its status has been reduced by the other dogs in the kennels and it will be subdued until it re-establishes its ranking back at home.

KENNEL COUGH

This illness got its name because it spreads rapidly among closely confined animals. The first five days are worst, although the coughing may persist for 10 to 20 days. An annual booster vaccination is needed and good kennels will want proof that one has been given before accepting a dog. (See **Symptoms**).

KISSING (See **Licking**)

KOEHLER METHOD OF DOG TRAINING

I was brought up on this system which is used for police dog and service dog training all around the world, but it is not suitable for the average dog owner

Bill Koehler developed his method in 1946 and in 1962 he published a book about it which is currently in it's 39th printing and has never been revised. If it works...don't fix it.

The Koehler method does not assume that a dog has an innate willingness to please. The system believes that when a dog has obeyed a command, it has trained the owner to give it a tit-bit or praise.

Information on Koehler training: Dick Koehler and Tony Ancheta, Koehler Dog Training 599 Stanley Rd Westpoint CA 95255. http://www.koehlerdogtraining.com http://www.geocities.com/Heartland/Meadows/4159/koehler.html

KUMFI TRAINING EQUIPMENT

By George Grayson. (See **Acknowledgements**)

"I have around 200 pet dogs in my training classes every week. Some are very difficult indeed, especially owners with unsuitable dogs far stronger than the handler. Problem dogs are, of course, in the minority but they can take up a considerable amount of my time.

As a result of what I have learnt from my training classes, I have, in the last 10 years, designed the Kumfi Range of Training Equipment and Behavioural Aids which are used by hundreds of. trainers and clubs throughout the U.K. They include:

- The training lead. So very important with strong untrained dogs. It must be good to hold, not too thin. The lead should be adjustable, giving a maximum length of about six feet. The 3 in 1 Training Lead, patented and designed by me, adjusts with the aid of two rings to a standard 48" and a short 24" lead.

- The training collar. Although I used check/choke chains for years in the Police Force Dog Section, with domestic pet training sessions I use only my own designed Kombi Collar which is a half check, i.e. half chain and half adjustable fabric.

The reason for not using check/choke chains in pet dog training is twofold. Handlers are usually novices, they tend to keep the lead tight. All this does is choke the dog. The "Kombi Collar" cannot be put on the wrong way, it still has the checking capability, but does not choke the dog.

Some years ago, if a dog was a "puller", a strong or boisterous dog, the check/choke chain was put on, raised up just behind the dog's ears and the dog checked with this very painful method.

- The halter for dogs. Dogalter is similar to a halter for horses and is probably the most useful piece of equipment I have designed. It has the advantage of leading the dog by the head, makes controlling the dog so much easier and assists in teaching good Heel work. It has a very mystical calming effect on strong, excitable and indeed aggressive dogs.

To summarise:

a) The correct type of lead is important.

b) I have no objection to check/choke chains for service dogs or indeed trained dogs, but the length of chain is all important and for G.S.D's I use 3mm long linked chain.

c) I have no objection to soft choke collars for trained dogs but will not allow them to be used for novice handlers with young dogs.

d) I prefer the use of the Kombi Collar for young dogs and for pet dog training.

e) With strong, boisterous or anti-social dogs, I use the Dogalter in conjunction with the Kombi. The latter is for safety, the Dogalter controls forward movement. The Kombi assists correction and is a safety feature which stops the dog pulling its head out of the Dogalter by backing away.

For details of the Kumfi range of products send a SAE to: George Grayson, North East Dog Training Centres. P.O. Box 19, Northallerton, North Yorkshire, England. DL7 8AF. Tel. 01609 770792.

E-mail: georgegrayson@thisisthenortheast.co.uk

"I wonder if other dogs think poodles are members of a weird religious cult." — Rita Rudner

LABRADORS (See **Top Dogs**).

LAWS

Whether there is a law or not, all dogs should be microchipped and have vaccinations and inoculations with boosters every year (in Spain). All Dobermans, Rottweilers, German Shepherds, Mastiffs and other designated dogs should be fitted with a muzzle in public places where it is against the law to walk a dog off a lead.

A motor vehicle on a public road is a public place, therefore, a dog must be secured in the vehicle. A dog's head should not be allowed to hang out of a window. Don't drive a car with a dog running behind for exercise. A dog should not be allowed on a public beach.

LEICHMANIASIS

"Leichmania donovani is the causative agent in the eastern hemisphere and L. chagasi, in the western hemisphere. The parasites are transmitted as promastigotes by the bite of several species of phlebotomin flies (sandflies). In the mammilian host, promastigotes are engulfed by macrophages in which they transform into and divide as amastigotes."

Well, that couldn't be clearer, could it? So now you know all about Leichmaniasis according to the Bible of veterinary medicine, "The Merck Veterinary Manual."

To make matters even more confusing, the so-called sandfly is not a fly at all, but a mosquito, and it doesn't live on the sand of beaches. It is prevalent in Mediterranean countries, Brazil and China and has been found in Oklahoma, U.S.A. It is transmitted into a dog's bloodstream (cats are not affected) by the mosquito's bite and as yet there is no cure, the incubation period being months or even years.

Signs are rapidly growing claws, bleeding paws, fever and enlargement of the spleen, liver and lymph nodes. Given early detection through a blood test, the disease can be successfully contained for varying periods of time, depending upon the individual resistance of the dog. However, toxic effects are likely and relapses after treatment are common. Treatment with Zyloric tablets, given to humans for gout, has also been known to help prolong the life of the infected dog.

Interestingly, a recent report on global warming predicts that by the year 2025 southern England will have a climate like Southern France today. If this happens, much more money could become available to British scientists to find a protective vaccination or a cure for Leichmaniasis. It is the lack of funds for research in the poorer countries affected that has been responsible for the lack of progress in fighting this deadly disease

LICE – Mites and Mange

These live off skin, hair or blood and cause scratching, flaking skin, loss of hair, even baldness. Mites can affect the ear canal, the signs being a brown, waxy substance crusting around the edges.

LICKING

When your dog licks you, it is seeking attention and not salt as some believe.. Licking starts when puppies do it to their mother's jaws to get her to regurgitate food. Naturalist Desmond Morris in his book "Dog Watching", makes the point that mothers in primitive tribal societies chewed food into a soft paste and transferred it to their baby mouth-to-mouth. This practice, he says, developed into human kisses. If you want to believe your dog is kissing you, that´s fine, but you should think about what it might have been licking before giving you a "kiss".

Licking as attention seeking is unwanted behaviour. The dog licks and we respond by giving it attention and affection. So the dog learns to lick for attention, which might be the start to a dog becoming dominant.

A dog will often lick its lips when it is corrected for bad behaviour. In this case, the licking is a sign of submission. I look for this sign when taking the lead of a dominant dog and giving it a quick tug. Often a dog will also give a quick lick of the lips when wagging its tail to greet you when you return home. (See **Scratching and licking**).

LIFE SPAN

The smaller the breed, the smaller the litter and the longer the life. Toy breeds may only give birth to one or two pups and suffer considerable difficulties at birth. On the other hand, giant breeds such as the Great Dane, which has a short life span of around seven years, may have up to 14 pups in a litter. Interestingly, animal scientists believe that dogs inherit their characteristics equally from the sire and dam.

LIP LICKING

When your dog licks its lips, it is a sign of nervousness or submission. It will often do when you return home. It also happens when I am training a dog and is an indication that it has recognised me as the boss. If your dog never licks its lips, it probably sleeps where it wants and barks at all visitors and is the dominant dog in the household. (See **Ten Commandments**).

MAGAZINES (See **Publications**)

"Cat's Motto: No matter what you've done wrong, always try to make it look like the dog did it."

Unknown

MAGNETIC COLLARS

Magnetic collars, including the Bioflow range, for dogs and cats can improve the condition of some dogs with arthritis and swollen joints and give them a better quality of life.

MALES (See **Sexual Tendencies**).

MANGE

The contagious symptoms of mange, which are caused by parasites in the hair follicles, are scratching and raw skin. Consult your vet. (See **Lice**).

MAN WORK

This is when a dog is trained for defence or attack work with humans. When taught correctly, under proper control, it is a game which stimulates the dog's natural drives. With correct training and guidance from an experienced trainer, man work does not, and should not, make a dog aggressive.

MARROWBONES (See **Bones**).

MAT TRAINING

By Kevin McNicholas. (See **Acknowledgements**).

The purpose of this exercise is for you to be able to put your dog on a special mat anywhere in the house by training the dog to think of the mat as a pleasant and rewarding place to be.

The mat should be a towel or square of carpet, not the dog's usual bed or basket.

Use tasty treats or rewards such as liver pills, bits of chicken or cheese. You also need a four-foot webbing or rope lead to use throughout the following weekly stages.

Week one.

Place the mat on the floor a few steps away from you and your dog. Sprinkle a few treats onto the mat so the dog sees them fall. Let the dog eat some of the treats from the mat, saying "On your mat" repeatedly and quietly while sprinkling more treats onto the mat.

If possible try to ensure the dog does not see you dropping the treats. Stand up, do not bend over, and drop the treats surreptitiously from waist level. It is important that the dog's attention is on the mat area, not the owner.

Week two

When the dog has almost finished eating the treats, with one or two still left, use the lead gently to pull the dog away. Take the dog two or three steps away from the mat, then let it return immediately. When it reaches the mat start saying and repeating "On your mat". Surreptitiously, drop a few more treats, the aim being to trick your dog into thinking that the mat is a magic carpet that sprouts a never-ending supply of treats.

Third week

The dog should by now realise that the mat is rewarding. Hold it five or six steps away and allow it to race you to the mat allowing it to win.

Fourth week

Using the command "On your mat", encourage the dog to settle there, rewarding it with treats when it does so and increase the time it stays on the mat. Do not confuse it by using Sit or Stay commands.

In the following weeks, you can build up the exercise, rewarding the dog when it is on the mat and using the lead if it wanders off. When it stays for 30 seconds or more, introduce some mild distractions, randomly dropping more

food on to the mat without turning to face the dog. If your dog leaves the mat to join you at this stage, go back to the fourth week regime.

Continue to build up the distractions so that the dog stays on the mat even if a doorbell rings or someone new walks into the room. When your dog ignores all distractions you can remove the lead for you should have incorporated the "On your mat" command into its life."

©*Kevin McNicholas,* 1999. (See **Puppy – controlled**).

MATING

The female should be taken to the stud dog. Male dogs are often distracted if they are taken to strange premises. As a prelude, the dogs will sniff the area of each other's genitals. After a variable length of courting, the bitch should allow the male to mount, standing with her tail aside. The tie lasts several minutes.

Finally the dogs swivel round and remain in a back to back position, facing away from each other, joined in the genital "lock" where they should be left until they have uncoupled.

MEALS (See **Food**)

MICROCHIPS

Responsible pet owners use microchips to ensure that if their pets are ever lost and taken to a pound they will be returned as quickly as possible. Increasingly, it is becoming a legal requirement in Spain as local councils pass the necessary by-laws, and responsible breeders are using them to ensure the puppies they sell can be identified if lost or, for any reason, turned over to a shelter or pound.

The microchip, about the size of a grain of rice, is inserted between the shoulder blades with a syringe like instrument. It contains no batteries or chemicals and has an active life of about 25 years. The age at which this can be done varies with the size and development of the dog, as a certain amount of muscle tissue is necessary. With larger breeds, it can be done by 7 to 9 weeks of age, which is when most puppies go to their new homes. Most vets can insert microchips.

When scanned, the microchip will reveal a code that is unique to the dog. By consulting the appropriate chip registry database, relevant information can be obtained, including the dog's owner, breeder, emergency contact, even health problems and food requirements. Implanting the chip and registering the information is included in the cost. Dog clubs often have group microchip discounts.

The advantages of a microchip are that it cannot get lost or stolen like a collar, it cannot be worn off or removed like a tattoo and, as stated, additional information can be registered and, in some databases, changed.

The disadvantage is that they cannot be detected or read without a scanner and not all pounds or animal shelters have them. Another criticism is that some thieves of valuable dogs have become expert in removing microchips. When microchips were first introduced, some owners feared that the chip could move around the body, but nowadays a non-toxic coating is used to anchor the chip in place. (See **Name tags, Quarantine** and **Tattoos**).

MITES (See **Lice**)

MONGRELS

Before buying a pedigree dog, have a look at the dogs in the local animal shelter. Adopting a dog from an animal shelter will save a life and will not contribute to the prosperity of bad breeders or puppy farmers who perpetuate genetic diseases.

Dogs from shelters will not cost more to feed or be any less loving than their pedigree cousins. What's more, mixed breed dogs are not subject to more than 300 potential genetic diseases, the result of injudicious breeding practices and a perverted logic that places success in the show ring over soundness in temperament and configuration. This includes a much lower chance of a mongrel suffering from hip dysplasia compared to a pedigree dog. Think mongrel. (See **Hereditary diseases**).

MOON – FULL

Do dogs howl at a full moon? I asked one of my Internet forums. Here are some answers:

"They are not howling at the moon. They are howling at another wolf (dog). It so happens that the moon is out." *George Grayson.*

"After reading a lot about wolves and why they supposedly howl together in groups, I tried it with my dogs, as a sort of bonding thing. At first they looked at me with really odd expressions on their faces, sort of incredulous and apprehensive, but then they joined in. They had never howled up until that point. Also, my only dogs that will do this are German Shepherds. My Great Danes, Collies, and Poodles never joined in."

Joyce Carrin Sprague. Carrin.Sprague@reliastar.com

My GSD will howl at the moon but only if the rest of the family howls first. We do so periodically so she will not forget her distant wolf relatives! She loves it! The Labrador never joins in, though, but just sits and stares at us all as if we are mad! *Julie, JULIEBOT@aol.com*

MOUNTING

Both females and males will mount each other or a person's leg to masturbate. (See **Sexual tendencies**).

Case Histories:

Question: I have a beautiful Husky. He was castrated when he was six months old and yet he still tries to mount dogs, even male dogs. Is there something wrong because I thought that castrated dogs did not do this?

Answer: Castration will not make any difference to his behaviour. I have known castrated dogs that have penetrated females on heat. The mounting of male dogs is also a form of masturbation. I would speak to your vet. Maybe he will consider some female hormone to calm him down.

Question: I have a female puppy (about nine weeks old) and she has mounted my leg and started "humping". This is usually when we are in the middle of a play session. She has shown some dominance and aggressive behaviour which I am trying to stop. Is this a way of her trying to prove her dominance? Or is she possibly an oversexed pup?

Answer: This is quite normal behaviour in young dogs. She is masturbating. Next time she mounts, kick her off quickly. If you do not act now it will become an obsession and as she gets bigger and stronger she will not let go. When you then try to get her off she will get aggressive. She sounds dominant, but much depends on how you handle her and where she sleeps and feeds. Get her enrolled into a puppy social class where you can learn all about dogs. Train, don't blame.

MOUTHING
(See **Biting, Puppy - mouthing** and **biting**).

MUZZLES

Many hate the idea of putting a muzzle on a dog and assume that a dog with one on is dangerous. This is not necessarily so. They may be obeying a law which requires their breed of dog to be muzzled or they may simply be trying to prevent it eating all sorts of rubbish and even poison on a country walk off the lead.

The earlier a dog is taught to wear one, the better. It will prevent destruction in the home and biting by a nervous dog when visiting a vet and stop the dog from licking a wound.

There are many types of muzzles but the one you choose must enable the dog to breathe. I recommend the Baskerville which is marketed by the eminent Roger Mugford. It is a basket design which allows the mouth to open sufficiently to pant and drink. It comes in 12 sizes to ensure that a good fit is available for most breeds of dogs, and is available through The Company of Animals. PO Box 23 Chertsey, Surrey KT16 OPU, UK.

A plastic box muzzle covers the whole mouth, which prevents the dog from drinking but allows it to pant more efficiently, important in hot weather. An efficient muzzle that protects against poisoning is the double-ended, plastic muzzle, but some determined dogs will push the muzzle into soft muck and lick what percolates through. (See **Walkies**).

MYTHS

Myths about canine health and behaviour still exist despite researchers having proved them wrong. How many dog owners have ignored signs of illness because they believed their dog's wet cold nose indicated it was healthy? Or how many have been bitten because they assumed a wagging tail meant a friendly dog?

Here are some of the myths with a cross-reference to the appropriate text heading if you want to learn more.

- A cold, wet nose does NOT necessarily mean a dog is healthy. (See **Nose**).

- Dogs do NOT always eat grass because they are sick. (See **Grass**).

- A wagging tail does NOT mean the dog is friendly and happy. (See **Tail wagging**).

- Dogs are NOT completely colour blind. (See **Sight**).

- Raw eggs are NOT good for dogs. (See **Eggs**).

- A female does NOT have to have one litter of puppies. (See **Spaying**).

N.A.D.O.I., National Association of Dog Obedience Instructors. (See **Organisations for Trainers**).

NAIL CUTTING (See **Grooming**).

NAMES

The wrong name for a dog can cause problems. I recommend that names end with an A, E or Y. The name can then be used with a sing-song voice, warm and friendly, or a little quicker, sterner and sharper. This enables the voice to reflect the owner's mood so that the dog can recognise whether the use of it is loving or a reprimand..

What's in a name anyway? Personally, I do not need to know the name of the dog I am training, although I ask, to be polite. The basic instructions of Heel, Sit, Down, Stay, Away and Recall can be implemented using body language.

For example, when walking off with a dog I will shake the lead very slightly, no more than a flick of the fingers. This is enough for the dog to know I am walking off. All starts are made with the left leg so that the dog can see the leg go forward. When the lead is not shaken (I emphasize that the shake is so slight that many do not see it), the dog knows not to move from the Sit, Stay. In the early stages the shake of the lead is changed to a slight movement of the left forefinger. Now the forefinger is the trigger for moving off at Heel. A lot of bodywork and knee nudging is required to achieve this.

NAME TAGS

The microchip is now generally accepted and it is compulsory in most parts of Europe. In the UK, the tattoo has been used by many breeders and show people. So, once again, the U.K. is the odd man out in Europe, not yet having adopted the much more sensible microchip.

Name tags should also be attached to every collar, irrespective of whether the dog has a microchip or tattoo. The best type is the metal one with the dog's name and your phone number engraved on it.

Some pet shops and vets sell a barrel type tag. You unscrew this and put your details inside, but they are not suitable for dogs or cats because they can accidentally twist open while being worn, and the information is lost. (See **Microchips** and **Tattoos**).

NARCOLEPSY

A sudden and overwhelming desire to sleep, which can occur at any time and is not to be confused with normal sleeping habits.

NATIONAL CANINE DEFENCE LEAGUE

The N.C.D.L. was founded in 1891 and is the UK's largest dog welfare charity. The aims are:

1   "To protect and defend all dogs from abuse, cruelty, abandonment and any form of mistreatment, both in the U.K. and abroad. The charity seeks to achieve this aim through the work of its nation-wide network of rescue centres, education and advocacy work and welfare campaigns.

2   "The charity is committed to the belief that no healthy dog should ever be destroyed and that all dogs should be protected, wanted, suitably homed for life and cared for by responsible owners."

It is supported by donations, legacies and fundraising events held by animal lovers and receives no state funding.

The following figures for 1999 demonstrate what an effective job the N.C.D.L. does.

Re-homed or adopted:	7,042	65.0%
Lost dogs re-homed with their owners:	1,716	15.9%
Dogs in care by N.C.D.L.:	1,433	13.3%
Dogs fostered:	403	3.7%
Dogs put to sleep:	122	1.1%
Dogs died:	53	0.4%

The N.C.D.L. has carried out numerous campaigns, such as obtaining amendments to the Dangerous Dog Act, fighting puppy farming, publicising the necessity for neutering and cleaning up dog mess in public places.

National Canine Defence League, 17 Wakley Street, London EC1V 7RQ. Tel. 0171-837 0006; Fax. 0171-833 2701

Excellant Internet site: www.ncdl.org.uk Very comprehensive. List of contacts. "Bark back" page for questions.

NEUTERING
(See **Castration**, **Sexual tendencies** and **Spaying**).

NERVOUSNESS
This can be inherited or created by an event or events. The obvious signs of a nervous dog taking fright are whining and whimpering, running away and hiding, or burying its head under cushions. Others include lip licking, shaking, the hair on the hackles rising (the equivalent of shivers down the spine), tail drooping, sometimes between the legs, ears down and even urinating, especially with females.

Nervous dogs are particularly susceptible to noise or sounds from outside their territory, barking incessantly to send the intrusion away. Sometimes a nervous dog will flee if approached.

Either the nervousness has been inherited or there has been a lack of early socialisation with people and other dogs. Take the dog to a social class. Walk it on a lead in towns.

NEW HOME – saying goodbye
As soon as you know you have to find a new home for your dog, start cooling off the relationship. No more sleeping in bedrooms should you have made this mistake in the first place.

When the time comes it is best to say "Goodbye" very quickly and go. The dog will pine for you for a few days but will soon adapt to the new family pack.

Dogs react to what is happening now. They do not live in the past and do not think about the future. It is best not to visit the dog.

> *"Outside of a dog, a book is probably man's best friend; inside of a dog, it's too dark to read."*
> *– Groucho Marx.*

New Year's Resolutions

I do not need suddenly to stand straight up when I'm lying under the coffee table.

I will not roll my toys behind the fridge or put my head in it.

I must shake rain water out of my coat before entering the house.

I will not eat the cat's food, before or after the cat has eaten it.

I will not be sick in the car – too often.

I will not roll on dead seagulls, fish, or any other decomposing mess.

I will not lick my human's face after eating animal mess.

I will not eat any more socks and then deposit them in the garden after processing.

I will not chew humans' toothbrushes and not tell them.

I will not insist on having the car window rolled down when it's raining.

I will not bite the policeman's hand when he reaches in for the owner's driving license.

I will remember that the dustbin man is not stealing our rubbish.

I will be kind to the postman and only tear up bills.

NOSE

A cold nose is no indication of a dog's state of health. Normal canine temperature ranges from 101-103° F. A dog with a temperature can still have a cold wet nose.

OBEDIENCE versus BEHAVIOUR

By Dennis Fetko, PhD. (See **Acknowlegements**)

Many dog owners confuse obedience and behaviour. Obedience means the direct response to a specific command. If the dog Sits or Stays when commanded to do so, that's obedience. Behaviour means everything else; what the dog acts like when it's not under a specific command.

Many people who have dogs with behaviour complaints enrol in obedience classes and are disappointed, no matter how well the dog obeys commands. The reason: the dogs had a behavioural complaint but underwent obedience training.

Most dogs are abandoned because they are destructive or dangerous. Behaviour training, concentrating on the unwanted act instead of commands, can make problems disappear.

We often hear that obedience training cures all complaints because it establishes the owner as the dog's superior authority. That's a logical theory with little basis in reality. No matter how completely the dog accepts you as boss, it's unlikely its behaviour will improve if it isn't taught the correct act. If it is, you don't need the obedience command. We often punish ignorance, not defiance. That's a shame because what the dog does or does not learn is up to us. Punishing unwanted behaviour but failing to teach the correct act is stressful, harsh and counter-productive.

To overcome this, some owners use counter-command. They use obedience commands to replace unwanted acts. They train jumpers to Sit upon command because dogs cannot Sit and jump at the same time. But this approach has negatives. First, if the dog enjoys jumping onto you, being made to sit instead results in something it wants less. You have just punished the dog for obeying your command because sitting prevents a greater pleasure. And must the dog obey everyone that commands it to Sit? If not, it might Sit when you enter but jump onto others. If so, is it wise to teach your dog to obey every intruder?

It is more successful to teach the dog to simply stay off people, without commanding Sit. But don't confuse obedience with good behavior. And enjoy your wonderful dog.

OBESITY

About 25% of dogs are overweight. Being overweight will place greater stress on the heart and could lead to an earlier death than a dog kept to a sensible weight. Overfeeding is not a kindness. It could well shorten your dog's life.

You should check your dog's weight when you buy worming tablets at the vets in order to work out the correct number of tablets you should give it. This is the time to ask your vet for advice about the dog's weight. Beware, though. I have heard some vets are reluctant to tell an owner that the dog is overweight for fear that the owner will take the dog somewhere else where there will be no criticism. (See **Food**).

ODOURS

If your dog has a strong doggy odour, there could be many causes and there are many solutions. It can be caused by the dog rolling in decomposing organic material. This is a throwback to the past when a wolf out hunting would disguise its scent by rolling in the dung of its prey. A good bath will cure the problem today.

A smelly dog might be due to excessive skin oil. Usually a dog shampoo will do the trick. Some dogs will require weekly baths. Between baths you can use dry shampoo. If there is no problem, shampooing can be detrimental because it removes natural skin oil.

If your dog has a skin problem, consult your vet about the best medicated shampoo because there are different ones available depending on the problem. Just buying any dog shampoo might be counter-productive. The food you are using could result in an excess of oil in the skin and coat. Try a food with a lower fat content. Some contain a yucca plant extract that results in less smelly stools and urine. "Eagle" is one brand that includes yucca in the formula.

Better general nutrition could be the solution. If you are buying a cheap food from a supermarket, try feeding a better quality dog food, such as a Super Premium like Hills Science Diet or Euakanuba, Purina or Pedigree. Extra vitamins, minerals and particularly biotin have been found to help dogs with odour.

Excessive body odour could indicate an illness. Really offensive odour could be a sign of cancer, seborrhea, mange and a variety of other diseases. See your vet.

Yeast infections and other infections in the ears are quite common and cause odour. Seek professional advice. If your dog smells in the hindquarters, the problem could be hair matted around the rectum.

The anal sacs are another problem area. Located to the left and right of the anus, they produce a sour or rancid, smelly, watery secretion that is brownish in colour. The sacs usually empty to give your dog's stool its identifying smell.

Sometimes they empty explosively when the dog is frightened or stressed. Other times the anal sacs do not empty at all. This could be a reason your dog is scooting along the floor, dragging its rear on the ground. Time to see your vet.

At the other end of the dog, offensive mouth odours could be due to gingivitis or periodontal (gum) disease. Again, see your vet. Mouth odour can also be a sign of corprophagy, or stool eating. Some dogs eat their own stools as a way of acquiring enzymes they need. Other dogs will eat horse manure, cow manure and dog and cat faeces because they taste good to them.

Finally, you can cover up minor body smells with one of a number of colognes for dogs, but do not use a human cologne.

OLD AGE

As with humans, old age in dogs affects eyesight, hearing and activity. An old dog might also not be so tolerant of young children. A dog's lifespan is around 10 years, longer for small dogs, shorter for the large breeds with exceptions at both ends of the scale. Never forget an older dog does not need much exercise and cannot tell you about its aching joints.

OLD DOGS, new tricks?

It is commonly believed that you can't teach an old dog new tricks. Don't confuse the word "Trick" with a circus term. In fact, you can teach an old dog obedience often quicker than a young dog..

OVERWEIGHT (See **Food** and **Obesity**)

PANTING

A dog only sweats only through its paws and tongue. Panting helps the sweat to evaporate. Dogs grew thick hair on their bodies when they lived in a cold climate and needed the hair to keep warm. There was, therefore, no need for sweat glands on the body. (See **Summer safety**).

PARASITES

There are quite a few of these nasty things, the principle ones being **Fleas**, **Lice**, **Mites**, **Mange**, **Ticks** and **Worms**, all dealt with under the appropriate headings. (See **Symptoms**).

"Some of my best leading men have been dogs and horses".
Elizabeth Taylor

PARVOVIRUS

Dogs of all ages are affected by this disease but it mainly occurs in puppies. If it is not fatal, there can be a quick recovery. Vaccination is included in the annual booster.

PATTING

People usually pat dogs when they are happy with them, but the dog can think otherwise. The basic signals of communication were taught when the puppy was with its mother and siblings. One is nudging by the mother when the pup 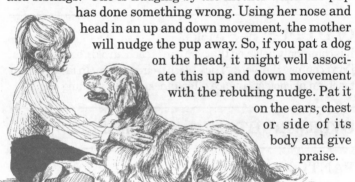 has done something wrong. Using her nose and head in an up and down movement, the mother will nudge the pup away. So, if you pat a dog on the head, it might well associate this up and down movement with the rebuking nudge. Pat it on the ears, chest or side of its body and give praise.

PAWS

Dogs sweat through their paws that have only four toes, the fifth (called dew claw) having been sacrificed for speed in running. (See **Dew claws**).

PEDIGREES

Not worth the paper they are written on unless you are entering shows. (See **Breeding**).

PENS (See **Crates**).

Photographing a puppy

Remove film from box and load camera.

Remove film box from puppy's mouth
and throw away in bin.

Remove puppy from bin.

Mount camera on tripod and focus.

Find puppy and take dirty sock from mouth.

Place puppy in pre-focused spot and return to camera.

Forget about spot and crawl after puppy on knees.

Focus with one hand and fend off puppy
with other hand.

Get tissue and clean nose print from lens.

Take flash cube from puppy's mouth and throw away.

Put cat outside and attend to the scratch
on puppy's nose.

Try to get puppy's attention by squeaking
a toy over your head.

Replace your glasses and check camera for damage.

Call someone to help clean up mess

Pour a drink

Resolve to teach puppy to Sit and Stay.

PHANTOM PREGNANCIES
(See **Sexual tendencies**)

POISONS

Ordinary household products contain many of the substances that poison animals every year. They include insecticides to kill ants, fleas, termites, wasps, pesticides against rats and mice, herbicides to kill garden weeds, cleaners used in homes, fuel and other petroleum products used in cars, heaters, and even lighters.

The combination of being common and dangerous means that pets which share our homes, gardens and cars are particularly vulnerable, depending on the amount of toxic ingredient in the substance. It is vital in any potential poisoning situation to take the container with its label of contents to a vet. All poisons do not necessarily have the same ingredients.

Salmonella Poisoning

Feeding dogs raw meat and uncooked bones, raw eggs or chicken, allowing them access to rubbish bins full of rotting garbage or having a bird feeder within snacking range, can result in salmonella poisoning.

Commonly classified as food poisoning, salmonella is a group of about 2000 related bacterial strains. It causes gastrointestinal infections and can be very dangerous. All livestock carry the bacteria which is transported via the retailer to your home.

Dogs eating bird droppings or birdseed that has been touched by the infected birds are at risk. Animals who are carriers of the bacteria spread it to other animals and humans via their faeces. Although susceptibility depends upon the animal's immune system, the strength of the particular strain and the amount ingested, salmonella in its slightest form is a very painful infliction.

Prevention includes cooking all raw meats (including poultry) and using a cooking thermometer to determine minimal acceptable temperatures to kill the bacteria - meats 170° F. (82° C.), poultry 185° F. (90° C.)

- Thaw all frozen meat and poultry in the refrigerator instead of outside.

- Secure all possible sources of rubbish.

- Wash all preparation surfaces, utensils and your hands in hot, soapy water to avoid contamination of other foods.

- Keep your dog away from animal's faeces and bird feeders.

- Disinfect bird feeders with a mixture of 250ml bleach to one litre of hot water. Be sure to rinse thoroughly before refilling the tray with seed.

Pest Control

Pesticides can be dangerous, but there are alternatives:

- Marigolds will repel many garden pests such as beetles.

- Daffodil bulbs or garlic plants keep mice and moles at bay.

- Basil in pots near your outdoor sitting areas will deter flies and mosquitoes. Spearmint acts in the same way for ants.

- Ladybirds eat aphids and make pesticides unnecessary.

- If you want a harmless ant repellent, wash kitchen tops, cabinets and floors with equal parts of vinegar and water or pour a line of cream of tartar at the place where ants enter the house. They won't cross the line.

- Strip old fruit from trees to stop caterpillars from laying their eggs.

- Flea and tick repellent can be made by boiling half a litre of water. When cool, add either a thinly sliced lemon or one of a combination of herbs such as fennel, rue and rosemary. Stand the mixture overnight and spray or sponge onto your dog. This only keeps fleas and ticks off pets. It will not make residents leave.

193

- Put cedar chips around clothes or dried lavender sachets in drawers and closets to repel moths.

- Place whole bay leaves in several locations around the kitchen to repel roaches.

Signs of poisoning

Signs appear from six to 72 hours after the poisoning and include fever, vomiting, dehydration, constant diarrhea, weakness, depression and loss of appetite, burns around the mouth, reddening of the skin, staggering, twitching, convulsions, even coma. Get your dog to a vet immediately.

POLICE DOGS

By Grant Teeboon, a senior police dog handler with the Royal Australian Air Force for the last 20 years. (See **Acknowledgements**).

"There has been a massive increase of legal actions by criminals against canines.

Having been a police dog handler for 20 years and listening carefully to my counterparts on the other side of the globe, it is clear that the avoidance of litigation is fast becoming a battle that must be fought by the handler on the street.

About 40 percent of Internet posts to Police K9 lists involve enquiries about how to handle/avoid litigation and about how current local policy will affect their ability to withstand a challenge.

In these trying times where everyone is being asked to do more than before with less money and resources than before, it is the handler who suffers. Dwindling resources and cutbacks on training time and allowances forces the handler to take the shortest route to train his dog, not always the best policy.

Our Police Forces and their dogs used to be called America's / Australia's / Britain's finest. How much longer can they tolerate the shrinking of their support structure before they become "The best we could do with the resources we had"?

Differing methods of police dog training

The Koehler Method is by far the most common training method used throughout the world for police and service dogs. The recent trend in the public sector to change over to "force free" training methods has also encroached into the police and service sector. Notably Steve White from Canada has trained at least two police dogs using predominantly clicker methods. While Steve seems more than happy with the results, the mainstream will wait for a while longer to embrace this new technique.

Concerns have been raised about the level of commitment and the dog's ability to withstand force used on it by an attacker. It certainly appears that clicker training may at least be able to supplement the existing training, but I doubt that it will ever replace current methods entirely.

Support your local Police K9

Increasingly in the States, police K9 units are being forced to be self-funding. With everything from public displays, baseball cards of the K9 handlers, donations from public and commercial sponsorship, the K9 unit is being asked to carry more and more of its own financial burden.

Drug dogs are surely paying their way with the millions of dollars worth of drugs being found, but patrol dogs and tracker dogs are paying their way by a service that is not recognised in cash terms. The preservation of human life and the sheer deterrent value of a police dog is being overlooked in favour of a revenue making asset.

The message that this sends to the K9 handlers of the world is a distressing one. It reeks of the old days when some traffic officers had to meet their "quota" of tickets to raise the revenue for their existence. Cutting back on the funding of K9 units is like buying cheaper and cheaper parachutes... one day when you really need them, their performance will have been so degraded by cutbacks that their performance level will become unacceptable, a death knell for any unit.

Why is it that the management of these organisations cannot see that we have to maintain a certain safety level that cannot be impinged upon? Would you like your family to trust their lives with an airline that spent less than all other airlines on maintenance and safety? That may be over simplifying it a bit, but the principle is still valid. Police forces everywhere are putting too much focus on revenue gathering and not enough on "deterring" the criminals before they start to generate their own revenue.

Have you ever wondered if the release of a police dog on an offender is considered as the use of deadly force? Statistics recently quoted in the US show that there has only been one fatality caused by the release of a police dog. Most courts within America now recognise that a bite from a police dog is not the same as deadly force. Incidentally, the man who did die was hiding beneath a parked car and refused to come out. The dog was used to extract him and during the struggle the man received a bite on his neck from which he subsequently died.

Grant Teeboon http://www2.dynamite.com.au/gtboon/
ICQ: 12854070 "JAWS, with PAWS, enforcing LAWS".

POLICE DOG SELECTION

By George Grayson. (See **Acknowledgements**).

"I am often asked when obedience training should start. My answer is the day you get the dog. The two fundamentals are a training plan and training equipment.

I am often told that the articles I write for publications in the U.K. are 'Equipment Related'. I am not afraid to admit this. Without being correctly and adequately equipped, training is much more difficult. Time and effort can be wasted and the end product (i.e. the quality and standard of training) might be inferior.

In my lectures to handlers I train, I repeat the same phrases:

- You only get out of a dog what you put in.

- A dog can never ever be any better than the handler makes it.

- In training there is no such thing as a perfect dog – problems will arise with any dog.

- A good and efficient handler who works and takes pride in his dog will always have a good dog.

- With an inefficient or poor handler, his standard will be reflected in the dog irrespective what qualities the dog has.

A programme of training should be prepared before the acquisition of a puppy. Although a handler might prefer to start with a young puppy, there are always the obvious dangers that the puppy would genetically not have the right character, temperament or working ability.

These factors cannot be positively assessed until the puppy is about eight or nine months old. There is also the added danger, particularly with a German Shepherd puppy, that hip dysplasia could develop later, even though all necessary known precautions have been taken. Acquiring a dog for training at the age of about eight to 12 months eliminates a lot of these problems.

In selecting a puppy from a litter, I like to know the history of the particular line of breeding. If possible, I would buy from a repeat mating and from a bitch whose previous progeny I had seen develop.

Selection of a puppy from a litter is not easy when they are only six weeks old. I always removed the bitch puppies if I was seeking a dog, then I usually removed the smallest from the litter. The handler was always given preference to select the one he wanted, unless I had strong objections.

For obedience training of Service Dogs there is an anomaly that a long check/choke chain is usually required for practical use with criminal work for releasing the dog. Yet, teaching heel work, a long check/choke chain can be a disadvantage, i.e. the dog is easier to correct and the hand is kept on the lead, not a long length of chain.

I used long link 26-inch chains for training, shorter for smaller bitches, but a longer chain is preferable to slip a dog for a chase. There is of course a right way and a wrong way to put on a check/choke chain. The chain should pass over the top of the neck of the dog.

POLICE DOGS - web site

Police dogs sometimes give their lives protecting their handlers. Visit the Police Dog Homepage and then go to the very large Valour Section and you can read the stories of how these police dogs gave their lives... and in some cases how their handlers gave their lives, too.
http://www.policek9.com/rollcall.htm

POODLES (See Top Dogs)

POOP SCOOPS

The single most hateful thing about dogs for non-dog owners and responsible dog owners is excrement scattered over pavements and public places, especially where children play. Around 900 tons of excrement are deposited each day by the 6.8 million dogs in the UK, according to Department of Environment figures based on pet food sales.

It really is the responsibility of dog owners to clear up the mess left by their dogs and not give more reasons for the anti-dog lobby to demand greater restrictions to the detriment of all.

Remove it with a poop scoop or plastic bag with the hand inside the bag, turned inside out, and place the bag in a dustbin. Please.

POMERIAN (See **Top Dogs**)

POPULATIONS

According to R.S.P.C.A. statistics, (other sources vary)the worldwide dog population is more than 200 million. The following are the countries with the largest number of dogs:

U.S.A.	60 million.
France	10.8 million.
Russia	10 million.
U.K.	7.2 million.
Japan	7 million.
Italy	5 million.
Germany	4.5 million.
Australia	3.1 million.
Spain	2.9 million.
Scandinavia	2 million.
Belgium	1.6 million.
Holland	1.4 million.

(See **Statistics**)

POSITIVE REINFORCEMENT

This is giving a reward (a positive thing) after a dog has obeyed you as opposed to a scolding or physical punishment (negative reinforcement) when the dog has done wrong.

PRAISE

Praise is an important form of reward but it is often over-done. All animals need praise but it should only be given at the right time. When a dog is corrected, it is vital that the very second the unwanted behaviour ceases, the dog is praised. Praise is given by treats or the voice: "Gooood Dog" in a singsong voice. You should not correct a dog unless praise can be given instantly.

PREGNANCY – avoiding

If you are not deliberately breeding and you have not had your dog spayed before her first heat as is generally recommended and the bitch gets pregnant, or you fear she has been mated when on heat, go straight to your vet. Injections are available to avoid a pregnancy. An injection is much better than having to put down unwanted puppies or to find good homes for them. (See **Puppy – birth**).

PRESENT LIVING

As stated elsewhere, dogs are present living creatures. They don't remember past events except when a trigger happens which the dog links with a bad experience (not the actual event) in the past. The trigger can be a sound, smell or an action which, if you can establish what it was, should of course be avoided. Depending on what the bad experience was, it can result in aggression by the dog or simply fear.

Dogs also do not think about the future but they will often know when it is time to be fed, associating the feeding bowl with a pleasurable experience. So, being present living animals, it is useless to reprimand or punish (which is an unproductive reaction anyway) after more than three to five seconds. By then the dog will have forgotten what it has done. (See **Instinct, Intelligence** and **Triggers**).

PROCESSIONARY CATERPILLAR

The processionary caterpillar is a danger every spring in Southern Spain where there is an abundance of the pine trees they use for nesting.

The white, fluffy nest they build in the autumn, contains dozens of developing caterpillars and a pollen-like poisonous substance can be blown off the nests by the wind.

More dangerous for dogs, however, is when the caterpillars have developed and seek new territory by crawling along the ground in a long line, one behind the other, hence the term "processionary".

Some dogs are fascinated by this moving line of the black and yellow furry creatures and will be tempted to sniff and lick them, thus absorbing the caustic acid which can cause frothing at the mouth and severe burning of the lips and tongue.

The dog should be rushed to a vet because the poisoning can result in serious wounds or even prove fatal.

PRO DOGS

Pro Dogs is a national charity in the U.K. that promotes the good name of dogs and defends their interests. It also runs an insurance scheme and grief counselling.

National Head Office:

Rocky Bank, 4 New Road, Ditton, Aylesford, Maidstone, Kent. ME20 6AD. Tel. West Malling (01732) 848499.

http://www.k9netuk.com/charities/prodogs.html

PUBLICATIONS (U.K.)
NEWSPAPERS

DOG WORLD – Somerfield House, Wotton Road, Ashford, Kent, TN23 6LW. Tel. 01233 621877. Fax. 01233 645669. E-mail: newspaper@dogworld.co.uk

OUR DOGS – 5 Oxford Road Station Approach, Manchester, M60 1SX – Tel. 0161 228 1984. Fax. 0161 236 0892 E-mail:: www.ourdogs.co.uk

MAGAZINES

ALL ABOUT DOGS – Suite C, Heathmans Road, London, SW6 4JT. – Tel. 0171 384 3261 Fax: 0171 384 3264

DOGS TODAY – Pet Subjects Ltd, Pankhurst Farm, Bagshot Road, West end, Nr Woking, Surrey, GU24 9QR. Tel. 01276 858880 Fax. 01276 858860

DOGS MONTHLY – RTC Associates, High Street, Ascot, Berkshire, SL5 7JG – Tel. 01344 628269. Fax. 01344 622771.

MAD ABOUT DOGS – 101 Baginton Road, Coventry, Warwickshire, CV3 6FR. – Tel. 01203 416946. Fax. 01203 416053

PET DOGS – Ashdown Publishing, Avalon Court, Star Road, Partridge Green, West Sussex, RH13 8RY. Tel. 01403 711511. Fax. 01403 711521 Web site: www.petdogs.com E-mail: victoria@ashdown.co.uk Lynda@ashdown.co.uk

YOUR DOG – Roebuck House, 33 Broad Street, Stamford, Lincs. PE9 1RB.

Tel. 01780 766199. Fax. 01780 766416

E-mail: countrypursuits@compuserve.com

Here is the background to "Dogs Today" magazine by the editor *Beverley Cuddy*. (See **Acknowledgements**).

"Dogs Today" is a unique breed of dog magazine. It isn't part of a magazine empire. It is produced by a small team of people passionate about dogs. Within a glossy, easy-to-read format, it aims to help people acquire dogs that better suit their lifestyles, encourage breeders to produce better pups and then help new owners to bring their dogs up using the most modern approaches to diet, health and training. It's the undisputed leader of the pack with an audited circulation of over 37,000. It's also the only pet magazine that has received a magazine equivalent of an Oscar. "Dogs Today" aims to entertain and never lecture, while at the same time giving pet owners all the information they need.

As a teenager, I showed Beardies and campaigned my first three up to Champion. I gave CCs for the first time at just 22 and became the secretary of the Bearded Collie Club. But when one of my pups nearly died of parvovirus, I realised I'd turned into a pet person. Other show people couldn't understand why I kept Sally, a sickly, shy pup when it was obvious she'd never make it in the ring.

After writing for "Our Dogs" and working at "Dog World" as a sub-editor for a year, I spent three and a half years at the Kennel Club, first as information officer and then as assistant editor on the "Kennel Gazette". None of these jobs seemed to have any relevance to me now that I identified with the majority of pet owners.

After a year working as a bored journalist, I got the job of launch editor on the new pet magazine "Dogs Today". After two years of erratic management, "Dogs Today" was due to close with losses of £300,000. At that stage I bought the magazine for £1.

Industry experts thought I'd been robbed as I stood no chance of turning the title around! A year later we won the

Small Publisher of the Year award, the magazine equivalent of an Oscar. Readers knew we were in trouble and they went out and sold subscriptions to their friends. Contributors wrote for free until we were able to pay. As well as magazine 'Oscars', there have been a couple of entrepreneurial awards.

"Cosmopolitan" magazine made me one of their young women of achievement for saving the magazine and I've twice been invited to the Women of the Year lunch. For several years, I've written the only national newspaper column on dogs - in the "Mail on Sunday".

Six years later, "Dogs Today" is number one and dear old Sal (now aged nearly 15) still comes to work with me every day. I'm now 36. My partner is illustrator Kevin Brockbank - a regular contributor to "Dogs Today"! Both my parents also work on the magazine. It's a case of love me - love my dog mag!

PULLING ON A LEAD

One eminent dog behaviourist I know, Dick Russell (sitstay@premier.net), believes that pulling on the lead is a behaviour TAUGHT to the dog by the owner. He reasons that if you ask a friend to hold a hand out in front, palm out, fingers straight and you put your hand against theirs and push, their reflex action will be to push back.

The same thing happens with a dog. It strains forward against the lead while the owner pulls back. This action is, in fact, forcing the dog to pull forward, resisting the pressure of the owner's pull. So the problem is self-perpetuating, with the owner responding by pulling back

Since going for a walk is usually rewarding to the dog and a tight lead is the condition imposed by the owner, the dog will tolerate it to obtain the walk. In that sense the pulling is being rewarded.

Dick says a walk on a loose lead is easily accomplished with a pinch collar. The dog is rewarded with praise when

A dog strains forward against the lead while the owner pulls back. This action is forcing the dog to pull forward, resisting the pressure of the owner's pull. The problem is self-perpetuating

walking on a loose lead and negative reinforcement is applied with the pinch collar. Only a short, sharp correction should be made. There should NEVER be any tension except when the correction is made.

Incidentally, my behaviourist friend states that in his opinion the pinch collar is the world's ONLY humane training collar, and countries where it is illegal need to get "the foolish law changed". (See **Collars**, **Exercise** and **Walkies**).

PULSE RATE

When the animal is at rest the pulse rate is around 70 beats a minute in large dogs up to 120 beats a minute in small dogs. Excitement or fear can increase these figures. A human heart beats 70 to 80 times a minute.

PUNISHMENT

This only teaches the dog that the event will result in punishment. It does NOT teach it to stop doing whatever it is being punished for. So it is totally negative. Correction training using praise and rewards is far more effective. (See **Aggression**).

PUPPIES

Puppy – ages

Seven to 12 weeks. This is the correct time to take from the litter and to start socialising your puppy at a training class after its second set of injections. A good trainer will want to see proof of this having been done before allowing the puppy into the class. (See **Puppy – training**).

Eight to 12 weeks. This is the "fear imprint period" when anything bad happening to the pup can be recalled (not remembered) if a similar trigger caused by sense, smell or sound occurs a long time afterwards.

12-18 weeks. This is the time when it is most important to expose the puppy to the outside world, to people, children and traffic. If this is not done at this age, it can result in abnormal behaviour later.

Puppy – birth

Pregnancy may range from 59 to 65 days, the average pregnancy being 63 days. The smaller breeds tend to whelp earlier than the larger breeds. A bitch will destroy a pup if malformed, ill, or a weakling.

The average litter is five pups with around 30 minutes between each birth, but litters of up to 20 pups have been recorded. (See **Pregnancy**).

Puppy - buying

Buying a puppy is a long-term commitment and responsibility. So please consider the following points carefully.

Cost:

The main expenditure, apart from vet fees, will be the food bill and this will obviously depend on the size of the dog. The average cost of a good meal for a medium sized dog is around £15 to £28 a month. In addition, you will need a crate or bed, lead, water and food bowls and toys. Allow for kennel boarding fees of £5 or more a day. The highly recommended and worthwhile cost of going to a training and social class can vary from £2 to £7 a week. There will also be grooming and clipping fees for long-haired dogs, and I recommend pet health insurance to cover the imponderable cost of veterinary fees. This will be between £90 to £125 annually with the cost of medication not covered, which could be quite expensive for an older dog. Be sure to read the small print. With cheaper policies, there could be an excess of around £50 on vet's fees. (See **Insurance**). One of my dogs - she is 10 years old - has recently been diagnosed as having arthritis in her hips and her tablets cost £10 a fortnight. Finally, you may wish to join the club for your breed, which could cost an annual fee of around £60.

All this adds up to about £600 or more a year.

Time:

Dogs can take up a lot of time and attention, particularly as puppies when they will need to go outside almost hourly because they have very weak bladder control.

Lifestyle:

This is possibly the most important consideration of all because you will need to choose a breed that will suit you and your lifestyle.

The average life span of a dog is 13 years. Are your current circumstances likely to change during this time?

Will owning a dog become a problem if a family is started? You may have to move from a house with a garden to an apartment (where there could be restrictions about owning pets), or go to another country.

Will you be able to devote a lot of time to a puppy for the first few weeks? Are you going to be away from home for long hours during the day?

Dogs that become lonely and bored are more likely to bark and become destructive.

If you are out a lot, it may be unwise to buy a puppy. Get a mongrel from a rescue centre or a pedigree that needs re-housing from a breed rescue organisation.

Do you go away frequently? If so, will you be able to take the dog with you? If not, can you afford the kennel fees? Will you have time to attend training classes? Will you be able to take the dog for at least one good walk a day?

Breed:

So you have decided you can cope with a dog. Next, think carefully about the breed you should have, not necessarily the breed you would like to have. Again your lifestyle, type of accommodation, facilities for exercise and the spare time available are key considerations.

Find out as much as you can about different breeds. Get advice from a vet or dog behaviourist or owners on the breeds you are considering. Research the breeds by reading books or visiting some of the many breed sites on the Internet or phoning one of the many breed clubs. They could be giving shelter to an older dog that could save you the trials and tribulations of puppy training. (See **Breed characteristics**).

Selection:

When you have made your choice of breed, contact a breed club secretary to find out the names of local reputable breeders so that your name goes on the list for the next litter. A reputable breeder will only sell a puppy between seven and 12 weeks old. Younger than seven weeks is far too soon to take a puppy away from its mother. Older than 12 weeks can result in behavioural problems.

You will want to see the mother and, if possible, the father of the puppies. Indeed, you could enquire about their parents as well to ensure there is no hereditary hip dyspla-

sia. Have they been x-rayed for this crippling disease so common in some breeds? Have their eyes been examined for defects? Has there been any testing for deafness? Ask to see the inoculation certificate, though you probably won't have to do this with most breeders who will have automatically carried out this basic requirement.

You should be able to handle the puppies. Don't necessarily select the one that "chooses" you by coming forward. This could be a sign of potential dominance. Don't choose the one that lingers behind the pack or remains in a corner. This could be a sign of a nervous dog.

Females will grow up to be smaller than the males, but if you want a male dog you should find out how many males and females were in the litter because, generally speaking, if there are more females than males, those males will have more female genes in their makeup and inherit more female passive characteristics than male aggressive ones.

How much contact with adults (men and women), children and noises have they had? Have they been raised inside the home, with all the associated human contact and noises, or in an isolated kennel? As an insurance, you should also ask for a written agreement that the purchase is subject to a satisfactory examination by your vet within 48 hours.

Finally, as the RSPCA and National Canine Defence League advocate, never buy a dog from a pet shop, retail outlet, street market or from any other place where you cannot see the mother.

As stated earlier, the excellent alternative to buying a puppy is to visit your local animal rescue organisation or a pedigree breed rescue society to discuss adopting a rescue dog (Ask for a signed veterinary health certificate). You could be saving a dog that would eventually be put down. By buying an adult dog, you will know exactly what you are getting and will have the added satisfaction of doing a good deed. (See **Mongrels**).

The certificate of pedigree you will get from a breeder is not worth a great deal. It merely lists the puppy's antecedents but not the genetic diseases it might have had, though it can include details of tests carried out on the parents. A mongrel dog from an animal shelter will not have a certificate but will probably not be so vulnerable as pedigrees to certain problems. (See **Breeders, Exercises, Castrating** and **Spaying**).

Puppy – buying a purebred

This excellent advice comes from *Ann Thibault*, a highly respected U.K. breeder (See **Acknowledgements**).

- Research the breed you are interested in purchasing. What was it bred for? Large or small, each breed has particular traits that are part of the package.

- Visit at least three kennels. Spend time at dog shows. Talk to people knowledgeable about the breed. When going to look at puppies, leave your cheque book at home. A concerned breeder will want to interview you several times to make sure the pup is going to the best possible home.

- Make sure you are aware of health problems in the breed. Are hips x-rayed? Elbows? Heart and eye clear of problems? Make sure you are aware of particular breed problems before you buy.

- Get a contract with the purchase of your puppy. Read it carefully. This is your recourse if there are problems.

- Are you prepared to devote the time, effort and money to care properly for your pup? The initial purchase price will be the least amount of money you spend.

- Adorable puppies grow into adults quickly. Obnoxious, untrained dogs are the product of their environment. Your pup's education should start the day you bring it home. There is no need to wait until six months to train your pup. There are classes for puppies that begin at 12 weeks. Enroll in a course that will show you how to manage your pup as it grows into an adult.

- It's a fact that people spend more time shopping for an appliance than they do for a dog that will live in their home for the next 10 to 15 years. Don't fall into this category. Make a wise and informed purchase.

- If buying a dog sounds like a lot of work, you are right. You would not buy a car based on colour or looks. Make an informed purchase. © *1998 Ann Thibault.*

That is good advice, and I would add two points:
- Never be talked into taking two pups, even if the breeder does try to convince you that they will be company for each other. Two siblings could be a disaster All the breeder is trying to do is get rid of two of the litter as profitably as possible.

- Visit your chosen litter a couple of times and don't be afraid to refuse a pup if you change your mind. This will not worry a good breeder, whose only concern is that the puppies go to a good home.

Puppy - buyers packs

My good Internet forum friend *Diana Barbara*, a well-known Labrador breeder in Sussex (See **Acknowledgements**), gives the following puppy pack to each buyer:

- A Kennel Club registration certificate,

- A five generation signed pedigree,

- A 5 kilo bag of the brand of puppy food used in the kennel,

- A piece of the bed that the puppies have laid on in the last week or so,

- A "Bringing your Wylanbriar Puppy home" leaflet with information on feeding, worming, introducing the puppy to other animals / children, early training and so on,

- Recommendations about books to buy,

- Breed club contact numbers,

- Copies of the hip and elbow scores for both parents and an eye certificate

- A six-week free insurance cover note,

- A pack of puppy-sized chew bars,

- A copy of the signed puppy sales contract.

Did your breeder match, that I wonder?

Puppy – development

When a puppy is born, it cannot see, hear or smell and for the first two weeks relies only on a sense of touch until the eyes open. By three weeks, all the pups can see and hear. Tails begin to wag when the pups are suckling, teeth appear and infant barking starts.

Growth is rapid, and by four weeks old a puppy can be seven times its birth weight. At around seven weeks, they must be weaned because the milk supply stops. During this time it also starts to hear and smell things and the teeth appear.

Some puppies are more aggressive than others from a very early age. Others react to situations and develop a fighting response. These aggressive tendencies can easily be re-trained later, but it takes time to redirect those dogs that were aggressive from an early age. (See **Teething**).

Puppy - eliminating

Start by feeding three times a day with a good quality puppy food. Avoid over-feeding or making sudden changes in diet because both can cause diarrhoea. Allow 10 minutes for each meal and remove anything left after that time. Keeping to a feeding timetable helps you to predict evacuation times, and you can take action accordingly.

If you follow this intensive programme, you could have a happy, reliable pet in three days that's right, THREE DAYS - and it's easy, but you will have to be alert during all the puppy's waking hours for those three days.

You may have suffered before with other dogs you have owned. The frustration, the damage to your home, the smells, and the temptation to get rid of the puppy because "it wouldn't learn." The real problem was that the owner couldn´t learn how to deal with the puppy or didn´t have the patience to do so.

Housetraining or housebreaking is easy, but only if you do it the right way. The wrong way - yelling, screaming and hitting your dog - creates lasting bad feelings between the two of you and often fails. The right way is quick, easy, stress free and results in a proper, loving relationship between you.

Puppy – preparation

Be prepared before you bring your puppy home. You need two essential tools for house training besides the basics such as a leather lead, leather collar, and proper food for the age of your dog, a food dish and a water bowl.

The first tool is one of several products which contain enzymes to remove all traces of the inevitable messes on the carpet and elsewhere that will occur, and the second is a "crate", similar to a baby's playpen, to house your dog when you can't be there properly to monitor it (See **Crates**).

Some may think the crate is cruel but think about it. In the wild, where do dogs or wolves live? They seek out small dark dens or caves for shelter and once inside they select a tight, secure area to sleep.

Your puppy, like its wild ancestors, wants to feel secure and safe when it goes to sleep. So provide a secure, cave-like den in your home with a crate. The normal puppy's instinct is to keep the den clean and it will be prevented from destroying your treasured possessions and be safely confined when not supervised. But never leave a pup in a crate for more than two hours, except at night.

You could help your puppy to relax in its new surroundings by asking the breeder for a small piece of cloth or bedding that has been in close contact with the litter to give it a familiar smell.

Crates are made in different sizes so you should select one based on the present size of your puppy. Don't worry about having a crate for its full-grown size. You won't need it when the dog has grown up, although I recommend that the crate is retained for the dog to have a private space. If you want to do this you can buy a crate for the full-grown dog and get spacers to make it smaller for the puppy. A good pet shop owner can help in choosing the right size crate but, as a general rule, it should be just big enough so that your dog can turn around in it.

Use an enzyme product sold at pet stores (following the instructions carefully) whenever your puppy soils in the house. "Nature's Miracle" or "Piss Stop" work well. If you do not use these products, your dog will be attracted back to the spot where it made the mess. No amount of scrubbing or cleaning, not even with the strongest of bleaches, will completely remove the scent.

Only enzyme products will break down the odour to its component parts. Make sure that you saturate the soiled area completely. If urine is on a carpet, the enzyme product must cover the whole area. Pour more on than you think is necessary, allowing it into the carpet padding. It won't damage the carpet if you use too much. After a few minutes, you can soak up any excess with some paper towels.

For the first part of its life, your puppy has no control over its functions, just like a human infant. During the first 14 days of their lives, the mother stimulates the puppies to urinate and defecate by licking them, and she will then clean up the mess.

Initially, a puppy will believe it is alright to urinate and defecate anywhere outside its crate. Your job is to train it to go outside the house. If the puppy does soil some part of the house and you do not catch it in the act, it is too late to correct it, even if it is only a few seconds later. Don't get angry. The puppy will have already forgotten what it has done and will not understand why it is being punished. If you punished too late, all you are doing is teaching the puppy to fear you.

When you first bring the puppy home, take it outside to a grassy area. Use the same door each time. Say repeatedly "busy, busy, busy", or some similar word in low soothing tones. As soon as it has done its business, repeat "busy, busy, busy", adding "that's a gooooood dog. What a gooooood dog you are. That's a gooooood puppy." Your tone of voice should be happy and upbeat. The puppy will not, of course, understand what you are saying but it will know that you are pleased, especially if a tit-bit is given as a reward. Do not give orders like "hurry up" or "be a good dog." Keep to one simple word. Play with it for a while as another reward before taking it inside and putting it into the crate.

You can put an old towel in the crate. The puppy, used to lying against its mother or siblings, will be comforted by something soft. Don´t be alarmed if the puppy cries and whines when you go out. Remember, it is natural for young pups to do this when left by the pack. The answer is to ignore it for five or 10 minutes before leaving it and for the same period when returning, even if you have just gone upstairs. This will make the pup realise that its crying and whining does not bring rewards. The same applies to adult dogs (See **Ten Commandments**).

So, hopefully, the puppy has slept all night in the crate without crying or whining. Get up early because the first thing it will want to do when it awakes is to eliminate. If it is free to roam around the hall or a room it will go at what it considers a proper distance from the puppy bed. If it is confined to a crate it will hold on as long as it can.

Take it outside, when it will usually do its business quite quickly. There are a high percentage of pups, though, that will start to sniff around or get otherwise distracted and will forget why they are outside. When you bring them back in the house, they suddenly remember and you have a clean up job to do.

If the pup is easily distracted, take it out on a lead. Stand in one spot until boredom causes the puppy to do its business. Then take the lead off and let the puppy play. This is the reward for going outside and, within a few days, it greatly speeds up the process. If it does not perform, put the puppy back in the crate. Fifteen or so minutes later, take it out again. In time it will perform.

Some pups will need to go more than once. Only observation will tell you if yours is one of these. If it is, stay with the puppy until it has finished.

Now give the puppy breakfast. After a while, it is going to need to go out again. The time varies between puppies but for each individual it is more or less fixed. Put the puppy on grass again at this time.

Other predictable times when a puppy is going to need to relieve itself is when it wakes from a nap, after it has eaten or drunk water, whenever it has had a play session, at night before going to bed and then, depending on the puppy, about every two to four hours in between. It may signal the need by starting to sniff the designated area or by turning in a tight circle.

After a couple of days of being taken to the grass and being praised and rewarded for using it, your puppy will catch on because dogs are creatures of habit.

Clean up after your puppy because many dogs refuse to walk in an area fouled by faeces. Put your hand into a plastic bag, scoop up the faeces, turn the bag inside out and seal it or use a brush and a receptacle. Make this a standard practice to deter flies and mosquitoes if you live in an area where they are prevalent.

While in the house, you need to watch your puppy's every moment. If you need to go to the bathroom yourself, or do anything else, put it in the crate. The point is to see when it squats and apply a punishment. I use a bean bag by putting some beans into the toe of an old sock. Make several so that you always have one handy. Throw it to hit, not to hurt.

Should you find a pile or a puddle that you did not see the puppy deposit, simply clean it up. Showing it to the puppy and punishing it will not help. It may even result in the puppy starting to destroy the evidence. You can imagine how it will do this. Given time, most dogs will start telling you when they need to go out.

How long should you use the crate? My answer is, forever. However, if you want to substitute a conventional basket, you should use the crate until your puppy has gone 90 consecutive days without even once squatting in the house.

House training a puppy is attention intensive. It takes as much effort as training a child.

The difference is that when the puppy is trained, you can enjoy it. If you ever get a child trained, it marries and leaves home.

Do not teach a puppy to do its business indoors on newspaper. Once taught to go in a particular place on a particular surface, it will be hard to change the habit.

Finally, do not allow your puppy to sleep on your bed, in your bedroom or even go upstairs. Install a baby gate at the bottom of the stairs and save yourself many of the problems that arise from dogs having been given such freedom. (See **Dominance** and **Ten Commandments**).

If your puppy has any stool or bladder problems, do not hesitate to see a vet. Intestinal parasites can affect the stools, and bladder infections can occur, the symptoms including frequent urination of small amounts, unproductive straining, or licking of private parts.

Puppy - mouthing and biting

If you watch a litter of puppies playing, you will see that they spend much of their time biting and grabbing each other with their mouths. When you take a puppy from the litter and into your home, the puppy will play bite and mouth you. This is normal behavior, but it needs to be modified.

The first thing is to teach your new puppy that human flesh is much more sensitive than other puppies and that it hurts us when they bite. A puppy has very sharp teeth and a weak jaw. So the puppy cannot cause severe damage. An adult dog has duller teeth and a powerful jaw. So an adult dog can cause significant damage if it bites.

Any dog will bite given the right or wrong circumstances. If a small child falls on an adult dog or sticks a finger in the dog's eye, it is not surprising if the dog bites.

It is simple to teach a puppy bite inhibition. Every time the puppy touches you with its teeth, say "OUCH" in a harsh tone of voice. This will probably not stop the puppy from mouthing, but over time should result in softer and gentler puppy biting.

The commands to teach a puppy not to mouth are easy and fun. Hold a small handful of the puppy's dry food, say "take it" in a soft tone of voice and give the puppy one piece of food. Then close the rest of the food in your hand and say "off" in the same soft tone of voice. When the puppy has not touched your hand for three to five seconds, say "take it" and give the puppy a bit.

Now the puppy has been taught that "off" means not to touch. Do this before every meal for at least five minutes. After a couple of weeks of training, this is how you should react:

a)   Unexpected mouthing (you don't know the puppy is going to mouth until you feel the puppy's teeth):   say "OUCH" in a harsh tone of voice.

b)   Expected mouthing (you see the puppy getting ready to mouth you): say "OFF" before the puppy can mouth you.

c)   The puppy is mouthing you because it wants to play. If you have time to oblige, make it go into the Sit or Down positions with a reward. If you do not have the time, then you need to do a time out (crate, or otherwise confine the puppy, so the puppy can't continue to mouth you).

That is much easier and more humane than yelling "go away" at the puppy.

Puppy – problems

If your puppy has any of the following behaviour problems, seek professional help (often the problem can be solved in a single session on a one-to-one basis):

•   Mouths you excessively,

•   Seems unable to learn,

- Growls at you at any time.

- Guards its toys and food.

- Shows excessive fear.

- Is withdrawn.

- Hides from or is shy of people.

- Runs away.

- Barks excessively for no obvious reason.

- Chases children or other animals.

Puppy – punishing

As the late John Fisher suggested in his excellent book "Think Dog", puppies and dogs do not think like a human and for this reason we must try to think like them.

How does a mother punish her puppies? She never shouts or barks at them. If annoyed, she will use eye contact and facial expression to convey disapproval. If this does not work, she will try a low growl followed by a louder one, with a show of bared teeth. As a last resort, she will make a mock attack.

Despite the squeals of the pup, little or no contact is made. As soon as the pup responds, it is rewarded with licks. This procedure of correction and reward is repeated time after time during the puppy's formative first few weeks and is instinctively remembered for a lifetime.

So how do we humans punish a puppy? Eye contact and a firm "no" will ensure that the puppy will soon recognise your facial expression when you are displeased and the word "no" replaces the growl of the mother. As soon as the puppy stops misbehaving, stroke it briefly to emulate the mother's lick.

Remember, too, as with all dogs of all ages, it is useless to reprimand or punish more than a few seconds after the act. A dog has a retention span of only around three to five seconds. After that, it will not understand why it is being punished.

So if you come home to a mess or scene of destruction, it is useless shouting or smacking the puppy. It will only learn that the human, or pack leader, has come back to the den in an incomprehensible, aggressive mood. It is better to completely ignore the situation and not even speak to the puppy or dog for five minutes. Think puppy.

Puppy - training

Start socialising your puppy through a training class after it has had its second set of injections at around eight weeks.

At my classes, where I have a big open space under the Costa del Sol sun, I aim to work with them off a lead with the other dogs. I start the walk on lead. All those that pull go to the back. There is no reward for dogs that pull or try to lead a big pack. After a few stops and making the pups Sit, they are set free and the owners are told not to call their dogs. If the pups run ahead, I make the owners change direction so that the pups return to follow the pack.

The owners are told to bend down with their legs and arms open and quietly call their dogs when I blow my whistle. There are always a number of older good dogs who do an immediate Recall and the young ones follow. All the dogs get a cuddle and are freed again. The lesson is repeated many times with constant changes of direction, the most vital part being the Recall after which the pups are not put on a lead.

If there is a special class for puppies under five months in your area, join it because they can allow for a pup's attention span with short, positive, motivational sessions.

A mixed-age social class is not always suitable for puppies. If they are introduced to badly behaved adult dogs, they can emulate the behaviour or be scared for life.

There is an art in introducing young pups to other dogs and only an experienced trainer would know how to do this.

So, if a mixed-age class is your only option, go along first without the puppy and ask advice from the trainer, noting the methods and whether there are any other pups being trained. If you don't like what you see go, elsewhere.

At home, the dog's name should precede every command to act as an attention trigger. Whisper the command in a pleasant but firm, not harsh voice. Starting this way, you will never have to shout a command.

Only give a command once, using it when you know the puppy is going to do what you want. If the pup starts walking away from you, say "Away". If it come towards you, say "Come". When it gets up, say "Up". When it lies down, say "Down". This way the pup can never be wrong.

If it does not obey, hold the collar and push its bottom into the sit position and praise. Take the appropriate action if the other commands are not obeyed. Keep training to a few minutes, three or four times a day. This is enough to make progress without overwhelming or boring your dog.

Eye contact is important. Before any obedience exercise, you must get the dog's attention. When you call its name and it looks at you, praise it. If it will not look at you, use a squeaky toy or treat to attract attention.

You will need a collar and lead. Few pet shops or vets understand what is required. If they did they would not stock half the products they offer. Most collars and leads are not suitable for training. Check with a knowledgeable trainer. Use a half-check buckle collar (not a choke chain), and a leather or rope lead, soft to the hands (not chain type leashes or Flexi lines).

Possibly the most important command is the Down, particularly when you are walking and a large dog approaches. Do not pick up the puppy. Put it in the Down position and allow the other dog to sniff the pup, holding the lead slack. If held tight, this could indicate that you are nervous. The large dog will understand that the pup is being submissive and not attack. (See **Down** and **Tracking**).

QUARANTINE

The U.K. Government has announced a pilot scheme to start early in 2000 to dispense with quarantine for dogs travelling between European Union countries and the U.K.

The conditions are that the dog must be:

- Microchipped.

- Vaccinated against rabies.

- Blood tested at an approved laboratory to show that the vaccine has given sufficient protection. The blood sampling must be carried out at least six months before entry into the U.K. However U.K. resident dogs, vaccinated before the pilot scheme becomes operational, will not have to wait six months before being allowed back in the U.K.

- Issued by a private, authorised vet with an official health certificate recording details of the animal, its chip, vaccination and blood test.

- Tested for tapeworm and ticks 24 – 48 hours before entering the U.K. by a vet approved by the Government of the departure country.

Vets will send the blood test to the one (at the time of going to print) approved U.K. laboratory in Weybridge. Nobody knows how long a delay may occur. The same applies to tests in the European Community – in Spain for instance, there is only one approved laboratory in Granada.

So, for those in the European Community, a trip with your dog to the U.K. will have to be planned at least eight months in advance, with entry into the U.K. taking place within 24 – 48 hours of the tests for tapeworms and ticks.

The cost in the U.K. of microchipping, vaccination and the blood test has been quoted at around £150 with, perhaps, another £20 for the tapeworm and tick test in France for car travellers. Dogs travelling will require a booster vaccination each year.

The authorised routes are expected to include Calais to Dover and certain routes into Portsmouth from France, the Eurotunnel by road and certain (but not all) air route into Heathrow which rules out charter flights.

The countries qualifying for the pilot scheme are:

Andorra, Austria, Belgium, Denmark, Finland, France, Germany, Gibraltar, Greece, Iceland, Italy, Liechtenstein, Luxembourg, Monaco, Netherlands, Norway (not Spitzbergen), Portugal, San Marino, Spain (not Ceuta or Melilla), Sweden, Switzerland and the Vatican. The situation with Ireland is to be clarified.

All of which means that people are unlikely to take dogs on holiday with them for it would be cheaper and simpler to put them in kennels. However those leaving the U.K. to work or retire in one of the listed countries and for those wanting to return to the U.K. after living in one of those countries, will no longer have to be parted from their pets by outdated quarantine regulations.

Further information: Ministry of Agriculture Helpline
Tel: (44) 0181 330 6835 (9 a.m. to 5 p.m., Mon – Fri.)
E-mail: pets@ahvg.maff.gov.uk.
Web site: http://www.maff.gov.uk/animalh/quarantine/default.htm
(See **Microchips, Rabies**).

QUESTIONNAIRE

When a person seeks my advice, either personally or on the Internet (the site address is: www.thedogman.net), I ask the following questions so that I can identify a reason or reasons for the behavioural problem. The answers to these "loaded" questions give me all the information I need to assess the situation and to start a behaviour modification programme.

- What is your name and e-mail address?

- What is your dog´s name, breed and age?

- Is it a dog or bitch, and is it neutered?

- Did the dog came from a private breeder, pet shop, rescue centre, or elsewhere?

- Did you see the mother and father of this dog? If so, what was your opinion of them?

- What is the name and phone number of your vet and when did you last visit him?

- When did you acquire your dog?

- Is this your first dog?

- How many humans, including children, are in your household? Give ages.

- Is your dog house trained?

- Where does the dog sleep? In the bedroom, on the sofas, in doorways and thresholds?

- Does the dog eat before or after your meals?

- Does the dog leave its food, guard the bowl, beg or steal?

- Is the dog a fast or slow eater?

- How does your dog react to being groomed? Does it tolerate it, struggle, mouth, or bite?

- What are the dog's favourite games? Tug of war, rough and tumble, possession, killing toys?

- Does the dog use its mouth or play bite?

- Does the dog jump up on you or guests?

- Does the dog mount (leg, cushion or child)?

- Does the dog demand attention by nuzzling hands, barking, crying or biting?

- Does the dog pull on the lead?

- How does it react to other dogs in the street or park?

- Does the dog come back when called?

- Is the dog destructive? Where and when?

- How do you correct or chastise?

- Does your dog have any problems?

- Do you ha.ve any other information to give me?

RABIES

The rabies disease exists worldwide except in those islands or countries with rigorous quarantine regulations, which means most of Europe and is the reason for the change in the British quarantine laws (see **Quarantine).**

All warm-blooded animals are susceptible but it is mostly found in dogs, cats, bats and wild carnivores. The disease is transmitted by biting. A key symptom is the development of aggression, hence the danger of being bitten by a dog or other infected animal. Bites on the face or head are extremely dangerous because the closer the bite is to the brain, the more quickly it will be affected.

Contrary to popular opinion, frothing of a dog's mouth is not a symptom of rabies. Simple indigestion or nausea can cause frothing and unfortunately many innocent dogs have been killed because of this erroneous belief.

The incubation period is usually from 15 to 50 days but can be up to several months. Dogs in Spain must be vaccinated at three to four months and have an annual booster. (See **Symptoms**).

RACING DOGS (See **Greyhounds**)

RECALL

One of the most frequent complaints I get from owners is: "As soon as I let my dog off the lead it won't come back." So they resort to angry shouting and, when that does not work, many give up. They do not understand why their dogs, who followed them everywhere when they were puppies, suddenly change.

Most dogs do not get sufficient exercise, their only activity being taken out to relieve themselves. From the dog's point of view it is taken out to perform and then is taken straight back. It is being punished. If it has a few sniffs to smell out if other dogs have been around in its territory, it is rebuked. A simple change in our behaviour can alter all this. Don't take it home as soon as it has performed. Let it explore a bit and sniff.

Recall training should start in the home. Make it fun. Whenever you call a dog, always bend down in a crouched position. Open your legs and arms. This is a warm posture, not the aggressive one of somebody standing tall and shouting. Bending down reduces height and the open arms trigger the idea of returning to mother when a puppy.

Call your dog in a soft, loving voice. When it comes to you, give it a treat and a cuddle so that it realises that coming back is rewarding. Then release the dog and walk away. Repeat the lesson – time and time again. Using a film can half filled with liver pills to create a rattling noise helps because the reward on return is available in the can.

When going for a walk, take a toy like a ball and encourage the dog to drop it by giving a treat. Make it learn it must drop the ball to obtain the treat. Now comes the real object of the exercise. Put the dog back on the lead and continue the walk for a minute. Then let it off the lead. After a few repetitions your dog will learn that the lead is no longer a threat, no longer a signal that the walk has come to an end.

Put it on and off lead as much as possible, play games and then both of you will enjoy the walk. And guess what? It will always come back. Take the dog out to different places but always be consistent in your handling. Teach the dog to respond no matter where it is.

Another tip. When the dog is a puppy, keep your elbows bent so that the pup does not learn the length of your arms. Do not praise until the pup is close enough to be handled with bent elbows. Then when you need to catch the dog quickly, you have an extra few inches of arm-reach that the pup does not know about. Otherwise the dog rapidly learns how long your arms are and can stay just outside reach.

What do you do if the dog refuses to answer to the Recall? Is this something that only happens in situations of great distraction? Where does it happen? At what distance from the owner is the behaviour more likely to occur?

Based on these questions, I would choose a course of action. Either retrain the Recall and eliminate all other options - don't allow the dog off the lead during the training process if you can't enforce the Recall - or teach a different behavior such as Down at a distance.

If the problem only occurs at a significant distance from the owner, you might try teaching the Recall and/or Down at a distance with a whistle. The sharper sound will sometimes get a better response than a voice command when a dog is distracted.

Running away is not unusual when on a walk off the lead. Get a long training lead, giving the dog room to roam quite some distance. Have some treats in your pocket or, better still, put some treats in an empty tin and rattle it. As soon as the dog comes back, give him a titbit. It will learn to come to you when called or when the tin is rattled. In time you will find you can do away with the long lead.

When out off the lead, dogs should not chase or worry livestock. The answer is to accustom them to big "dogs" like horses and cows by taking them near on a lead and making them go into the Stay position. Practise, practise, train, train. (See **Down** and **Stay**).

REPEATING COMMANDS

Many owners are inclined to repeat shouted commands to their dogs. Often I hear 'Sit, Siiit, Siiiiit' - and the dog does not sit. Repeating a command teaches a dog to wait for more commands.

RESCUE CENTRES

If you got your dog from a rescue centre and do not know its background, there are some basic rules to follow.

Dogs react to the present time. They do not live in the past. Unlike humans, they have no recall of past life. However, if they have had bad experiences they can have an instinctive reaction to a variety of situations. The owner needs to identify the trigger and remove it or reassure the dog when the situation re-occurs.

This trigger could be activated through a smell, sound or a particular event like a rapidly raised arm which, in the past, preceded a thrashing. The dog does not know why it reacts, it just knows that the sound, sight or smell preceded a bad experience. (See **Instinct** and **Triggers**).

It takes a dog only two to three days to adjust to a new home, two weeks to start to try to establish dominance and around three months fully to settle.

Most humans feel sorry for the dog, believing it has had a bad life. So it can be spoilt with the consequence that the dog's status is raised. Always remember that during this time it is finding out where it stands as a new member of the human pack.

Two critical factors are when it is fed and where it is allowed to rest and sleep. If it is fed before the rest of the family "pack", it thinks it is an Alpha because all Alphas, or leaders of the pack, eat first. If the dog is lying down and the rest of the pack walk round it rather than making it move out of the way, this will also raise its status.

Further, when going out for a walk it should not be allowed out of the door of the home first because this is the privilege of the leader of the pack. For the same reason, it should not be allowed to lead the walk by pulling on the lead or pull to a tree or lamp post for a sniff. (See **Ten Commandments**).

Dogs from a rescue centre often drop their stools in the house. It only takes a few weeks for a dog to learn in the kennels that the concrete ground is the place to drop stools. The change in diet from a shelter can result in the stools becoming loose or firm. Either way, the answer is to add some cod liver oil in the food to act like a laxative.

About 30 minutes after feeding the dog, take it into your chosen grassy place in the garden or outside. Encourage it with a word like "busy" to encourage it to do its business as soon as possible.

When the dog has performed, praise it. The odour on the ground will encourage it to use the same area again. If you have taken it out, do not go back home straight afterwards otherwise the dog will associate being "busy" as the end of the walk.

American research

Millions of pets are put into shelters in America each year. The following reasons for relinquishing dogs were defined by a National Council on Pet Population Study and Policy (NCPPSP) survey published in the Journal of Applied Animal Welfare Science (JAAWS), in which researchers went into 12 selected animal shelters in the United States during one year:

- Moving
- Landlord not allowing pet
- Too many animals in household
- Cost of pet maintenance
- Owner having personal problems
- Inadequate facilities
- No homes available for litter mates
- Having no time for pet
- Pet illness(es)
- Biting cats
- Allergies in family
- House soiling
- Incompatibility with other pets

According to the study, most of the surrendered dogs (47.7%) were between five months and three years of age, most dogs (37.1%) having been owned from seven months to one year. Around half of the pets surrendered were not neutered. A third of them had not been to a vet. Animals acquired from friends were taken to a shelter in higher numbers (31.4%) than from any other source. The number of male and female dogs was more or less equal.

Significantly, 96% of the dogs had not received any obedience training.

Moving and changing a lifestyle were the main reasons given by pet owners when surrendering their animals to shelters, according to two other studies conducted by Colorado State veterinary epidemiologist, Dr. M.D. Salman, and sponsored by the National Council on Pet Population Study and Policy.

Horrifyingly, most of the pets (64%) were put down instead of being adopted into new homes. The studies also found that 62% of pet owners who surrender their animals to shelters were under 30 years old, and more dogs were taken to shelters than cats and all other animals combined.

"Euthanasia of domestic pets in the United States is an epidemic," Dr. Salman concluded.

About 1,000 shelters in the United States responding to a Shelter Statistics Survey accepted an estimated four million pets each year. This survey also revealed that, on average, 42.5% of pets that entered animal shelters were submitted by animal control authorities and nearly 30% were surrendered by their owners. The remainder came from other sources. Three million (about 25%) of the dogs taken to shelters over a three-year period were adopted by new families. Only 1.2 million (10%) were reclaimed by their owners.

Out of the 70 reasons pet owners gave for relinquishing their dogs, 15% said they were ill or old and needed to be put down; 7% said they were moving; 5% felt they had too many animals; 4% said owning a pet cost too much; and 3.5% said the animals had soiled the house.

"Some of the reasons pet owners cited for giving up their pets to shelters could be resolved through educational or other types of programmes," Dr. Salman concluded. "Most of the problems are really not with the animals but rather with the pet owners, who might not be prepared or knowledgeable enough about the realities of owning a pet."

msalman@vth.colostate.edu

RESPIRATORY RATES

An average dog takes 10 to 30 breaths a minute at rest or more when exerted. Smaller animals tend to breathe more quickly.

RETRIEVING (See **Training programmes**).

REWARD OR PUNISHMENT

Which is more powerful, reward or punishment?

This depends on the behaviour of the dog. I do not believe we can correct or punish a dog without an instant reward. A wolf will correct her pups quickly and sharply. The unwanted behaviour instantly stops, the bitch then licks her pup.

This is a lesson about communication. As soon as an unwanted behaviour ceases, we must give a reward immediately. The voice can be sufficient: "Baaad dog. Goood dog."

Other rewards can be given depending on the individual animal and what has been accomplished. Although food is condemned by some, titbits such as liver pills or pieces of biscuit can be used as a small treat. Any toy that a dog likes can be used as a reward as well. However, most dogs appreciate being fussed, petted and talked to in a friendly voice. "Good dog" could be the best reward of all.

ROBOT TRAINING

It is an interesting and important fact that dogs can be trained to act like robots. This can account for a number of apparently incomprehensible reactions. The subject was raised on one of my forums and *Grant Teebon* (see **Acknowledgements**) posted this response:

"Robot trained dogs are very reliable, especially when they can perform under heavy distraction to the same level. A lot of our police dog training is geared toward getting this `robot´ like response.

We also rely heavily on "association of equipment" with police dogs. When my dog is wearing a choker, he associates that we are doing obedience training and not bite work.

Conversely, if I put him on a flat collar, he 'knows´ we are doing bite/patrol work and he is in the 'on-guard´ mode.

Trainers should be aware of the possibility of this 'literal association'. If a dog is trained only at one location, then he will probably associate that location with the training and might not perform anywhere else. I have seen a classical example of literal association causing a dog to seize up completely. I overheard the trainer saying "I don´t understand it. We've been practicing this for weeks and he´s been working perfectly. We even went out and brought him a new lead and collar because we were sure he´d win today.

I introduced myself and told the owner that I suspected the dog had an "association of equipment" problem. Subsequent questions showed that in the dog´s whole working life, it had always worn the same old lead and collar, which were looking a little the worse for wear.

I suggested to the owner that he should do another run through using the old equipment during the lunch recess… and, you guessed it, the dog did the work perfectly. I told the owner how to "wean" the dog off the old equipment and how to introduce the new stuff to avoid the problem.

Literal association problems in training can relate to equipment (works on one lead but not another), location (works at one place and not another), people (performs a behaviour, such as jumping up, on the person who taught him but not on others), etc.

Like any dog training problem, it is best avoided in the planning stage but sometimes even the best of us can let one slip through, so you have to be able to recognise the signs and adapt your training to solve the problem.

A literal association problem is NOT a fault in the dog, but rather a fault in the training as done by the handler/ trainer. It is usually very easy to solve once you have identified the cause." (See **Training programs**)

ROLLING IN DUNG

Many dogs seem to enjoy rolling in dung. There are several
theories as to why they do it. The most popular claims it is
a way to disguise their scent, a throw-back to wolves that
roll in the dung of their prey to disguise their own scent
and remain undetected as they close in on them.

ROTTWEILERS (See **Top Dogs**)

ROYAL SOCIETY for the PREVENTION of CRUELTY to ANIMALS (R.S.P.C.A.)

The first animal welfare society in the world, the Society
for Prevention of Cruelty to Animals, was formed in 1824
after the world's first animal anti-cruelty law had been sponsored by Richard Martin, M.P., two years previously. In 1840,
Queen Victoria gave permission for the Royal pre-fix.

Today it investigates more than 100,000 cruelty cases a
year and treats more than 270,000 animals a year in its
hospitals and clinics, finding homes for about 80,000 a year.

The running costs, met completely through charitable contributions, are £40 million a year. An excellent web site: www.rspca.org.uk.

RUMP RUBBING

Rubbing the rump along the ground could be caused by swollen rump glands. See a vet.

SAYINGS

Dogs have not only entered our affections but they have also entered our language more than any other animal, as the sayings below illustrate.

Barking dogs seldom bite. True, because usually a canine attack is carried out silently, but this proverb which is found in Latin, French, Italian and German refers to blustering people.

Barking mad. Angry.

Barking up the wrong tree. This is derived from raccoon hunting, which took place in the dark. Dogs were trained to identify the trees in which there were raccoons and then bark. If they got it wrong, they were barking up the wrong tree.

Bark worse than its bite. "His bark is worse than his bite" is a popular saying, which is true in the sense that, with humans, barking at, or being aggressive to, somebody is worse than being bitten or sacked. But barking, or howling, by dogs is a call for the pack to return, either because they are lonely or lost.

So, in effect it is a sign of fear, not aggression. When aggression is tinged with fear, a dog growls a warning, but when it truly intends to be aggressive, it snarls, stares at you and raises its tail high. The attack, when it comes, is silent.

***Die like a dog*..** Miserably, shamefully.

Dog's body. Junior officer, lowly servant. Sailors' name for dried peas boiled in a cloth.

Dog box. Railway van.

Dog cheap. Not expensive.

Dog collar. Clerical collar.

Dog days. Days of great heat. The Romans called the hottest weeks of the summer "caniculares dies". Their theory was that the Dog Star, (known by its Greek name, Sirius, but called Canicular by the Romans) rising with the sun, added to its heat and that the "dog days'' were from July 3 to August 11. With water scarce, dogs slobbered and a slobbering dog was believed to be carrying rabies. In fact, in extreme heat, dogs are sensible enough to find a shady spot in which to snooze. Canicularr is the Latin diminutive of canis, dog

Dog's dinner. "Done up like a dog's dinner", being overdressed, dates from the 1920s.

Dog ear. Turn down the corner of book.

Dog face. U.S slang for a soldier since World War Two, possibly reflecting the "hang dog" expression of enlisted men.

Dog fall. Two wrestlers hitting the ground together.

Dog fight. Fight between aircraft.

Dog hole. Mean room.

Dogged. Obstinate, tenacious, persistent. To follow like a dog, pursue or track. To drive or chase a dog or dogs (1591).

Dog in the blanket. Rolled currant pudding.

Dog in the manger. A person who prevents others enjoying or using something which is useless to him.

Dog leg. Going back and forward.

Dog's breakfast. Slang for a mess or something that has been bungled.

Dog's life. A life of misery.

Dog's nose. Gin and beer or some other mixture of alcohol.

Dogs of war. These were the horrors of war: fire, sword and famine. "Cry havoc and let slip the dogs of war", Shakespeare. Now used in relation to mercenaries.

Dog Star. Sirius. Brightest star in the firmament in the constellation of the Big Dog - Alpha Canis Majoris.

Dog sleep. Light and fitful.

Dog tired. Tired out.

Dog watch. A short half watch at sea of two hours from 4 to 6 p.m. and 6 to 8 p.m., thus enabling seamen to dodge a full watch.

Don't keep a dog and bark yourself. Let an inferior person do the job.

Every dog must have his day. A change of luck or success will come one day."Let Hercules himself do what he may, the cat will mew and the dog will have his day".
Hamlet v. i (1600)

Give a dog a bad name and hang him. Power of slander.

Go to the dogs. Be ruined.

Hair of the dog that bit you. A sip of the drink you got drunk on the night before. The phrase originated in the 1700's when it was thought the hairs from the dog would help heal a bite.

Help a lame dog over the stile. Be a friend in need.

Hot Dog. A phrase coined in 1901 by the American cartoonist "Tad" Dorgon because he could not spell Dachshund. Harry Stephens, the concessionaire at the St. Louis Browns ballpark, created the idea of putting a hot Frankfurter, known as a Dachschund, inside a roll, and the cartoonist make fun of it by drawing a dog between bread. Not knowing how to spell Dachshund, he called it a "Hot Dog", a name which rapidly caught on.

In the dog house. In disgrace. Traditionally applied to a husband who has displeased his wife. Also slang for double bass. Used in jazz circles since the 1940s.

It's a dog's dinner. A mess.

Let sleeping dogs lie. Let well alone. "It is nought good a sleeping hound to wake". Chaucer (Troilus and Cressida iii (c. 1374)

Love me, love my dog. Accept my friends as yours. If you love someone you must love all that belongs to them. "Qui me amatu et canum meum", St Bernard, 1150.

Mad dogs and Englishmen go out in the mid-day sun. Noel Coward.

Not a dog's chance. Not the least chance.

Put on dog. Assume air of importance.

Raining cats and dogs. Raining very heavily. In Northern mythology, the cat is given the power to have great influence on the weather. Witches rode on storms and supposedly assumed the form of cats. Dog is the signal of wind, as is the wolf, both of which were attendants of Odin, the storm God. So a cat is a symbol of pouring rain and the dog a symbol of strong gusts of wind with the rain.

Sea dog. A pirate in the time of Queen Elizabeth I (1659). A luminous appearance near the horizon believed to foretell bad weather (1825) and an old salt, long used to the sea (1840). Light near the horizon portending a storm.

Shaggy dog stories. Very long and rambling jokes.

Sick as a dog. Very sick.

Tail wagging the dog. An unimportant issue preceding the important one.

Throw to the dogs. Throw away, sacrifice.

You can't teach an old dog new tricks. You can't change an old person's ways. (See **Old dogs – new tricks**).

SCENT (See **Smell**)

SCHOOLS
(See **Behaviourists**, **Good Citizen Test** and **Training**).

SCRATCHING AND LICKING.

Dogs that ritualistically scratch and lick could have an allergic reaction to an ingredient in their food. The body defence mechanisms could be triggering cells that release histamine into the body.

These cells occur in their greatest numbers on the feet and the legs, around the ears, eyes and nose, on the root of the tail and on the chest and abdomen. Frantic licking or scratching in these area's, especially shortly after eating a meal, will eventually damage the skin and leave it open to infection.

Some of the licking and scratching is so extreme that it gets to the point where the dog or cat cannot sleep. They just lick or scratch. These compulsive disorders seem to be linked with genetics, increased release of endorphins and altered levels of neurotransmitters, particularly serotin and dopamine, in the brain.

Tail chasing and tail chewing in Bull Terriers, flank sucking in Doberman's, hind end licking and sucking in Schnauzers have been documented,

If you find your dog is scratching or licking excessively, your vet should be able to determine if this is an allergic reaction to food or whether the behaviour has a medical cause.

Parasites, skin problems or arthritis could result in excessive licking. Liver disease could also cause unusual behaviour and bowel or anal problems could result in hind end licking.

After physical causes and instinctive behaviours are ruled out, a vet or animal behaviourist could take a detailed history to find out what is triggering the behaviour.

Some of the common causes include a new baby or spouse in the family, moving to a new home, holiday periods like

Christmas when the animal gets less attention, and even children leaving home to go to boarding school.

The dog could need more attention and exercise. It could be suffering from frustration at being left alone in too small an area or being confined for too long or being given harsh or inconsistent punishment.

The simple act by an owner of shouting "Stop licking" could be enough to cause stress in the dog's mind, not because it understands what is being said, but by the manner in which it is shouted.

Stress levels can be reduced by maintaining regular schedules for feeding at a set time, habitual and increased exercise and consistent use of commands followed by immediate reward of "Good dog".

Sometimes, drug therapy is required to correct the dog's problem because it is difficult to achieve with behaviour modification alone.

Now what about you scratching the dog? If a male dog is scratched between its front legs, the same sensation is created as when a dog mounts a bitch and thrusts against her back. Before mounting a female, the chest is rubbed on her rear as a pleasurable experience. Scratching or tickling behind the ears is also sexually stimulating because ear licking, sniffing and nibbling are part of the sexual preliminaries of mating. So give your dog a scratch from time to time. (See **Licking**).

SEARCH and RESCUE DOGS.

By Natalie Ray, a trainer in search and rescue for 11 years. (See **Acknowledgements**).

"The aim in training dogs to perform Search and Rescue (SAR) work is that the dogs are taught that finding people is the best game in the world. Another feature is that they are taught to follow the "drift" of the human scent as it lies on the ground, and trail, not track,(in tracking, dogs are trained to follow the scent of crushed vegetation also) to find the lost subject. Dogs trained to "Airscent" or follow the drift of the human scent on the air currents, are used to a great extent. They can be cross-trained to locate drowning victims, and deceased persons.

To start a dog in Trailing, there are exercises called "runaways." The dog's handler is the first person that the dog will find. While one person holds the dog, allowing it to watch, the handler calls to the dog while running away. The handler teases the dog, gets it excited, says "good bye", and "Come find me" and runs away 50 to 100 yards (depending on the dog's age) before dropping to the ground.

The person holding the dog then releases it with a command to "Find". Of course, the dog runs right to the handler, where it is rewarded with its favourite toy, food, or praise. The idea is to get the dog extremely excited about this new game.

These exercises are usually done in sets of three, depending on the dog. Only on the first runaway is the dog allowed to watch the handler run away. After that, the exercises become progressively more difficult, training the dog to follow the scent on the ground.

To train Airscent, the subject goes upwind of the dog. The handler then places the dog so that the scent of the person hiding is blown directly to the dog. The dog is given the command to "find", and rewarded when it does so. The areas are increased in difficulty as the dog progresses. Other variables are added in time to make the dog work through problems. Dogs can be taught to look under and into things, and that human scent can be underwater, too.

Dogs being trained for SAR are highly socialised to all different types of people –° babies, elderly, Alzheimer's patients, and mentally retarded people, for instance – because they "smell" different to the dogs.

Exposure to as many different things the handler can manage is crucial in a SAR dog's training. As always, obedience is also a major factor, as you must always have control of your dog. Your life, your dog's life, or someone else's may depend on it.

After the parents have been checked, dogs are selected on temperament, drive, lack of fear and body structure. You don't want to put hours upon hours of training with a dog, only to be unable to use it due to health problems. Size is not important as long as the dog can be lifted into trucks and carried if it is injured.

Training, training and more training is vital until what you want to do becomes automatic. I also keep myself in shape by jogging, lifting weights, and riding an exercise bike. My dog jogs with me and I have become a licensed Medical First Responder.

I carry a pack that contains a first aid kit (both human and canine) and food and water for both myself and the dog. It averages about 40 lbs. Usually. I have a large plastic box-like container that I keep packed and contains all my gear, including my pack, so I can put that into my van with the dog crate, and anything else I grab, and go. Time is usually crucial, especially if there's a chance the victim may be still alive.

There are many good online sources of information on SAR dogs, two of which are:

http://www.drizzle.com/~danc/FAQ/sarfaq.htm

http://www.zmall.com/pets/dog-faqs/lists/www-list.html

SENSES

A dog's hearing is about the same as a human for ordinarily sounds but it can hear high-pitched sounds five times better, and beyond our range. Their sight is not so good. They see colours in pastel tints but can detect far-away movement in a grey landscape and they see well in poor light.

The ability to smell is much the same for basic human smells but around 40 times better for things like sweat, drugs and explosives. Dogs lose out with taste, however, for humans have about a third more taste buds. (See **Hearing, Instinct, Present living, Sight, Smell** and **Taste**).

SEPARATION ANXIETY

Separation anxiety can be genetic or the dog can be nervous. It occurs when you go out or leave the dog alone in a room for a long time. This nearly always results in chewed or torn-up furniture or carpets and is always the fault of the owner. You must have a cooler relationship. The dog must not be allowed to follow you in the house from room to room. As you walk through a door, close it behind you, creating a short period of separation.

When you leave home, do not look, talk, or touch the dog for at least five minutes before going out, and do the same when you get back, whatever has happened. Soon the dog will learn that, if you do not greet it when you return after it has been chewing, it has not been rewarded and chewing is not the key to bringing you home. (See **Ten commandments**).

Case History:
Question: During the past few months I have taken up part-time work. My beautiful 12-year-old Labrador has been soiling in the house. Any idea what is wrong? The vet says he is fine.
Answer: I am afraid this is called separation anxiety, which is more apparent in older dogs. Your dog has become too attached to you. Older dogs when left alone are apt to become stressed and lonely. I really do not know of any treatment for this type of problem because I think it would be pointless to apply any form of behaviour modification. This could well be a good time to bring a second dog into the family. If it is a puppy or a young dog, it could do your dog a lot of good.

SEXUAL TENDENCIES

The female

Bitches are more affectionate and easier to control than the male dog. They are about 30% smaller than the male and, whatever their breed, tend to be more gentle with children and, some say, more loyal to the owner, but they are more likely to try to be dominant than males in the home.

The bitch will come into season about every six months and it will last for around three weeks. At that time the female is receptive to mating and her scent is extremely attractive to dogs that will instinctively try to mate, being attracted by the scent from up to a mile away.

A sign that a bitch is coming into season is that she will produce a discharge, initially a bloodstain, that will be deposited wherever she sits or lies. She will also spend much time licking her vagina.

Your home will attract the local male dogs and they could camp outside for the whole three weeks and howl during the night to attract the bitch´s attention. The female will attempt to escape if at all possible, so keep all doors closed and secure, especially when greeting your guests. I have known bitches that have chewed their way through doors during the night to get to the male dogs.

Do not underestimate the great heights that male dogs can climb and jump to reach a bitch on heat. During this time the male dog can be extremely aggressive and could well attack you if you tried to send him away.

Phantom Pregnancy

Bitches that have not been spayed can have a phantom pregnancy. They will go through all the stages of pregnancy both mentally and physically. The breasts will enlarge and she will produce milk, even storing items to treat them as her babies. This is stressful for the bitch.

245

If there are signs of a phantom pregnancy, take the bitch to a vet because there is a treatment to dispose of the milk. The vet can, of course, also spay the female, after which she will not have another phantom pregnacy.

If you are not going to breed from your bitch, have her spayed a few months before her first season. Veterinary colleges have endless scientific proof that the female will live longer and the likelihood of mammary tumours is reduced to a negligible factor. She will certainly not put on weight if you do not overfeed her. (See **Spaying**).

The male

The adult male has an instinctive urge to escape and wander free from home for periods ranging from an hour to several days or weeks.

Often a clear sign of a dominant, house-trained male, is when he starts to lift his leg in the house and urinate on walls and furniture. He does this to scent-mark his territory and to affirm his dominant status. This type of dog should be castrated.

Owners of dominant dogs should spend time re-enforcing their own dominance and insisting on absolute obedience. (See the **Ten Commandments**).

Male dogs that are confined and not allowed to roam can develop sexual frustration and will mount the human leg and even mount children who crawl on the floor. This is intolerable and dangerous to a child. (See **Mounting**).

Discuss the problem with a vet who might suggest either using a female hormone to try to counteract the condition or to castrate the dog.

I recommend castration for all dogs that are not to be used for breeding. A castrated male dog is happier, being freed from frustration. He will be more pleasant to have around, less likely to fight other males and more submissive to the wishes of the human pack leader. A castrated dog retains all his other instincts. He will guard, hunt, work, and retrieve.

The best time to castrate is around five to six months before he starts to lift his leg. It is a minor operation from which the dog will have recovered within 24 hours.

Male dogs, which have not been castrated, are often disturbed and can get excitable when a lady owner has a period. Castrated dogs can also be affected in this way because the mating time in all herds and packs is when there is a show of blood with the accompanying scent.

SHAMPOOS (See **Grooming**)

SHEEP DOGS

During a walk off lead, a dog might well run forward, then drop behind, go to one side or another. This is an instinctive, elementary way of herding the owner. Training a true sheep dog is a matter for a professional and here one of the best, *Barbara Sykes* (see **Acknowledgements**), explains how it is done:

"When searching for a Border Collie puppy for sheep work it is essential to know the background breeding of both the dam and the sire for at least seven generations. Are they compatible, is there any inbreeding or known defects, is the temperament good, are they eye-tested? There is a list of questions and they are not dissimilar from those needed to be answered when choosing a puppy for a pet.

The average Border Collie does not need a high-energy diet. With a pet dog it can lead to hyperactivity and destruction and in the working dog it encourages the development of chasing rather than herding. Sheepdogs are not encouraged to use their teeth on anything other than bones, their instincts are of the pack and if they are encouraged to be destructive they will develop the chasing rather than the herding instinct.

Their first introduction to sheep must be happy but controlled. A Collie always remembers the "first incident", so if it chases and grips on the first day this will set the pattern for the second day. Although they need to see sheep on a regular basis, I believe they should also be allowed to enjoy their youth. The time for serious training should not be until they are at least one year old.

They should, however, be obedient from puppy-hood. The Recall, Down and Stay commands are mandatory, for without these they will assume control of the shepherd and at all times he must remain pack leader.

Many sheepdogs allowed to develop naturally on a sensible diet, trained correctly and worked sensibly, are still capable of light work when they are 12 and 13 years old, and love every minute of it. It is a proven fact that dogs trained early and working from a young age need to be retired far sooner than the dogs allowed to develop freely.

Most working dogs live outside. It is not practicable to have them inside when they have been working on the land, but they need a warm, rain-free pen and a small secure sleeping area with plenty of warm bedding. Mine have greyhound bedding in summer to keep pests at bay, but in winter they refuse to use it and prefer straw. All my old retired dogs live inside

Many of the traits and characteristics mentioned above will be recognisable in the pet Collie. For this reason it is necessary to remember the Border Collie is a sheepdog and in order to establish leadership over him it is essential to understand him and his instincts. A Border Collie is clever and manipulative and quickly learns how to work a human being. But a human being who, kindly and firmly, becomes pack leader will have years of fun and companionship from their Collie."

"Understanding Border Collies" by Barbara Sykes. Published by Crowood Press, hard back – price £14.99 (p.& p. extra). Available from the either of the above or all good bookshops

SHELTER DOGS (See **Rescue centres**)

SHOWS

Showing your dog at a Dog Show has been the subject of many excellent books, so I do not intend to deal with any details here. Some people enjoy it and some dogs might well benefit from it. There are a whole series of rungs up the Show ladder, from the friendly local event to the ultimate: an award at Crufts. The sad thing about some of the Show people is the seriousness with which they undertake that climb and the deep, personal jealousies that can arise between contestants. Sometimes I wonder where the fun of owning a dog has gone.

Furthermore, in his book "Dr. Mugford's Casebook", the eminent Dr.Roger Mugford asks "How can man improve upon natural selection? Essentially, only by playing at God, and especially when trying to breed better dogs. There is an enormous moral and philosophical responsibility to be borne by those engaged in 'the sport' of dog breeding.

He states "To me the use of the word "sport" implies that breeders are somehow doing it for fun, that their satisfaction is of greater importance than the production of viable, healthy progeny that will go on to bring happiness to their prospective owners."

Show dogs are caged up for long periods waiting for their short "performance" before the well-meaning judges. They use criteria set by a committee, with all the compromises that involves, based on looks rather than temperament, which is of much greater importance to most pet owners.

Dr. Mugford cites the horrifying situation, brought about in the 1960's, when one top champion, tail-chasing Bull Terrier was used to sire nearly half of all that breed's litters in the country, with the result that there was a flood of whirling Dervish Bull Terriers madly chasing tails in homes all around the country.

SHYNESS and STRANGERS
By Lynn Aitchison (See **Acknowledgments**)

Dogs are natural interested in, but wary of, anything new or unusual. During early life, puppies should be exposed to as many new experiences as possible. They will then be able to cope with unusual events in later life.

If you have a puppy, try to take it out and about as much as possible, and introduce the puppy to lots of different people.

Shyness can occur for many reasons. Perhaps you got your dog from a breeder who had "run on" the puppy for a few months to see if it would grow up to be "show quality". This might mean that you have a young dog that has lived all its life in kennels and never experienced the world outside. This is not to say that the breeder did not love the puppy. However, where a breeder has many dogs, it is not possible to give each puppy the range of experience it would have got in a family home. There can sometimes be a problem with puppies that are born in rescue centres, as they will have been in a kennel for their first weeks of life. Even the most caring staff at these centres do not have the time to devote to proper socialisation.

Wariness of strangers or new situations may just be that the dog has not had the opportunity.

A shy person is not a problem. A shy dog is not a problem, unless the dog is so shy that you have to avoid stressing the dog, or is so nervous that it lunges out fearfully.

Before starting any reassurance training, it is worthwhile to get a veterinary check. Perhaps your dog has a sore spot on its body, and is scared of people patting it on the sore bit.

The treatment begins.

Assuming that there are no physical problems, let´s start to work with the shy dog. Examine your own behaviour. Have you "taught" the dog to be nervous? It is very easy to do this, so do not feel too upset at this suggestion.

When a dog whines, tries to pull away, flattens its ears against its skull, cowers, it is a natural reaction of humans to reassure the dog. We act protectively, and speak soothingly, pat the dog and even pick up smaller breeds. By doing these things, we are actually rewarding the dog for being scared! The dog will think that this is how you want him to react. Just what we did not want.

Dogs learn a great deal from our reactions. If we are scared, the dog will be scared. If we act excited, the dog will get excited. For the fearful dog, if we act "cool, calm and collected" and completely ignore whatever has scared the dog, the dog will learn that there is nothing to be afraid of. As soon as you notice any sign of the dog acting confidently, then you can praise and pat him.

Build up confidence.

Do not force your dog to do something if he is scared. If you can take him to training classes, and he wants to hide under the chairs, then let him. Give him plenty of time to look around and peek out. Gradually coax the dog out with a food treat, asking him to come out by another centimetre each time. Avoid pulling him out and do not keep the lead tight as this will add to his fears. If possible, ask people to get down to the dog's level. Try kneeling on the floor and tucking the dog's tail end between your legs. In this way, your body acts as a protection and the dog will not be as scared of something coming up from behind.

If your scared dog has previously lunged forward at people, you might find yourself holding the dog on a tight lead. Tightness around the throat will add to the dog's stress, and the dog will be even more likely to lunge. If you are worried, put a muzzle on the dog. Let him get accustomed to the muzzle around the house first. Suddenly putting a muzzle on a scared dog will only make him freak out even more.

Stay just outside lead's length of the stranger. Keep the lead slack, but hold the end of the lead firmly. If he does lunge out, he can only get to the end of the lead, and the stranger will still be safe. Try passing a couple of food treats to an obliging stranger so that the dog will see the person as a friend. Get the stranger to toss the treats near to the dog and avoid looking the dog in the eye. Strangers should not be allowed to force their attention on the dog. It should be left to the nervous dog to make the first approach.

If the dog does lunge, check how close to the stranger you were, and do not go as close the next time. Using a head collar can really help here because the dog can be reassured by the feel of this. Ask the dog to sit, and praise him as soon as you can. It is all a matter of timing. We do need to let the dog know that lunging is not acceptable. Make sure you never praise, reassure, pat or speak nicely to the dog whilst he is trying to strain forward.

The same system is used for the dog that hides behind your legs whenever a stranger approaches. Do not force the dog to meet the stranger, but let him peek around your leg if he wants. I know this is a bit embarassing if your dog is a large supposedly "aggressive" breed or that long awaited puppy you are so desperate to show off! Taking time now will pay off in the future. Talk to the stranger in your "cool, calm and collected" way, and the dog will soon realise that you are not scared of the stranger. Use the food treats in the same way as for the lunging dog, and let the dog make the first move to say "hello". Think of your dog as an actor about to make his first big stage appearance. Your dog is nervously "waiting in the wings". He will make his debut when he is ready.

Try not to feel "sorry" for a nervous dog. We want these dogs to learn to cope with life. At my Puppy Playgroup, I often see puppies hide under the owner´s chair on the first visit. Usually, they start to come out when the "coast is clear" at Week 2 and are running with the pack by Week 3.

One very persistent spaniel went round every owner at a class, acting scared and trying to persuade anyone to lift her up away from the other puppies. She was a really cute puppy, and it was hard to resist her fluttering eyelashes! Once she had been right round the group and had no success, she decided maybe these other puppies could be worth investigating after all, and gradually started to join in and play. Had anyone succumbed and lifted her, she could have remained nervous of other dogs for months.

So, in summary, keep calm and stay cool. Give the dog plenty of new experiences, but do not force him into situations he is obviously scared of. Praise when he is good, ignore the nervous behaviour."
Lynn the Dog Lady – Tel: 0131 669 1108.
E-mail 101333.3137@compuserve.com

SICKNESS

Humans regard vomiting as a nauseous experience, and therefore think a dog also suffers before and afterwards. This is not so. For a dog, vomiting is a simple, symptom-free act. Indeed some dogs have been known to vomit just to get some more food. Sounds horrible to us but not to a dog. (See **Grass**).

SIGHT

Dogs do not depend much on colour, which they see as pastel tints. Their eyes contain a variety of photoreceptors, or light detectors. Some are like rods, which enable dogs to see in poor light, and some are like cones, which are for colour vision. A dog's eyes have significantly more rods than cones, a legacy from their wolf ancestors who needed to see well for hunting in the dim light of dawn and dusk.

Once it was believed that dogs saw only black and white. Researchers at the University of California at Santa Barbara have found otherwise. Their studies revealed dogs could distinguish between a red ball and blue ball, white light and coloured light, but are unable to distinguish between colours from greenish yellow through orange and red. They are certainly more sensitive to movement, being able to pick out a moving object 300 yards away, but it could not see a stationary object at that distance or even nearer. It could not distinguish a stationary object, such as a rabbit, from the generally grey landscape.

Dogs also have a wider range of sight depending upon breed. The human visual field is 180°, but most dogs can see around 250°, depending upon the formation of the face. Those breeds whose eyes are wide apart have bad binocular vision. If the eyes are closer together, the dog will be able to judge distances better.

They also have different reflective cells in the back of the eye. A flashlight photograph will result in yellow or green eyes whereas in humans they are red. (See **Blindness**, **Cataracts** and **Glaucoma**).

SIRIUS

Popularly known as the Dog Star, Sirius is in the constellation of the Greater Dog (Canis Majoris), the brightest of the fixed stars. The appearance of Sirius just before the Nile floods was used by the ancient Egyptians to devise a 365-day calendar.

SMELL

A dog has around 200 million sensitive cells in its nose compared to a human's five million, so its sense of smell is around 40 times better than ours. A dog's sense of smell is made even stronger by an organ in the roof of the mouth that humans do not possess. This enables it to "taste" a smell, turning a weak smell into a stronger one.

This sensitivity to smell, especially butyric acid emitted in sweat, enables a dog to pick out the ball belonging to its owner from several balls thrown by different people. It also enables Bloodhounds to track an escaping convict up to 100 miles.

Trained dogs can also detect the odours of heroin, marijuana and cocaine hidden in suitcases even if surrounded by something strong smelling such as perfume. Other dogs can be trained to detect the acid in nitroglycerine and the sulphur in gunpowder for work with explosives. Dogs are even used to sniff out truffles in the ground. Some believe their sense of smell makes them suitable for infra-red detection, which helps them find humans in snowdrifts.

A dog, however, is not so sensitive to some smells that humans regard as important. A dog doesn't water at the mouth when a roast joint sizzles in the oven, nor does it get much pleasure from the smell of a rose. Thinking that a dog does appreciates these things is another sign of anthropomorphism. (See **Anthropomorphism** and **Nose**).

SPAYING

I recommend that bitches be spayed shortly before the first heat if they are not to be used for breeding. She will live longer and not suffer mammary tumours or have phantom pregnancies where a dog imagines it has pups and produces milk. Neither will she have the mood swings from which all unspayed bitches suffer.

A female does not have to have one litter of puppies. The myth that they need to do so could be responsible for the death of thousands of dogs each year as unwanted animals are euthanised in overcrowded shelters. The RSPCA reports that of all dogs born, half will not live to see the age of two years. They grow too big, out of fashion and develop behaviour problems due to incorrect feeding, no training or socialisation.

Having a litter is not necessary for a female to feel "fulfilled". If the reproduction hormones are eliminated through spaying, the bitch feels no urge to reproduce.

As with castrating a male dog, there is no need for a spayed female to put on weight if she is given the same food level and exercise as beforehand.

Thank goodness the pet profession and humane societies throughout the world are doing excellent work in educating people about the importance of spaying and castrating. Fewer dogs and puppies will have to be put down and there will be fewer strays. (See **Excuses**.)

STATISTICS

In the UK, 5.1 million households own a dog, just beating the 4.9 million households with a cat. This is according to a Pet Food Manufacturers' Association survey that showed one in two households owns a pet of some kind. There was just one dog in 77% of the households, with the remaining 23% having two or more.

Most popular breeds were: Yorkshire Terriers, German Shepherds, Labradors, Retrievers, Cocker Spaniels, and West Highland Whites.

The highest percentage of pet ownership was found in families with children and in households with four or more members. The most popular pets of all were goldfish.

(See **Populations**)

STEALING

This is attention seeking, especially rewarding if the dog is chased. The kitchen, with its worktops where cutlery, gadgets, washing and wiping-up cloths and many other mouth-filling items are left, besides food, is the most attractive area in the house.

Making it a "no go" area is difficult. Liberally dabbing every item with foul-tasting (to a dog) Tabasco, or something similar, is not practical, although spraying the edges of worktops with a special repellant can work, but not after the worktop has been wiped down.

Possibly the best solution is noise aversion. Blowing a whistle can be effective, but I would recommend having one or two empty drink cans containing a few nails, screws, small coins or pebbles ready at strategic points to thrown down beside the fleeing dog. The fright should make it drop what it's stolen. Then praise it. (See **Aversives**).

STICKS

Beware of throwing sticks. Should they break or be bitten into small pieces, they can lodge in a dog's mouth or throat, sometimes even vertically, holding the dog's mouth open.

STINGS and BITES (See **First aid**)

SUBMISSION

Signs of submission are rolling onto the back, paws hanging limply and licking the lips. Sometimes a dog will crawl up to a dominant dog to lick its face, in the same way puppies do to get food from its elders. A wolf pack returning from a successful hunt after having eaten to satisfaction, would bring back morsels for the puppies left behind. Some claim that this habit is now survives in the domestic dog when it brings back a stick or ball. Another sign of submission is keeping the tail between the legs to cut off the scent of the anal glands. While an angry dog will have erect ears, a submissive dog will keep the ears flat. (See **Aggression**).

SUMMER SAFETY (See **Heat danger**)

SWIMMING

Swimming is an excellent exercise for dogs. Breeds like Labradors and Newfoundlands are water dogs, sometimes used for sea rescue work. Introduce the dog to water when young by throwing something for it to retrieve. It´s best to keep your dog out of the sea because salt water and sand are not good for its coat.

SWIMMING POOLS

Swimming pools can be dangerous. A dog must learn where the steps are so that it can get out of the pool. Never tie a dog on a line near a swimming pool. If it should jump into the pool it might not be able to reach the steps and could drown. If you have a ladder but no steps, attach a chair to the ladder to provide a platform on which the dog can get out of the pool.

SYMPTOMS

Here are the basic signs of good health.

- *Body Temperature.* 100.5 - 102° F. (38° - 38.5° C.), but may be as higher in stressful situations, such as at the vet's surgery.

- *Pulse.* 70 beats per minute in large dogs, 120 beats per minute in small dogs. These rates are based on the animal being at rest. Excitement or fear may increase the rate. (A human heart beats 70 – 80 times a minute).

- ***Respiratory Rate***. 10 - 30 breaths per minute at rest or maybe higher after exertion. Smaller animals tend to breathe faster.

Here are some symptoms, one or more of which means a quick visit to the vet:

- Abdominal swelling

- Bleeding from any orifice

- Difficulty in breathing

- Difficulty in passing urine or motions

- Drinking excessively

- Excessive coat loss producing bare patches

- Fits or collapsing episodes

- Frequent coughing

- Irritation of the eyes/ears or discharge from them

- Lameness or paralysis of limbs

- Loss of appetite. Listlessness

- Persistent scratching or biting of the skin

- Persistent sneezing

- Persistent vomiting or diarrhea

- Thick discharge from the nose

- Unexplained weight loss

The following symptoms of the main illnesses suffered by dogs are listed here as a matter of interest, not for you to make a diagnosis. More information about the various illnesses are given in the relevant place throughout this A-Z section.

- **Distemper:** Diarrhoea, fever, vomiting.

- **Heartworms:** Gradual weight loss, listlessness, cough made worse by exercise.

- **Hepatitis:** Fever, vomiting, loss of appetitie.

- **Kennel cough:** Coughing, sneezing, wheezing, runny nose and eyes.

- **Leichmaniasis:** Enlarged liver, spleen and lymph glands. Rapidly growing nails, bleeding paws.

- **Parvovirus:** Vomiting, stomach pain, fever, watery diarrhoea.

- **Rabies:** Lock jaw which causes foaming from mouth, aggression, seizures.

(See **Cataracts**, **Deafness**, **Glaucoma**, **Health signs**, **Heart worm disease**, **Heat dangers**, **Hepatitis**, **Kennel cough**, **Leichmaniasis** and **Parasites**).

TAIL CHASING

Tail chasing is a sign of boredom in a puppy. If the habit persists in an adult dog it could be caused by the irritation of swollen rump glands, which can result in rump rubbing along the ground. Visit a vet. Tail chasing can also be caused by a genetic fault perpetuated by bad breeding. (See **Show dogs**).

TAIL DOCKING

Tail docking is legal in the UK as long as the docking is carried out by a qualified vet at the appropriate time, usually at four days old. The R.S.P.C.A. wants to change this law.

The British Veterinary Association has ruled that docking should be carried out only for valid medical reasons. Unfortunately, this ruling is a disciplinary one only and so far the BVA have failed to take disciplinary action against vets continuing to dock. Docking will only stop in the UK if and when a new measure is passed by parliament banning it outright.

As the law stands at present, docking is only illegal if carried out by a lay person.

Official standards for various breeds have been revised, so that a dog with a tail cannot be penalised.

TAIL WAGGING

Tail wagging is a complex business, often the result of conflicting emotions. Dog to dog tail wagging is a form of communication, the important thing being how the tail is wagged.

The tail of a dominant, aggressive dog will be upward and the tail will be wagged rapidly with short swings. The dog is hostile but also a little afraid that its aggressiveness will be challenged.

A submissive dog will hold its tail lower and swing it widely from side to side. It is friendly but fearful of being attacked.

In the dog world, there is more to it than this. When two dogs meet and smell each other´s bottoms, wagging the tail releases scents from the anal glands that humans cannot smell. These scents provide identification to dogs much as humans remember faces. High tail wagging will increase the ejection of scents. Low wagging decreases it. A truly frightened dog will put its tail between its legs to try to prevent any scent escaping.

So your dog greets you, when you return home, by wagging its tail. It is happy to see you but it is also a little fearful that you, the dominant dog returning from the "hunt", might not reciprocate. Perhaps when it was a puppy and had chewed up something in the house, you "barked" at it quite fiercely.

This mixture of happiness and fear was first established when tail wagging by a puppy starts at around four weeks old and the litter is feeding from the mother.

There is the happiness of being suckled and the fear of the siblings with whom a sense of rivalry is already taking place, a battle for dominance. Your return to the home could trigger the memories of being previously told off because that basic instinct formed at four weeks old is always there.

Finally, do you know why a dog has so many friends? It wags its tail instead of its tongue.

TASTE

Taste is not such an important sense to dogs, despite claims to the contrary made by the manufacturers of pet foods. Dogs have around only 3,000 taste buds compared to the 10,000 of a human, so their taste factor is seventy percent lower than ours.

Smell is far more important to dogs, which is why the manufacturers of dog food make sure their products smell good to a dog. (See **Smell**).

TATTOOS

Some say the prongs used for tattooing can hurt a dog, while others say their dog lay quietly while being tattooed. A tattoo is not the best identification for a dog. It can easily be altered and can fade or become indistinct.

TEETH

Believe it or not, there are special toothbrushes for dogs and a range of non-foaming tooth pastes with a variety of tastes. If the teeth are badly stained, ask your vet if he has ultra-sonic cleaning equipment. Most dogs have to be anaesthetised for this treatment.

TEETHING

Teething can be a painful experience for a growing puppy. Often the baby teeth are swallowed, and the only evidence of teething is the desire to chew virtually anything. This chewing relieves the pain because it releases endorphins that help deaden it.

In this way the dog learns that chewing is a rewarding experience and starts chewing everything in sight.Take away as many temptations as you can with taste aversives. (See **Aversives**).

TELEPATHY

(See **Extrasensory perception** and **Instinct**).

TEMPERATURE

Usually 101.5° to 102° F. (38 ° to 38,5° C). If it goes over 104, go to the vet at once, especially if it is being sick or has diarrhoea. Dehydration is a danger, so provide plenty of water. (See **Symptoms**).

TEN COMMANDMENTS

This is a summary of advice given under various alphabetical entries in this book.

If you have an unruly dog, the following guidelines will help you establish a proper pecking order between you and your dog. Any owner who is having an aggressive behaviour problem with their dog should not rely on these guidelines alone. The list cannot replace a consultation with an experienced trainer or canine behaviourist registered with the A.P.D.T., F.D.T.C.B., B.I.P.D.T. or A.P.B.C. (See **Trainers' organisations**).

You may think some of these items are petty but they are all important because their effect is cumulative in reinforcing your dominance, and the dog will be happier with a firmly established status.

1. Don't allow your dog on the bed or the furniture. Don't even allow your dog to sleep in the bedroom because it will then regard itself as a high-ranking member of the pack. If you have made this fundamental mistake, and I know a lot of owners do let their dogs sleep in their bedrooms, move the dog's bed nearer the door. After a couple of nights put the dog outside the door so that it knows it is still close to you. The next step is to move it downstairs or into another part of the house and to create an area that it will regard as its den.

2. Don't feed your dog before you have eaten your own food or have pretended to eat some of its meal. The junior member of a pack eats last. If the food is not eaten after five minutes, take it away. A dominant dog will leave it to come back to later, knowing that nobody will touch the food of a pack leader.

3. Don't let your dog control your territory. Go first through doorways and passages. If the dog tries to go through first, close the door on it sharply and close other doors in the house to prevent free roaming in your territory.

Make it wait for a signal to get in or out of the car and make it move if it is blocking your way.

4. Don't be inconsistent. Keep the rules constant. Either the dog is allowed a particular privilege or not and all members of the family should enforce the same rules.

5. Don't give a command that you can't enforce and always give a reward or praise for obeying.

6. Don't play tug-of-war with your dog. Play "fetch games" where you start and end the game with possession of the toy. You must ALWAYS win and never leave toys lying around. Doing this is a signal that the dog owns the territory.

7. Don't reward the dog for bothering you. Ignore nudging, whining or bringing you toys. Make your dog obey a command, like sit, before giving it attention. If you give attention first you are giving it a reward. The possible exception is first thing in the morning when the lower rank in a pack greets the higher rank.

8. Don't let your dog decide what handling is appropriate. Handle your dog's ears, feet, tail, etc. and groom it as long as you choose.

9. Don't neglect your obedience training. Practise many short Downs and one long Down per day. Incorporate obedience training into your dog's daily routine. Make it Sit before feeding and Stand for grooming, etc.

10. Don't let your dog control the direction and pace of your walks. Train your dog to walk on a loose lead in the direction you choose. If your dog is off-lead and not paying attention to you, go in the opposite direction or hide and make it find you. (See **Conformity**).

TERRIERS (See **Hunting dogs**)

TERRITORY MARKING

Male dogs urinate in frequent, short bursts because they are using their urine, with its distinctive "calling card" odour to other dogs, to mark their perceived territory. They cock their leg to deposit the urine as high as possible off the absorbent ground to ensure a wider distribution of the smell. Another dog, sniffing the deposit, will "read" the scent and know which dog has passed by. (See **Sexual tendencies** – the male).

THUNDERSTORMS

Some dogs take fright well before a storm starts. This is because they can detect a change in barometric pressure and / or the arrival of static electricity.

TICKS

These are nasty, potentially dangerous things because they can transmit a whole variety of diseases into a dog. These can result in nose bleeding (because blood clotting is inhibited), rashes, fever, loose or bloody faeces and difficulty in breathing.

Prevention is better than cure but, as stated under **Fleas**, some collars, claiming to repel ticks, have been found to contain undesirable chemicals.

There has been a lot of research into new, harmless chemicals and collars containing Amitraz are successful in repelling ticks and controlling mange.

A small dose of garlic in the dog's food can also help but don't overdo this as excessive garlic can cause gastro-enteritis.

The only completely safe answer during the tick season is not to take your dog into the countryside, particularly where sheep and goats carry ticks which drop into shady grass areas for you or your dog to pick up on the legs.

The tick, like a small spider the size of a nail-head, will crawl up to attach itself around the dog's head or on the ears. There it will grip with its tiny claws, which are like minute fish hooks, and begin to suck blood. Generally there will be at least two together, one male and the other a female. The tick will swell as it sucks up sufficient blood to feed the eggs it will lay on the dog.

Shampooing and grooming can help to remove them as they travel up the dog's body but, once established, the best method is to dab them with alcohol, wait for a few moments, and then pinch them off. If the tick is near the eyes, use olive oil. You have to give both treatments time to soak in as the tick breathes through two holes near the claws.

Make absolutely sure they are dead by burning or squashing or putting them in a small jar of olive oil. Treat the area where they have been found with iodine or an antiseptic cream.

And don't forget to examine yourself. Ticks attach themselves to humans as well and can transmit nasty diseases. Keep your ankles and legs covered in tick country.

TIME OUT

Just as an ice hockey player is sent off for a foul, time out can also work for a dog, but it must be applied at the right time, which is immediately after the unacceptable behaviour. Some advocate wrestling the dog to the floor and holding it there in submission for a minute or more. A much better method is to isolate it in a small room such as a toilet, rather than engage in floor-to-floor combat.

As soon as the dog has quietened down, which should not take longer than a minute or two, it should be let out, fussed and loved. However, perhaps better training would have avoided the cause for time out in the first place. Discuss the problem with a dog trainer.

TOP DOGS

The American Kennel Club was founded in 1930. It has 145 breeds registered and lists the following as the top ten breeds in popularity.

1. ***Labrador Retrievers*** are in the gun dog group and come from Newfoundland, where they were originally used for retrieving fish. This is why they love water. They have a short coat, are very good tempered and keen to please. They are dependable, adaptable, easy to train, and are good with children and other pets. They need lots of exercise.

2. ***Rottweilers*** are in the working group. An ancient breed, they served with the Roman legions. The modern ver-

sion stems from Germany. They are self-assured and have a natural guarding instinct. Not aggressive or vicious by nature, they are good all-round family pets and excellent guard dogs. They need training from three months old, and are not suitable for an apartment.

3. *German Shepherds* are in the working group and come in a variety of colours. Highly intelligent and responsive, they need an owner committed to early training. They are one of the most versatile and popular dogs, in the world but indiscriminate breeding has damaged its reputation.

4. *Golden Retrievers* are gun dogs. They are responsible, stable and affectionate and are excellent with children. They are trained as guide dogs for the blind.

   They love water and fetching sticks and balls, and they need to be with the owner as much as possible.

   A Golden Retriever will be your shadow.

5. *Poodles* are in the utility group and have a dense coat that needs regular brushing and clipping. Originally used as gun dogs to retrieve game from water, they are now one of the most popular companion breeds, always eager to please, and make excellent watchdogs. They are easy to train and affectionate with children.

6. *Beagles* are the smallest of the scent hounds. They have long ears and the tip of the tail is white. They can be black, tan or white or a mixture of these three colours. They have enormous energy and are very loving and friendly. They need a garden with a strong fence because they tend to wander off if they can, following an interesting smell. They are easy to train and good with children, but can be obstinate.

7. *Dachshunds* come from the hound group originally bred to hunt badgers and are considered a German

breed. They like to be heard as well as seen. They are intelligent and need training from a very young age. They are not ideal for young families.

8. **Cocker Spaniels** are gun dogs and are believed to have originated in Spain. They come in a variety of colours. They are popular family dogs and, if trained correctly, can be very loving and good with children. They need lots of exercise and extensive grooming.

9. **Yorkshire Terriers** are from the north of England and were originally bred to control the rat population in the early 19th century. They need daily brushing. They are popular with people living in apartments but are not easy to train. They make good companions for the house-bound, but need supervision with children.

10. **Pomeranian** is the smallest of the Spitz breeds originating from the Baltic. Poms have a double coat and require frequent brushing. They are good for the house or apartment and need little outdoor activity. Keen watchdogs, they are very affectionate and can be good with children. Although small, they have the temperament of a large dog.

TOYS

Beware of squeaky toys from which the squeak mecanism can be extracted by the dog and swallowed, and avoid toys that are so soft they can be torn up. Unfortunately, many vets are persuaded by animal toy salesmen to stock toys which are totally unsuitable for dogs

There are balls and squeaky toys in every vet's surgery, pet shop and store. Most were made for children, but manufacturers pop them into pretty, doggy-type presentation packs.

I do not recommend any type of ball other than those from the indestructible *Kong* range. Marketed for the last decade by Roger Mugford, these balls have undergone scientific testing and research. They cost from around £4 to £13, depending on size

The Kong is moulded at 300 tons to give just the right amount of resilience for a dog´s teeth. It has an unpredictable bounce that makes it an excellent exercise and fetch toy. The natural rubber taste and smell encourages chewing. Better your dog chews a Kong than chew your furniture.

Another form of Kong is a thick, twisted piece of heavy rope between the strands of which tit-bits can be inserted for the dog to retrieve and for you to have a bit of peace. Obtainable from some vets and good pet shops from £8 to £10. More information is available at: www.companyofanimals.co.uk

Rawhide chewies have chemicals that can cause hyperactivity and cause behavioural problems. Try and get a specially smoked marrow bone which you can stuff with some cheese after the dog has extracted the marrow. Another good product is the *buster cube*. Most good pet shops have them. You also can stuff these with goodies.

Never allow a dog to play with a ball that is small enough to be swallowed for it could get stuck in the throat. If this happens, ideally you need two people to go to the rescue. One should hold the mouth open as wide as possible without obstructing the nose, while the other tries to pull the ball out with their fingers or by using something like cooking tongs. If you fail, rush the dog to a vet.

Always pick up toys when they are not being used. They are yours, not the dog's. Start a game by producing the toy. End it by taking the toy away. (See **Ten commandments**).

TRACKING
By Ron Lawrence, Canberra, Australia.
(See **Acknowledgements**).
"First let me say - without intending to brag but in order to establish my credentials to discuss this subject - I presently have two Australian Obedience Champions that require me to teach the tracking exercises. Secondly, these two dogs

have never failed a track. I don't know of any other trainer who can say that. I do know what I am doing.

I recommend the Glen Johnson book because it describes how scents age and it describes what the dog is actually tracking on differently aged tracks. It also gives an excellent training plan/regime which describes double tracking, scrubbing, step and line tracking, etc.

Before I go into how I teach my dogs to track, may I say I don't teach the dog to scent or to follow a track (only he knows how to do that). I teach the dog to do it when I ask him to and to follow the particular track that I want him to follow. I will only describe one method. The others are in my home page for anyone really interested in the subject.

Puppy Training
Find the Toy Method/Game. This game is simple and fun. As usual, we start out with a simple exercise and build on it (Shaping). Select the dog's favourite toy. Play with him with it, hide it behind your back, bounce it in corners, get the dog excited about the toy and the game. Throw the toy a short distance and have him Retrieve it. Praise him for every step in the Retrieve process. Do this until the pup Retrieves reliably. Next, put him in a Sit Stay (or held by another member of the family) and place the toy somewhere at the end of the room where he can see you do it.

Send him to Retrieve it. Praise him enthusiastically for every step in the Retrieve. Do not worry if you do not get a Retrieve. The find and chase is the important part at this stage. Once this is going well, place the toy at the end of the room out of his sight and send him to Retrieve it. If the dog can't find the toy after half a minute or so, help him at this early stage. Always show excitement when he finds it and give him praise or a treat when he does it well.

Now let him see you place it under a cushion or some other object in the room. Send him to Retrieve it. When he is doing this well, place it under an object out of sight and send him to Retrieve it. He will have to start using his nose at this point.

Once the pup is finding the toy in the most devilish of places, put the toy on the floor in the room next to the one you've been playing in, perhaps in a connecting hallway (a squeaky toy increases the pup's desire to find it).

You can have the dog sitting with his back to you. He may by now be scenting your tracks or air scenting. He is learning that it will be somewhere that you have been, so he will start to use his nose on the track. Once he is retrieving the toy from the next room, move to other rooms. Come back to him via different routes/doors and place it in a sink that he can reach. And on it goes.

Next, progress the game outdoors. As a bonus, this training method/game can also be used to "proof" the formal obedience exercises and reinforce the obedience exercises: Sit Stay, Down Stay, Retrieve, Scent Discrimination, and Seek Back Lost Article, as well as Tracking.

It should be taught to every pup that is destined for obedience and tracking work by about three months of age. The retrieving exercises in obedience and tracking will become child's play, the bond between you and your dog will be strengthened and your dog will love you for it.

Find the Family Member.
This method is conducted in the same way as the Find the Toy Method, except a family member hides for the dog to find, i.e. plays Hide and Seek. In this game, the dog learns what Tracking is all about, i.e. to track a particular person. The game may be reinforced by having the family member reward the dog with the reward (its special favourite toy) when he is found. As with the Find the Toy Method, this method can be played both inside and outside. The greater the distance from the dog, the more the game is like a tracking exercise.

Do not be too concerned with what senses (sight or smell) the dog uses to find the family member. Always praise him mightily, and praise him also every time he makes progress towards tracking (Shaping). The Tracking Command can be introduced with these games, e.g. Find or Get, Find Mummy, Find Squeaky, Get the Ball, etc.

If you are using a clicker, whenever I say praise in the above training, substitute click. You always find something in the last place you look."
Ron Lawrence, Canberra, ACT, Australia
winron@bigpond.com , ICQ 21453314
Homepage: <http://www.users.bigpond.com/winron>

TRAFFIC ACCIDENTS (See **First aid**)

TRAINERS' ORGANISATIONS

There are quite a few organisations for trainers/behaviourists with a whole variety of aims, objectives and qualifications. I hope most of them are listed here. If any have been missed, please accept my apologies. I recommend readers only to attend trainers and behaviourists who are registered members of the following organisations.

Association of Pet Behaviour Counsellors (A.P.B.C.)

Membership consists of pet behaviour therapists working exclusively from referrals by vets. There are excellent consultation centres all over the country run by highly experienced and qualified consultants. Secretary: Dr. Peter Neville, 257 Royal College St., London NW1 9LU. Write to: PO BOX 46, Worcester, WR8 9YS, England Tel/Fax: + 44 (0) 1386 751151 E-mail: apbc@petbcent.demon.co.uk

British Institute of Professional Dog Trainers (B.I.P.T.D.)

Bowstone Gate, Nr. Disley, Cheshire SK12 2AW. Tel. 01663 762772.

Federation of Dog Trainers and Canine Behaviorists
(to which I belong).

The FDTCB, founded in 1988, was formed originally to give those who worked as dog trainers and behavioural consultants an organisation that represents quality of service, the fundamental aims being the promotion of positive motivational methods plus education and training.

The FDTCB developed the now fully recognised educational qualification of Canine Studies Level Two City and Guilds 7622. This qualification is an in-depth course covering dog training behaviour, welfare and development.

The aims of the course are:

- to provide the industries serving dogs and dog owners and the public with a recognised qualification that stands for nationally accepted levels of quality through a broad range of knowledge skills.

- to provide a framework which includes individual study units for dog owners to pursue their own interests

Integral is the gathering of evidence that gives relevance and cohesion to the learning achieved by:

- broadening knowledge and appreciation of other professionals in the canine field,

- acknowledging and developing current skills,

- increasing knowledge and skills in the study of canine behaviour, training and development,

- appreciating the theoretical background of canine psychology and physiology,

- investigating and researching areas of interest,

- developing skills and attitudes conducive to personal and professional development,

The F.D.T.C.B has a comprehensive application form including numerous questions on training and behaviour.

Applicants may be visited if it is felt that additional information is required and they need recommendations from vets with whom they are working and details of cases they are working on, plus letters of recommendations from satisfied clients.

Information: The Canine Studies Co-ordinator, FDTCB 15 Lightburne Ave, Lytham St. Annes, Lancashire FY8 1JE, U.K:.
E-mail: fdtcb@natural.clara.net
Web site: http://www.k9netuk.com/training/fdtcb

Association of Pet Dog Trainers. APDT

Ian Dunbar (See **Acknowledgements**) writes: "I initially proposed the idea for the UK APDT at the APBC conference in March 1993, and John Fisher did all the work in creating it. At the APBC Conference, the audience was becoming extremely restless, expressing concern that the APBC was an elitist group accepting very few pet dog trainers as members.

Pet dog trainers were crying out for their own organisation. After suggesting the formation of the APDT, I collected some 500 names at the conference and the list increased to just over 700 trainers within a couple of weeks.

Initially, John and I worked together intensively. In June I gave the list of interested trainers to John and from thereon he took over and did all the work.

For a while, the UK APDT developed along similar lines as the Canadian and US groups but soon distinct differences emerged. The US APDT was primarily an educational and networking association open to all pet dog trainers, whereas the UK APDT opted to restrict membership to selected trainers.

The list of 700 was culled to approximately 70 to be "grandfathered" in as advisors to establish the criteria to accept other members.

The UK APDT still selects trainers according to quite strict criteria based on preferred humane training techniques, which do not permit the use of a variety of aversive training tools, such as throw chains etc.

Whereas in the US dog trainers are represented by two large organisations - NADOI and the APDT - in the UK at the moment there are a wide variety of smaller groups of dog trainers and behaviour counsellors.

To this day, the US APDT has remained an educational group open to all trainers. As such, it has attracted an extremely large membership, which is now well over 2,000. The APDT Annual Conference has become the largest and most comprehensive educational dog behaviour and training event worldwide, with over 1,500 trainers attending the latest ('98 Valley Forge) Conference.

Personally, I hope that the APDT remains an open educational group. How else can we train trainers to make the training experience more enjoyable for dogs? In terms of the future direction of the APDT, I think an additional focus will comprise the design and implementation of formal programmes for the education, assessment and accreditation of pet dog trainers. I do not feel that these two objectives need necessarily be mutually exclusive. All trainers may become members of the APDT and benefit from its networking and educational programmes and those that wish may take formal courses and examinations.

Since many trainers have 30 or 40 years' experience teaching dogs and their owners, I have always thought it would be a mite presumptuous for any minority group to assume they have the qualification, let alone the right, to assess critically the training expertise of others.

Even just a couple of years ago, the notion of accreditation and certification of trainers was a trifle premature, to say the least. Now, however, I think the time is nigh. Indeed, when recently polled by membership vote, the collective input of the current APDT membership was in favour of accreditation.

Regarding the use of shock collars, the vast majority of APDT members voted overwhelmingly that they considered them totally inappropriate for the general public. I agree wholeheartedly.

The National Assoc. of Dog Obedience Instructors is the oldest American professional organisation for obedience instructors, and the only one (to my knowledge) which requires proof of proficiency. Members are all committed to upholding the highest standards of the profession."
An e-mail list is available for members.
Web site: http://www.apdtuk.f9.co.uk
Other organisation for trainers include:

Dog Training Industry Association

The Dog Training Industry Association was formed as a result of a conference arranged by a number of leading dog trainers in the United Kingdom and held at Wetherby, Yorkshire, in 1995. It is the intention of members to hold a conference at least three times a year.

The object of the association is to ensure that the interests of private trainers, private dog training clubs and persons within the dog training industry are realistically and democratically represented throughout the U. K. The formation of the association allows for an interchange of information and ideas by very experienced people who are running a business within the dog training industry of the U. K. It also provides a platform for their views to be expressed and their interests to be better represented.

Information: George Grayson, North East Dog Training Centres, P.O. Box 19, Northallerton, North Yorkshire. DL7 8AF. Tel. 01609 770792 .
E-mail: dogtraining@thisisthenortheast.co.uk

Institute for Animal Care Education

Bowstone Gate, Disley, Cheshire, SK12 2AW.

Tel: 01663 762772

http://www.k9netuk.com/apdt/index.html

This is an independent body that promotes education within the animal care sector and promotes equality of standards across the wide range of qualifications which exist. It claims to be the only organisation that has the technical expertise required to award qualifications in this specialised area which focuses on the educational and welfare needs of the animal care sector. Details from: The Secretary, Institute for Animal Care Education, New Road, Framlington, Woodbridge, Suffolk, IP1 9AT. Tel: 01728 727727, Fax: 01728 724306

http://www.k9netuk.com/commercial/edu/acc/iace.html

ASPADS.

The Associated Sheep, Police & Army Dog Society (ASPADS) was established during the 1920's to promote Working Trials in the U.K. It is the largest Working Trials Society in the U.K. and has many highly qualified and experienced members

Web site http://www.aspads.org.uk/

TRAINERS (See **Behaviourists**).

TRAINING CLASSES

Training classes can help enormously. Their great advantage is they accustom the puppy or young dog to socialise with other dogs and owners to socialise with people having a common interest and often a common problem.

Many believe that it is good for all members of the family to train a dog. This is untrue and will cause confusion to the dog. Every member of the family will have his own idea. It is better that a dog should attend training sessions with only one member of the family who can afterwards show others what to do.

Training methods vary just as much as dogs and their owners. There are however, many accepted exercises that form a useful basis for most dogs and most owners. Training is based on the knowledge that a dog learns by association of ideas, not by reasoning. So we aim to create associations we want by correction and reward.

A puppy can be taken to training classes after it has had the first course of vaccinations. A training club will want to see the certificate. Don't believe those people who say you should wait until it is six months or a year old.

Beware of those who are regarded as experts when they have trained a dog of one breed to a very high standard. Faced with a difficult dog of another breed they would probably not know where to start.

How do you select the right trainer?

Go along to a class without the distraction of having your dog with you. Do people look as if they're having fun? Are the dogs wagging their tails and having a good time? What is the instructor doing?

Is he or she standing in the middle of the hall calling out commands to the handlers walking around the outside? Or are the class members being given feedback and tips for improvement as they're moving?

Look for those with problems. Does the instructor go over as soon as possible and give constructive advice, or does he or she let them flounder for a while? What sort of advice are they giving? Do they simply take the dog from the owner, give a quick demo and return the dog, or do they help the owner to improve his technique?

Ask the trainer why he uses certain methods or teach certain things. If he cannot explain his thinking behind his methods, he is unlikely to understand the learning theories himself and so cannot teach them to the class.

Most important, what sort of rewards do they use and why? This will reveal whether they prefer to use punishments or rewards in their training. Avoid those who punish, such as trainers who insist on using choke chains, hitting dogs or shouting at them, dragging them along on the end of the lead, pushing them into Sits and Downs, etc.

Finally, when you have found a trainer you like, never let him or her take your dog and do something to it that you would not want to do yourself, or something which hurts or scares your dog.

You must control what happens to your dog. Don't be afraid to speak up and say that you would rather not do a particular exercise or would like more information before continuing. Some trainers can be very dominant. Don't accept this type of behaviour.

If you're looking for a class in the UK, see **Training Organisations**. For instance, all members of the Association of Pet Dog Trainers (APDT) are assessed before membership is granted and everyone has to abide by the code of practice. Members train primarily through rewards and play training methods. None use choke chains or spike, prong or electric collars. To find a trainer in your area in the UK, consult your vet or go to the web site:

<http://www.netlink.co.uk/users/k9netuk/apdt/index.html>

Your trainer should be able to advise you about many things. But if you have a specific behavioural problem you might need an in-depth consultation and the training club is not the place for this. Speak to your trainer about a private session in your home. If they cannot help you, they will probably know someone who can.

Above all, remember that your dog is for life and its training should be an enjoyable experience. A well-trained dog is a joy to own, an untrained one quickly becomes a menace and a burden. Certainly all trained dogs have happy owners. It is a satisfying experience and not very time consuming. Indeed most additional training can be done while exercising the dog. If you do not have the time to exercise your dog, then you should not keep one.

A good trainer will also be insured to cover all the accidents that can occur when dogs and humans are present. If the premiums are too high, they may ask you to sign a disclaimer. Finally, never send your dog away from home to be trained. (See **Whistle training**).

Internet sites for training courses.
Canine/Human Interface Course, and the Advanced C/H Interface are excellent courses run by the Animal Care College, Ascot House, High Street, Ascot Berks SL5 7JG.
Go to http://www.corsini.co.uk/animalcare/courses.htm
Exeter University on Animal learning and Cognition:
http://www.ex.ac.uk/Psychology/teaching/handbook/2ndyear/animal.htm

TRAINING PROGRAMMES
Not all dog trainers use the same methods of training. They tend to use the method that happens to suit them best. It would be a foolish trainer who claimed that his or her particular method is the best one and all the other trainers are wrong. For this reason and because there is more than one good way to train dogs, two articles follow by two top trainers. The first is by *George Grayson* (See **Acknowledgements**).

Training programme 1
"Socialising at a very early age is always a first priority. There are views that temperament training and socialising should start with some dogs at six weeks. This is especially so for dogs for

the blind and disabled, where it is regarded as so important that it should be done even before the puppy is fully vaccinated.

Anyway, training starts the day you get your dog. Play training with a puppy, the Recall and the Retrieve can be done at a very early age.

I prefer house training to be assisted with an enclosed crate / cage / bed. It is much easier. Dogs may object at first but later they love them. Early lead training with a puppy lead and soft collar is also important.

At the age of about six months, more serious training can begin. Heel work is done using encouragement rather than correction. The dog should enjoy any exercise. I like to see a dog wagging its tail as it walks to heel.

The Sit, Stand and Down can be incorporated at the halts, but by placing the dog in these positions rather than forcing it. In my time with the Service, treats were frowned upon. Today I use them without hesitation in my pet dog training classes and if I were asked which was the most important aid for training now I would say the use of treats.

The Recall (visual command - the arms outstretched) is a most important exercise that can be started at a very early age with the use of treats. Sometimes dogs will come for a treat where they will not come to the owner.

The treat is an easy method of getting dogs to Sit (in front of the handler) without it being necessary to touch the dog. Bring the hands together and lift the treat just above the dog. Eventually the treats can be dispensed with, the dog just obeying the visual commands.

Another very important exercise that aids the Recall and encourages the dog to use the nose is hide and seek. Have someone hold the dog, hide a short distance away, call the dog and then praise when he finds you.

One of the best police search dogs I had was taught through the hide-and-seek method. The handler used a hard rubber ball and the dog was taught to "speak" on production of the ball and, after this, the ball was thrown as an incentive. This was extended to searching for a person and it resulted in a very keen search.

Aggression was introduced later when the search exercise was perfected. This was the most practical and efficient search dog I had in my 31 years with the Police Service. Trained this way, the dog won the UK National Police Dog Trials several times.

The Stays are important and again can be taught at an early age along with Down. The dog is put in the Sit with the handler facing the dog from the right of the dog, i.e. the dog is on the left. On the command "Down" the left hand is put on the shoulder blades and, if necessary, the right leg is lifted with the other hand to put it in that position.

The dog should not move his backside off the ground. The front legs should just go forward as the dog goes into the Down. On the command Sit, the dog should pull its legs in, again the backside not coming off the ground. With the command Stand from the Sit, the rear legs should be pushed backwards, either with the left hand or very carefully by touching the dog's hind-legs at the joint with the left foot, thereby making the dog move its hind legs backwards.

When brought back into the Sit, the dog should be in exactly the same place, having not moved forwards or backwards. As the dog progresses, the handler should go in front, facing the dog. The use of the selected hand signals can then be incorporated for each movement.

The Retrieve is probably one of the most important exercises for a working dog. Tracking and searching all depend on the dog's ability in this exercise.

My training plan starts when the dog is a puppy, fetching and playing with (not chewing) a variety of articles. The puppy usually attaches itself to one and this will be kept as the training article to throw, to praise and eventually to teach a controlled Retrieve.

Problems that may arise:

1. The dog not bringing the article back. If this happens, keep the dog on a long training lead. Throw the article a short distance, bearing in mind a moving article instills enthusiasm. Run out with the dog on the lead, bringing it back to retrieve to hand. Take the article off the dog before it is dropped, praise and forget the control at this stage.

2. The dog mouthing or chewing the article. Obtain a Retrieving Dummy as used by gamekeepers. It must be big enough to fill the dog's mouth to stop mouthing. I have used a dumbbell with an aluminium centre that stops mouthing".

Training programme - 2

Here is a second view on training programmes by *Joyce Stranger,* who has written many books on dogs. (See **Acknowledgements**).

"There is a great deal of controversy among dog people as to the age at which you should start training a puppy. There are many breeders and instructors who say you should wait until it is around nine months old before teaching it anything.

The age of maximum learning is from three weeks to 16 weeks. The puppy that does not hide from the hawk is a dead puppy. The wild pup is taught by his mother to know about danger.

No pup is born wise. Yet many people bring a puppy into the house and expect it to learn by either magic or telepathy. They teach it nothing. It is programmed to learn. So it does. It learns never to come when called, as no one taught it how. It learns that the only result of any misdemeanour may be a smack or a yell of NO.

It learns that when it jumps up everyone says DOWN. It learns that people are not particularly nice and are very unpredictable, and what makes someone laugh when it is 10 weeks old makes the same person furious when it is 10 months old.

When it is nine months old, the hopeful owner comes to dog class with a dog that now needs re-training, which is much more difficult. Also the dog has reached puberty and is the victim of raging hormones, and the last thing it wants to do is learn to be sensible.

Those who really know about dogs know that teaching begins the day the puppy comes home. Those dogs taught DOWN when they jump up have problems, as that word now means don't jump up, stand on four legs. So another word, such as FLAT or LIE has to be used. Few people understand why it is difficult to teach their dog Down. It is better taught when the pup first comes home.

If the pup is encouraged to sit and look up, instead of leaping up, it soon learns not to jump up at all. Anything we permit becomes part of its repertoire and is our fault.

So many people take the pup out on the lead and expect it to walk perfectly. This is like putting a learner driver into a car and driving straight onto a motorway. The pup must be taught how to walk.

One pup that came to me was so afraid of the lead it would not walk at all, but lay flat and refused to move. It preferred its owner to me, so I held the lead and he walked away. The puppy soon followed. Within a week it was happy, but had we dragged it or scolded it, there would have been a long resistance to being led.

It is fascinating to watch pups learn. A gun dog breeder I met has a huge pen beside the whelping kennel. This is totally enclosed. The first thing the puppies see when they open their eyes is an enclosure with very low undergrowth in which there are a number of pheasants and rabbits. These pups become so used to seeing game run around that they do not chase them when allowed freedom.

The older dogs are taught their lessons inside the game pen, having to ignore the animals moving around them. The pups are also taken into the big, enclosed yard en masse, and allowed to run off – only about two feet away - and then they are called back. Gradually this distance is extended, the pups learning to come at once, for a game and a cuddle.

Spaniels range in the field and this is being taught without the pups knowing it is a lesson. It also teaches them to come quickly when wanted at seven weeks old. They learn to Sit, Stand and to lie Down at this stage, too.

If games are devised for the puppy, it learns fast. We have to train for success. Failure depresses us and our dogs. The most important lesson a dog can learn is to Stay absolutely still in one place.

Even in the home, a glass might be broken, leaving splinters everywhere. The dog is told to Stay. The glass is collected safely and the dog is not injured. If it ran through the glass, it could well cut an artery and bleed to death.

The dog is told to Stay at the road edge, on the lead. The traffic is heavy and there is no chance to cross. He sees a cat on the other side of the road and takes off, pulling its handler and itself under cars. I have known a child killed this way. The dog that is taught to Stay and not move until told, lives a long life.

So many people, when teaching at first, tell the dog to stay and then call it. The handler MUST go back to the dogs. Otherwise it will soon become confused. I teach my dogs to come, in the early lessons, by running backwards with them coming towards me on the lead. Until they can do a Stay without any problems, I never call them to me when at a Stay. I go back. The dog does not move. In this way the Stay can be used to prevent many problems.

Greg could not bear his owner out of his sight. He seized her arms, to hold her to him. The owner was black and blue with several bites. The dog was taught to Stay, without any distractions whatever at first. When this was perfect, his handler moved slightly away from him, then further, putting a biscuit between his paws. She practised this several times a day.

Finally, he would sit with the biscuit while she went out of the room and shut the door behind her. She called through the door, "You can eat your biscuit," and he was freed from his position, without contact with her. The new skill gave him confidence.

She also put on her outdoor clothes several times a day, took up the lead and her purse, and then sat down and read a book. Going out did not then become a major occasion, and he never knew if she was leaving or not, which prevented a build-up of anxiety. He was completely cured.

Khan lived on a caravan site and devised a wonderful game. He chased those visitors on their way to the showers, seized their towels, ran off and ripped them up. As he was a Newfoundland he frightened small people. He was penned.

When the season ended, I went over several times a week. Khan was taught to Stay and not move even a whisker. Then the caravan site staff of 15 people filed past him, at a distance of about 20 yards. When he would stay still while this went on, they came gradually nearer and nearer till they could come up to him and stroke him without him moving. It was practised several times a day, moving up a stage very gradually over the weeks.

Then we repeated the 20-yard sequence with everyone swinging a towel, again at 20 yards distance at first. After 12 weeks they could walk up to him, still swinging the towel, and he did not move. He never chased or ripped up towels again, and everyone adored him. He was the site pet.

Pero was a rescue dog bought for security work. His problem was other dogs, joggers, and any kind of traffic. Again he was taught the Stay, this time in a large car park beside the Nature Reserve park where he worked. We started in May when it was not busy (this is a tourist resort).

There was a large pond on which there were many ducks that rushed to people for food. This triggered my dog, so Pero and Troy did Stays side by side, which helped Pero see that other dogs did this, too.

By August, we could sit both dogs at the edge of the car park and invite boys on bicycles or skateboards to circle them. Other dogs off lead ran up to them. Joggers passed them. The ducks were all over the place, as so many people brought food. Neither dog moved.

Pero is now a sound steady working animal. Troy can Stay among sheep and chickens. But it took a lot of practice and careful teaching. They did not Stay off lead until we had perfection on lead, no matter what happened.

It is useful practice because in a big busy car park in the height of the season there are all sorts of odd incidents that might trigger a dog to misbehave. Balls are thrown, children run and scream, people carry odd pieces of equipment. Any one of these might upset an untrained dog.

I have my own method of teaching the dog to Stay and my own rules. It must be a pleasant exercise. In some classes, it is often terrifying to the dogs in training. If they break, they are pushed into position and may be yelled at. They become anxious, wanting re-assurance, and are more likely than ever to break.

My owners are taught to have a toy or food in their hands, the dog on the lead beside them, looking up at the hand, which is held near the face. At first, we never say "Stay" so that the dog has not learned to disobey a command if he does move

They count to five, aloud. The dog watches those moving lips, hears the sounds and knows that this is an interactive exercise, with both dog and owner involved. It also makes the owner concentrate on the dog, and not think about supper, or some treat in store while the dog is supposed to understand he may not move.

Why? There is no possible point to the dog.

When the dog does not move for the count of five, but stays as if locked, then the handler is told to praise the dog, to give him the food, or the toy to hold, and then to unlock him with a cue word. The dog must never move until he hears this word. I say "that'll do." Others may say "enough" or give a command that means they can now move. This is done gently, without a lot of enthusiastic praise that may trigger the dog to be silly.

I like the Stay to be a very calm quiet exercise in which the dog is neither worried nor excited. I have seen 18 dogs at a show released from a Stay by excited handlers with lots of praise and jumping around. They all piled into one other. There was a massive fight and several dogs and people were bitten trying to separate them. They had been over stimulated.

When the dog is steady on a count of five, we go up to 10, and by increments of five at a time up to 30. When the dog can do a perfect on-lead Stay to a count of 30, it gets a certificate of competence.

The next certificate comes when the dog Stays for one minute without moving; the last certificate is given for on lead Stays for two minutes. The handler always counts aloud. The dog, by now, is watching the handler and does not notice if dogs around him misbehave and does not break.

When this is done as a class, we have all the dogs concentrating on their owners and ignoring their surroundings.

We start off-lead Stays by moving around the dog, still on lead, till he can understand that we move and he doesn't.

Then, with the handler one step away from the dog, we go back to counting five only at first, but the perfection comes quickly and we can often get an off-lead Stay for a minute in one lesson.

If the dog does move, say at a count of 12, then we go back a stage, and only count to 10, until he has learned to Sit still for that period. It is very difficult for a very active dog. He is never scolded. He is simply moved a few steps away from a place that has become unpleasant and told to Sit still again.

As the dogs progress, we make the counting quieter and quieter and when they know the exercise well, they don't need it. And then we can progress to out-of-sight Stays, again starting with the handler vanishing for one second and then returning; and gradually extending the time so that the dog knows it has not been deserted. It is important not to practise out-of-sight stays alone because the dog might move and you don't know it has.

Have someone else there watching the dog all the time.

I once did an out-of-sight Stay in a field I thought secure. I did not see the Collie that jumped the fence until it attacked my poor dog who was lying quietly and watching the place where I had just vanished to hide behind a bush.

That upset her so badly, we did not manage out-of-sight stays for months and she was never reliable in competitions when I was not there to re-assure her. She expected another attack because she had been quite badly bitten.

When doing their homework, I ask handlers not to teach the dog to Sit Stay and Down Stay in the same session, or in the same place, and we don't in class. We may do Sit Stays at the beginning of the lesson and Down Stays at the end, the dog always in a different place to that where the first exercise was performed.

Also I teach the dogs to go down from a Stand into a Sit, as then they don't slide from one position to the other. If the dog is running off and you want him to go down, he is not going to sit first and then Down. If not taught to go Down from the stand, he won't do it at all.

If the Down and the Stay are both well taught, it is often easier to stop a chasing dog with the command Down, followed by the command to Stay, than to call him. He goes down. You then have to go and lead him because when released he will often continue the chase. Dogs that learn to go Down at a distance on command in my classes have a trophy to commemorate the event. It is not easy. But it is well worth doing because it can save the dog's life. Many dogs chase birds over cliffs here and fall to the rocks below. The command of Down, then Stay, will prevent a serious injury or death.

Trained dogs do sponsored Down Stays for charity, for so much per minute up to 10. In this way we bought 10 Guide Dogs for the Blind in the past few years.

Rescued dogs often will not Stay off lead. They need to be near their owners because they are very easily upset and might feel they are being left again, especially if they were dumped.

There is no magic wand in dog training. Nobody reaches Wimbledon in tennis after one lesson. We did not pass our driving test after one lesson. It took time – a great deal of it. So why should we expect a dog, which does not have our mentality, to learn overnight?

There is nothing in the world like a well-trained dog. There is nothing so exciting as seeing it begin to understand what is needed and perform the action perfectly. Training will give you a reward beyond anything you have ever known. Enjoy your dog."

JoyceStranger@k9phoenix.freeserve.co.uk

Website: http://www.k9phoenix.freeserve.co.uk

(See **Robot training**)

TRAINERS – THE FAMOUS

Everyone has heard of Barbara Woodhouse, who brought dog training to the public's attention through TV.

I would hope that everyone has also heard of Dr Roger Mugford, Britain's leading animal behaviourist. He is the man who developed the new philosophy of the importance of relationships to dogs, having introduced the Halti and published several excellent books.

Way before anyone had heard of people like John Fisher, Peter Neville, Ian Dunbar, John Rogerson, Brian Appleby or indeed myself, Roger Mugford was teaching us all his philosophy, solutions and giving advice.

In 1979, he founded the Animal Behaviour Centre in Surrey, which designs and distributes functional pet accessories, which I use daily. (See **Behaviourists** and **Good Citizen Test**).

TOP TEN TRAINERS

"Dogs Today" carried out a survey in 1997 when it gave a free listing to dog trainers and asked all those who filled out the form to name their favourite trainer.

The top ten were:

1.	Ian Dunbar	7.	Peter Neville
2.	John Fisher	8.	Roy Hunter
3.	John Rogerson	9.	Konrad Lorenz
4.	Karen Pryor	10.	Gail Fisher
5.	Sylvia Bishop	10.	Kevin McNicholas
6.	Dr. Roger Mugford	10.	Charlie Wyatt

TRAUMATOLOGY

Increasingly, vets are having to specialise in particular areas of treatment for dogs. Traumatology is one such speciality, involving the examination of joints and bones.

TRAVEL

You could be asked for an up-to-date vaccination book when crossing the border into another country in Europe. Though it is unlikely, you could also be asked if you have a lead and muzzle.

TRICKS and FUN

Obedience training tends to be serious. Most people just want a dog to walk correctly and come when called. Further training, such as trick training, does not have to be serious and can be fun. Here are a few ideas:

Shake Hands. This is very popular. Simply make the dog sit. Ask for the "Paw" and tickle the leg in the hollow behind the paw. As soon as the dog moves the paw, give it a treat. After a while the dog will do this on its own to your enthusiastic praise.

Play Dead. When your dog is lying down, gently roll it onto its side and quietly say "dead". Make certain that the dog can see you. Do not walk out of its sight, otherwise it will lift its head. Keep saying in a soft tone "Dead". Stretch the word out: deeeeaaaadddd. You will be amazed how easy this is provided you say the words slowly. At first, do this for a few seconds and release the dog. Each time extend the trick to a few more seconds. Always be in a position where the dog can see you.

Good and Bad. This is a very good party trick. Offer your dog some food and say "Bad" in a hard voice. If the dog tries to take the food from your hand, gently tap his nose. When he backs off quickly, say in a soft voice "Good'" and offer the food. After a few minutes, the dog will stand back and wait for you to say "Good" or "Bad".

Sit and Beg. Most dogs can sit and beg. First make your dog sit and hold a treat just above his nose. The closer you hold this the better, for then it will not jump up. As soon as the dog raises its front paws, give it a treat. This will not take long, provided you get your timing right.

Crawling Get your dog in a Down position. Stand in front and place your hand on its shoulder to prevent it getting up. Hold a nice treat in front of it and say "Crawl". Your dog should follow your moving hand. You only want the dog to move a few inches to get its reward.

Hide and Seek Throw your dog's favourite toy. Repeat this, but turn its head so that it cannot see where you throw the toy. Then release the dog and ask: "Where is it?" in a sing-song way. After a while, put your dog in a Sit and Stay while you or a friend hide the toy. Then send him out and encourage it to seek by saying "Where is it?"

TRIGGERS

There are many triggers that can cause a dog's aggression to a human. They could be medical triggers such as toothache, a sprain or joint disease. They could be due to a sound, scent or action that resulted in a bad experience in the past - or even jealousy. Whatever the trigger might be, the antidotes are not to allow the dog to become dominant and to ensure it is socialised and trained.

URINATING in house while away.

A worried owner sent me an e-mail about his dog urinating in the house while he was away.. In the e-mail, he revealed that the dog slept in the bedroom and was allowed on furniture – two basic errors. I told him the dog was suffering from separation anxiety. This starts with either barking and/or urinating, and I warned that the next step could be destruction - and the stress could also have an effect on its coat.

I told him he must cool down the relationship. The dog is a pack animal. If it is allowed to be with the family in the bedroom and lie on the furniture, it gets angry when the family goes off hunting (to work) without it. So it should not be allowed in the bedroom, and should certainly not be allowed on the couch.

It should be fed twice a day and the food should be on the floor for five minutes only. He should also make sure the food is not too high in protein.

(See **Puppy – eliminating** and **Territory marking**).

VACCINATIONS

A "cocktail" of vaccinations should be injected by your vet once a year. It contains a very mild dose of the diseases so that, in theory, your dog creates anti-bodies to kill off the disease should it occur. One against rabies should also be included in Spain.

Are vaccinations really necessary? *(Catherine O'Driscoll* (See **Acknowledgements**) writes: ("Dog and cat owners are urged to vaccinate their friends every year against a wide combination of viral and bacterial diseases. Recently, however, there has been mounting concern over the frequency at which vaccines are administered. Owners have been claiming that side effects are higher than the vaccine industry acknowledges.

Of course you want to protect your dog against killer diseases. This is perfectly natural. But what if vaccines are actually replacing one set of deadly diseases with another set of equally deadly diseases?

There is mounting evidence to show that this is precisely what is happening in humans. One vaccine, for example, has been shown to contain a monkey retrovirus that switches off the part of DNA that protects from cancer. Not only is the retrovirus being found at the cancer sites of the people who were vaccinated, but it is also being found at the cancer sites of their children. The retrovirus is causing inheritable cancer.

The same vaccine - the Salk polio vaccine - was also said to be contaminated with a monkey immunodeficiency virus, SIV. Two separate and independent scientific papers linked this vaccine with the emergence of AIDS after mass vaccination campaigns in the Belgian Congo and amongst male homosexuals in New York.

Swiss scientists have also found an enzyme, reverse transcriptase, in the live measles and mumps vaccine. This was traced back to chickens whose cells were used to create vaccines. Reverse transcriptase, which copies RNA into DNA, has also been reportedly detected in yellow fever and some influenza vaccines prepared in chicken embryo cells. Merck, a vaccine manufacturer, is said to suspect that this signals the presence of an avian leukosis virus, a retrovirus that can cause a leukaemia-like illness.

However, these are vaccines prepared for human use. Where is the evidence to suggest that our animals might similarly be affected?

Unfortunately, veterinary vaccine manufacturers are not required by law to tell us how they cultivate their vaccines. In order to test the viral component of a vaccine, you need a license and licenses are only usually granted to vaccine manufacturers.

We do know, though, that parvovirus appeared in the 1970s - a new and deadly disease in dogs. The Oxford Concise Veterinary Dictionary theorises that parvo might have been caused by cats shedding the feline enteritis vaccine.

However, the UK quality national newpaper, "The Sunday Times", quotes scientists who claim that parvo was created when cats, who were infected with feline enteritis, were used as culture media for the distemper vaccine. Parvovirus appeared simultaneously around the world. If it were a naturally occurring disease, then it would spread slowly across continents. Instead, the emergence of the disease appeared more reflective of the sales practices of multi-national vaccine companies.

Veterinary vaccines must use largely the same manufacturing techniques as human vaccines. Therefore, the vaccines used for your pets could have been cultivated on cats, dogs, monkeys, hamsters, and chickens.

Dr Jean Dodds says: 'Immune-suppressant viruses of the retrovirus and parvovirus classes have recently been implicated as causes of bone marrow failure, immune mediated blood diseases, lymphoma, leukaemia, organ failure, Thyroiditis, Addison's disease and diabetes.

Viral disease and recent vaccination with modified live virus vaccines, especially those containing distemper, adenovirus 1 and 2, and parvovirus, are increasingly recognised contributors to immune-mediated blood diseases, bone marrow failure, and organ dysfunction.

Vaccine manufacturers warn, in their data sheets, that only healthy animals should be vaccinated. Yet vets routinely vaccinate sick animals. Not surprising when you see how little they are told.

Intervet, for example, a veterinary vaccine manufacturer, states in its data sheets that: immunocompetence may be compromised by a variety of factors, including poor health, nutritional status, genetic factors, concurrent drug therapy and stress.

Although Intervet says more than others, most people, including vets, would fail to ask what "immunocompetence may be compromised" actually means.

In fact, it means that any of the above factors may compromise the immune system. In order to successfully react to a vaccine challenge, the immune system must be functioning properly. If it is not, then the body will not be able to mount a defence against the live viruses being pumped into it, and the viruses could overwhelm the animal and kill it.

Drs Tom R. Phillips and Ronald D. Schultz tell us that: "Incomplete vaccine attenuation or vaccination of an immunosuppressed host can result in modified live vaccines causing the disease they are designed to prevent".

Because, I suspect, a human life is worth more in law than an animal's life, human vaccine manufacturers warn that certain types of people should not be vaccinated. Merck warns in "The Merck Manual" that patients with eczema, dermatitis, neurological deterioration, inhalant and food allergies, and heart disease should not receive live virus vaccines because live virus vaccines could kill them.

And, maybe because parents of children can sue for millions, but your pet is worth no more than a piece of furniture, veterinary vaccines are recommended for use on a yearly basis - despite the fact that, according to world expert Ron Schultz, and others, once immunity to a virus exists, it persists for years or life."

VETS

The treatment of humans requires at least 21 specialists to look after somebody from prenatal days to post-mortem. Yet there is only one person who must be everything for a dog. That is the vet or, as the Americans say with deeper respect, veterinarian.

Much progress in many directions of pet care has been made in the last few years and many vets have invested in modern equipment to enable your dog to benefit from new techniques.

So, with a good, modern vet you are paying, not just for the examination, but also for the time they have spent keeping up with the latest developments and for the equipment they have installed in their surgery.

Some of the larger surgeries have much the same equipment as a hospital operating room and there may be a group of vets working together, each specialising in different fields of veterinary care. On the other hand, there are older vets who work alone and have not studied the latest techniques. Should you have a complaint, the only redress is to change vets or make a complaint, with full details, to the local veterinary college.

A second opinion is sometimes most important, especially if an expensive course of treatment has been recommended for a long-term illness. A good vet will not mind. Indeed some will recommend it.

Make sure that your vet offers a 24-hour emergency service. Personally I would not use a vet who does not provide this important facility, but you must, of course, expect to pay a higher consultation fee out of normal working hours.

Indeed, consultation and treatment fees can vary a great deal between vets as a "Dogs Today" survey revealed. The cost for a basic series of treatments and medicines varied from £149.58 in Cornwall to £363.88 in London, a difference so great that not even higher rents and rates could account for it.

Keep your own medical history book. You will find a page at the back of this book where you can do this. Every time you go to the vet write down the problem and the treatment. One day you may decide to move home, change vet, or your dog may need emergency treatment. The vet is closed and so is his computer. Your dogs medical history record may well be vital.

Visiting the vet

Prepare your dog to visit the vet. It should have inoculations and boosters every year, worming tablets every three months, the only effective worming products being available from the vet.

A visit can be a problem if the dog does not like to be examined. It helps if, from an early age, you have accustomed your dog to be handled by yourself and different people. Reassure the dog and reward with praise and tit-bits.

Most vets will examine the dog on a table. So train your dog by lifting it onto a suitable table to get it used to the idea. Hold the dog in a comfortable position for a few seconds, praising and reassuring, then give it a tit-bit and gently lift it off. Never let a dog jump off the table by itself. Put a mat or cover on the table so that it is not slippery.

After a visit to your vet you may have to continue a course of treatment at home. This can include giving pills or liquid medicine (orally), applying ointments to eyes, ears and skin, giving eye or ear drops. Again, if the dog has been accustomed to being handled, all these tasks will be a lot easier. Pills can by disguised inside a small piece of butter, margarine or cheese.

Do not give dogs any medicine unless prescribed by a vet. Never accept advice from unqualified people including pet shop staff, dog breeders, dog trainers, behaviourists and the person a friend knows who had a dog with the same sort of symptoms.

Never put anything in your dog's ears. Look, but don't poke. If there are discharges or smells, go to your vet. Do not put any drops or ointment into your dog's eyes unless told to do so by a vet. Do not interfere with any lumps, bumps, wounds, cysts, rashes or anything else on your dog's body. Consult your vet.

Vets - after care

After surgery, it can be a problem to get a dog to rest and recuperate, especially if there are other dogs in the house. As soon as a dog starts feeling better, it will want to return to normal activity. Supervision and crating are the only answers while remembering that, unlike humans, sick dogs do not want to be pampered. (See **Health signs, Ill-health signs** and **Symptoms**).

VISITING

When you go visiting or on a trip, take the dog's basket or crate, your own water and a radio to play music near to the dog to help drown unaccustomed noises. (See **Drinking water**).

VISITORS (See **Jumping Up**)

VITAMINS

Theoretically, there should be no need to provide additional vitamins if a dog is fed a "complete" dog meal. However, the mix of vitamins provided in commercial dog food are for an average dog taking average exercise with an average appetite (whatever all those are).

For those dogs which do not fit within the average parameters, there may be a need to supplement the vitamin diet but that is a decision for your vet, not you. So don't start giving extra vitamins because a friend tells you it might be a good idea. It might be a bad one. (See **Food**).

WALKIES

Taking a dog for a walk is beneficial to the owner because he is getting some exercise. But what about the dog? The same old walk on a lead, around the same old built-up block with the same old smells is not particularly stimulating. So vary your walks if you can.

Better still, try to take your dog to a nearby open space where it can roam free with fascinating new smells to enjoy. A dog "reads" the territory it is exploring by smell. Give your dog plenty to "read".

In the countryside, be careful what your dog eats. If you have one that thinks a walk is an opportunity for plenty of "snacks", put a muzzle on it.

Better that the dog should be muzzled than dead. Those "snacks" can be poisoned, especially in the Spanish campo, or they could come across dead rodents or carrion that have been `poisoned. (See **Muzzles** and **Poisoning, signs of**).

There is a benefit to humans from walking a dog, apart from the exercise. You are far more likely to strike up a conversation and make friends with somebody than somebody walking without a dog.

Furthermore, walking in a public place with a dog is one way to ensure nobody will try to rob you. Lou Castle, who has contributed the section on Police dog training in this book, has handled hundreds of cases of robbery on the streets of Los Angeles and says that he has not known of one victim who had a dog with him at the time.

At all times on your walks consider others. (See **Poop scoop, Exercise** and **Pulling on a lead**,)

WATER PISTOL

Water is an excellent aversive, especially when applied from a water pistol or plant spray.

WEIGHING

Weigh small or medium dogs by weighing yourself first on your bathroom scales. Step off and pick up your dog, then stand back on the scales, and simply subtract its weight from your own. For larger breeds, ask your vet, who should be happy to weigh any dog.

WEIGHT (See **Obesity**)

WHISKERS

A dog's whiskers have sensory nerve fibres, or vibrissae, with obvious ones around the muzzle which can be moved voluntarily. They are an important method for a dog to evaluate distances around their heads and shoulders. My good friend Nina Bondarenko (bondi@mcmail.com) tells me some owners in the States cut off the whiskers on show dogs to make their "heads look cleaner".

Hunting dogs that have had their whiskers cut off sustained cuts, tears and bruises on their heads, ears and shoulders during the hunting season which proves that dogs need them to estimate proximity of things close to their heads.

WHISTLE training

The sound of a whistle is stronger than that of the human voice. I am grateful to my friend *Pam Mackinnon,* a well-known behaviourist from Scotland (See **Acknowledgements**), for giving me permission to reproduce her training techniques using a whistle.

"When starting whistle training, you must first decide what type of whistle you need. Whistling yourself will not prove as reliable as an artificial whistle because you may not be able to whistle when it is cold or windy. Also a human whistle is not as loud or as constant as, for example, a plastic whistle. Plus, no matter who takes Fido for his walk, if they have the whistle they can call him back without causing any confusion and so can be confident that he will return.

Do not select a "silent" whistle as you will not be able to hear how hard you are blowing or if Fido can actually hear it, e.g. when using it in strong wind, or even if it is blocked and therefore making no sound at all.

Imagine scolding Fido for disobeying a whistle command that was never actually given.

I prefer to use an Acme plastic whistle, 211 1/2 pitch (the lower the number on the whistle the higher the pitch). It is loud enough, of an average pitch, won't rust and is cheap to buy, usually around £4, and so it doesn't matter if it gets lost.

Whistle Recall

1. At every meal, as you put his food down, give multiple pips on the whistle - always use the same number of pips. This is the only time to use the whistle for the next couple of weeks. Fido is learning to associate the sound of the whistle with food.

2. After a couple of weeks, still using the whistle as in step 1, try blowing it when he is mooching around the house. So, give your pips and when he comes to you, immediately reward him with a really tasty titbit.

3. After a few days, when you are confident that he will always come to you around the house, try whistling him in the garden, always remembering to reward him with a tasty morsel.

4. When he is recalling well in the garden, go to the park when it is quiet with few distractions. If you are unsure of his reaction, you can put him on a long line.

5. Gradually increase the distractions and distance as his reliability improves.

Remember to continue using the whistle at mealtimes during every step to continue reinforcing his behaviour. Only stop when he is really reliable.

Whistle Stop

Fido should already know the command for Sit. You can now introduce one long pip on the whistle followed by his usual Sit command. As a general rule, when adding a new command always try to place it before a command/cue that Fido already knows.

For example:

new cue	+old cue	= desired response
(whistle)	(voice & hand signal)	(sit)

To Sit Fido must Stop, so essentially a "whistle Stop" is a "whistle Sit".

You can teach Fido to lie down at the sound of the whistle in exactly the same way as the whistle Sit/Stop. You can of course do this instead of a whistle Sit/Stop or in addition to a whistle Sit/Stop by using a different whistle command.

In general, one long blast is usually best for an emergency command because it combines urgency with a direct command

Top training tips

- Plan ahead. What exactly do you want Fido to learn?

- Write down your training plan.

- Always reward Fido for doing the right thing, or trying to do the right thing.

- Break the exercise down into small sections, rather than trying to teach the exercise as a whole

- Make each step clear for Fido. Set him up for success. If he finds it too difficult, he will become too stressed and if he becomes too stressed he cannot learn.

- When training, only move forward a step once Fido has understood the current step.

- If training separate steps simultaneously, do not link them until Fido understands them all.

- You can always go back a step if Fido seems confused.

Internet address: pam.mackinnon@virgin.net

WOLF TRAINING

There are many instances of wolf cubs being brought up in a human environment as pets. However, they are unstable companions when they grow up because the dormant, yet still strong, instinct to hunt and kill can easily be triggered with dangerous results. The wolf exists in various variants around the world including the Dingo in Australia. Can a wolf be trained? The answer is "yes" according to this report by *Grant Teeboon* (See **Acknowledgements**).

"In 1979, when I first joined as a police dog handler and went through my basic police dog course, we had a Dingo named "Ding" trained up to police dog standard.

While he didn't look too impressive, he sure did just about everything the German Shepherds could do. He couldn't jump quite as high and he didn't have the weight to bring a man to the ground, but he was just as aggressive, agile and obedient as all the other police dogs.

One thing he would do that none of our Shepherds did was howl at night. I first heard this when we had him on the 'bush phase" of our dog course. It made the hair on the back of my neck stand straight up. We half expected the other 16 dogs that were there to join in, but they didn't

We have trained many breeds to police dog standard for comparison purposes. "Ding" was deemed a failure purely because he didn't have the body weight to bring a man down and had very little deterrent effect due to his size.

WOLVES (See **A Word About Wolves**)

WORDS

Remember, dogs do not understand words. It is the sound that it recognises, and too many sounds (or words for us humans) will only confuse it. Furthermore, a softly spoken, even whispered word can be just as effective. A quietly spoken "no" can have the same result as a shouted "NO". Timing and common sense are more important than the use of words. Having said that, there is no reason why you should not speak whole sentences of loving talk to your dog. It will not understand what you are saying,but it will sense the love in your voice.

WORMS

There is fortunately a simple solution to the problem of worms. There are daily, monthly or three-monthly tablets. The latter are obviously the easiest to administer. The main thing is not to forget to do it because all dogs have worms. (See **Heartworms**).

WORKING DOGS

(See **Blind, dogs for, Drug and explosive detection, Guard dogs, Guide dogs, Gun dogs, Hunting dogs, Police dogs, Sheep dogs** and **Smell**).

YORKSHIRE TERRIERS (See **Top Dogs**)

ZEST

The keen enjoyment or interest you feel for your dog ...and a good word with which to end this A-Z.

DOG RECORD PAGE

Dogs name: .... Date of birth: ....

Vet's name: ....

Tel. No. ....

Emergency Tel. ....

Treatment:

Date.	Diagnosis	Treatment

ACKNOWLEDGEMENTS
and PROFILES

Bereavement.

Dee Woodcock is a lifelong dog owner. She lives in Berkshire with David, her husband, and two much loved German Shepherds, Jenna, a home-bred bitch, and Ashla. She writes each month for "Our Dogs", "Dogs Monthly", and "Pet Dogs", and is behaviour consultant for "Dogs Monthly" magazine. She has a behavioural practice in Berkshire, and has written several open learning courses for the Animal Care College on canine psychology, nutrition, care and management, health care, pet bereavement counselling, and canine behaviour counselling. Recently she has written a book on pet loss.

Children and dogs.

Terry Ryan is founder of Prevent-A-Bite, author of "The Puppy Primer Program". Co-ordinator People-Pet-Partnership. College of Veterinary Medicine, Washington State University. Pullman, WA 99164-7010

Clicker training, Good citizen test.

Sheilagh B. Wilson is a 30-year-old trainer/behaviourist from Central Scotland. She runs Sheilagh's K9 Centre using mainly clicker training; however she will use the most kind and effective method necessary to get results. The centre concentrates on pet training and behaviour and classes include her own Canine Good Citizen and Road Safety Certificates. She also runs a fun agility class and aims to add social classes and real life situation training in the near future.

"Dogs Today" magazine.

Beverley Cuddy is the editor of "Dogs Today" magazine which she bought for £1 when the then management decided to close it down. Now it has a circulation of more than 37,000.

Her article covers her views on editing the magazine and how she has made it into an outstanding success story.

Electric collars.

Lou Castle is a police sergeant in the Los Angeles area of Southern California, USA. He is head K-9 trainer and instructor with one of the biggest departments of its kind in the USA. His base is surrounded by the City of Los Angeles, about 15 minutes north of the LA Airport. His other assignments have included SWAT team (as an operator, sniper, and team leader) vice, narcotics, traffic, rangemaster, baton instructor, use of force instructor and field training supervisor.

Flyball racing, Mat training.

Kevin McNicholas is one of the UK's most respected dog behaviour experts. He was one of the first dog trainers to understand and apply dog behaviour to every day dog training, the sort which we see around us today. His practical experience in many facets of dog training and behaviour is unsurpassed. Innovation, understanding, inventiveness and having FUN are the key to Kevin's dog training/behaviour philosophy. His methods move on and on, usually ahead of the rest of the following pack. He is a member of the Federation of Dog Trainers and Canine Behaviourists whom I always visit when in the U.K.

Human training, Obedience versus behaviour.

Dr. Dennis Fetko. <u>www.drdog.com</u>

Began obedience and protection training in 1960; Ph.D., Behavioural Psychology, 1981; full-time national and international trainer and behaviorist since 1976. Trained obedience, protection, police, stock, service, search and rescue, hearing ear and guide dogs. Combat paratrooper with awards for valour, merit and achievement. Works with dogs, wolves, cats, horses, elephants, marine mammals, captive exotics.

Kumfi training equipment, Police dog selection, Training programmes - 1.

George Grayson, a former inspector and officer in charge of the North Yorkshire Police Dog Section, now president of the British Police & Services Canine Association. Upon retirement in 1986 after 31 years' service, he founded the N.E. Dog Training Centres, based at Northallerton, N. Yorks where he is now mainly engaged in training domestic pet dogs and dealing with associated canine behavioural problems. He is also the designer of the Kumfi range of dog control products, which I recommend and use. President of the British Police Dog & Services Canine Association and a member of the Federation of Dog Trainers and Canine Behaviourists.

Police dogs, wolf training.

Grant Teebon has been a police dog handler with the Royal Australian Air Force for more than 20 years including five years as an instructor at the R.A.A.F's Police Dog Handler Training School at R.A.A.F. Amberley, Queensland. He is currently stationed at R.A.A.F. Fairbairn in the nation's capital, Canberra.

He also runs a K9 Behaviour Consultancy called "The Paw Man" specialising in dominant and aggressive dog behaviour problems. Grant gives seminars to civilian dog training organisations such as the Dog Obedience Trainers' Association and the German Shepherd Dog Club of Queensland on his favourite topics of K9 aggression and K9 human body language. He was Koehler trained by the R.A.A.F. but in his civilian sphere uses any method appropriate that works fast and is simple enough for the average dog owner to understand.

Puppy – buying a purebred.

Ann Thibault has taught private and group obedience classes since 1982 combining the importance of owner education, early training and dog behaviour. A monthly columnist for several Newfoundland club newsletters, her articles have been published both in the U.S. and abroad. Qualified to judge for the Newfoundland club of America, she is frequently called upon to counsel breed rescue. Currently working on a book about Newfoundlands and their behaviour. Ann and her husband, Ron, have more than 50 years combined experience in Newfoundlands. Their kennel prefix is "Storytyme". They live in Michigan with their three children and various Newfoundlands.

Puppy – packs.

Diana Barbara lives in Sompting, West Sussex, England. She and her husband, Arthur, have had Labradors all their lives. Since they began showing and breeding they have aimed for a steady, breed-typical Labrador Retriever. She helps Labrador Rescue in the South East of England, assessing dogs for them and visiting potential homes. She is also the secretary of the Hampshire Gundog Society, dealing with all administration and with a full committee, running three Kennel Club Open shows a year.

E-mail: Wylanbriar@aompuserve.com

Search and Rescue.

Natalie Ray. Born in Livingston, Montana, USA. Has trained in Search and Rescue for 11+ years, started in Colorado with Search and Rescue Dogs of Colorado. Was a K9 handler with Michigan Technical Rescue Operations Team and is now working with Michigan Urban Search and Rescue. She was sent to Michigan and to Papua New Guinea in 1998 after the tsunami's as a special attachment to Florida's Special Response Team. Mother of four girls...all of whom think she had them so she would always have a subject for her dogs to find!

E-mail:NRay01@aol.com

Sheep dogs.

Barbara Sykes, National and International trialist, grew up with Border Collies. She has always had an empathy with the breed and is passionate about maintaining the strong working instinct. At Mainline Border Collie Centre she trains sheepdogs and handlers and helps companion owners to understand their dog's "language".

Shyness and Strangers

Lynn Aitchison, a dog trainer from Scotland known as "The Dog Lady", has been involved in dog training since 1974, mostly with the Edinburgh & District Dog Training Club. For the past five years she has worked as an independent trainer and adviser on dog behaviour. She is an Associate Member of the British Institute of Professional Dog Trainers and a member of the APDT (UK), using clicker training as part of her motivational work with dogs.

Tracking.

Ron Lawrence, has instructed obedience classes at the highest level and given training presentations at Dog Obedience Clubs in the Australian Capital Territory and New South Wales. Hosted the Microsoft Network's (MSN) Dog Training, Trialing and Behaviour Forum in 1996-7. At the time of writing he had two working Border Collies under training, ie Rough OC and Ready OC, ET. Ron Lawrence, Canberra, ACT, Australia. winron@bigpond.com, ICQ 21453314.

Homepage: http://www.users.bigpond.com/winron

Trainers' organisations – APTD.

Ian Dunbar is renowned for his passive training methods, his pioneer work on the creation of the Association of Pet Dog Trainers and his many books, videos and TV programmes. He is a pioneer worker in the world of dogs whom I respect a great deal.

Training programmes - 2

Joyce Stranger has lived with dogs all her life. Four of her dogs had major problems, one being so difficult that she was told by "experts" to put it to sleep. It survived to become the 1,000th pets as Therapy dog, visiting schools and old people. As a result of her experiences with her own dogs she has, for the past 30 years, taught others how to civilise their dogs. For the last 10 years she has also given private lessons. She has written more than 70 books, six of them on her own dogs. One, a non fiction book for dog owners. "How to Own a Sensible Dog" has sold several thousand copies and is still in print.

JoyceStranger@k9phoenix.freeserve.co.uk

Website http://www.k9phoenix.freeserve.co.uk

Vaccinations – necessary or idiocy?

Catherine O'Driscoll is the author of "What Vets Don't Tell You About Vaccines". She lives with her husband John and five Golden Retrievers who are now protected by the homoeopathic alternative to vaccines. Catherine is a marketing consultant and freelance writer whose clients have, in the past, included pharmaceutical and chemical companies. The vaccine-induced deaths of three of her young canine friends had a major effect on her.

Whistles.

Pamela Mackinnon has been training dogs as far back as she can remember. She first got paid for it when she joined H.M. Customs & Excise and became a drug detector dog handler. After that she worked as a trainer for the charity Hearing Dogs for Deaf People. Her next move was back to Scotland, where she joined the ranks of the self-employed as a dog training and behaviour consultant.

DAVID THE DOGMAN

A great honour in the dog world was bestowed in 1999 on David Klein, or David the Dogman, the pseudonym by which he is known world wide among canine behaviourists, dog trainers, vets and those seeking his advice.

He was made an honorary life member of the British Police and Services Canine Association for his creation of an Internet forum for Service dog handlers world wide (police, prison and military) and for his previous work as a dog handler for the Israeli Police Force.

His deep association with the Internet is significant because many of the latest facts about dogs and modern training methods in this book have come from the knowledge he has gained from being probably more involved with Internet dog sites and forums than any other canine behaviourist in the world.

He was born in England in 1937 and has worked with dogs professionally since the age of 17 when he joined the Israeli Police Force as a dog handler in the Police Canine Section where he reached the rank of Sergeant. Like other police dog handlers world wide, he was known as "The Dogman", hence his pseudonym David the Dogman.

He has experience of most aspects of dog handling, including special scent work, involving the tracking of drugs and explosives, as well as air sea rescue and all forms of advanced defence work. He has trained dogs for the show circuit, including agility work, and to provide security companies with guard dogs besides being a consultant for rescue societies.

David the Dogman has lived near Marbella on the Costa del Sol in Spain for the last 13 years. He has his own radio and television programmes and special social classes and has recorded several videos which highlight his passive training methods. He also writes for newspapers and dog magazines.

He claims that with his silent training methods he can have any dog under his control in less than three minutes and can train it to walk to Heel, Sit and Stay without speaking.

He plays the organ in his spare time and in the early seventies created three world records for marathon playing to help the aged, infirm and children suffering from mental retardation. He was also the founder and pioneer of a hospice in Nottinghamshire in England, and holds a private pilot's licence and is a licensed skipper.

E-mail: david@thedogman.net

DAVID THE DOGMAN'S INTERNET SITES:

www.thedogman.net

There are dozens of links to this site which is visited by thousands from all around the world to obtain advice from the author. Because of this he knows the problems most people want answered. The site also contains many articles he has written which have appeared in newspapers and magazines all over the world. There are also links from this site and dog forums administered by David the Dogman.

www.canineworld.net

This site is owned by David who aims to make it the largest canine site on the Internet. Still being built, it is not as yet advertised.

www.k9netuk.com

The largest UK canine web site owned by Sue James featuring such dog magazines as "Dog Monthly", "Dog Training Weekly", "Working Sheepdog News", "Working Trials Weekly", besides the British Dog Breeders Council. The site has 400,000 visitors a month.

DAVID THE DOGMAN'S INTERNET FORUMS:
Dogs-Today forum

Free membership around the world to discuss dog related topics. This friendly, informal forum is associated with the popular U.K. magazine "Dogs Today" which makes special offers and there are competitions with prizes.

To subscribe send an E-mail to:

Majordomo@mailinglist.net with the message, "subscribe dogs-today" and your E-mail address.

For help or advice contact:

Administrator: Kirsty Firth

k.firth@lancaster.ac.uk.

All-k9 Forum

Free membership to those involved with dog training world wide. Latest methods discussed and opinions exchanged by a large membership of professional dog behaviourists, trainers and vets.

To subscribe send an E-mail to:

Majordomo@mailinglist.net with the message, "subscribe all-k9" and your E-mail address.

For help or advice contact:

Administrator: Sheilagh B Wilson

sheilaghsk9centre@falkirk.almac.co.uk

British Police and Services Canine Association

Discussion of all aspects of working dogs and an international exchange of information for professionals only. Administered by George Grayson (UK) and David the Dogman (Marbella, Spain) both life members of the B.P.S.C.A. This is an ideal forum for those involved – both presently and in and the past – in any kind of working dog, military, prison, police, security, rescue, drugs and explosion work. All trainers welcome

To subscribe send an E-mail to bpsca@mailinglist.net with a brief CV.

For help and advice contact: david@thedogman.net

TESTIMONIALS

From 10 of the world´s top canine behavourists and trainers.

Gill Minter, Animal Welfare Advisor For NCDL. National Canine Defence League.

"I have known David through the Internet for a long time. He offers specialist help through a clear understanding in dog behaviour and training, using positive, rather than punitive methods. As a nation who share our homes with beloved pets, we sometimes suffer from our tendency to dominate rather than understand, David helps us achieve this understanding through the Internet. Standing by his "Commitment, Firmness, and Kindness, David is not just "The Dogman" but an ambassador to dogs through the far reaching modern technology of the Internet. I'm sure the people he reaches through this book will feel the same and I wish him the best of luck."

Dr. Dennis Fetch, DR. DOG, *presenter of major TV and radio dog training shows in the U.S.A.< www.drdog.com>*

"I've been in contact with David the Dogman and have known of his dog training attitudes for years. His receptiveness to new methods while demanding valid, scientific bases is MOST refreshing and progressive. Knowing his scrutiny, I place high regard in his enlightened conclusions."

George GRAYSON, *Home Office Accredited Police Dog Training Instructor; Ex. Insp & O.I.C. North Yorkshire Police Dog Section, United Kingdom; Director of Training for N.E. Dog Training Centres, Yorkshire, ENGLAND; Managing Director of Kumfi Canine Products Ltd, Canine Training & Behavioural Aids; President of The British Police and Services Canine Association; Chairman of The U.K. Dog Training Industry Association; Co-ordinator (NE) Federation of Dog Trainers & Canine Behaviourists; Member of The British Institute of Professional Dog trainers; Member of the Association of Pet Dog Trainers.*

"I admire the work you do on the Internet and your replies to questions are always reasoned, sensible and very practical. You also obviously believe in positive, none punitive and persuasive methods of training and dealing with human and canine behavioural problems in a very passive way. I am sure your book will be a record of your work and of great benefit throughout the international canine world".

Ann DeRizzio, *President of the Federation of Dog Trainers and Canine Behaviourist, Member of the Federation of Dog Trainers and Canine Behaviourists:*

"When it comes to dogs, David the Dogman is a tireless professional. I am amazed at his enthusiasm and motivation. David is a man who gives 100% or I should say 200%. His dog related activities would leave a lesser person with canine burn out. David works in Canine overdrive".

Grant Teebon, *Senior police dog trainer, 20 years service, Royal Australian Air Force.*

E-mail: gtboon@dynamite.com.au

Homepage: http://www2.dynamite.com.au/gtboon

"I have known David for several years through his Internet interest group, specifically for K9 Professionals, called All-K9. David is the moderator of this elite group of professional trainers and behaviorists who discuss their ideas, methods and new problems daily on the Internet. Under David's guidance All-K9 covers the broadest possible spectrum of K9 training and behavioural situations, problems and solutions. His input into this resource is invaluable for both amateur and professional alike. There is no such thing as someone who knows everything about dog training, but those who admit they don't know it all, invariably seek out David the Dogman as a reference source."

Lou Castle, *Head Police Dog Trainer, Los Angeles, CA.*
UnclLou@aol.com
"A voice of reason on the Internet."

Sue James, *England. Webmaster of the U.K.'s leading all-round dog site. Sue@b-jam.demon.co.u*
"As webmaster for the UK's Leading all-round canine site, I have known David the Dogman for some time. David has a heart of gold where dogs are concerned, always ready to help other people with their dogs and offer assistance in behavioural matters. David has had his own problem page on K9netuk for about three years now, a popular page for people from around the world, and he also provides facilities for e-mail chat lists, where people can "meet" online and discuss their various canine interests together. In fact David the Dogman has become a household name and favourite of many dog lovers.

Ing. H. Hendriksen, *Head Trainer, Hondenschool ABOVO, (dogschool), ABOVO, W.Helmichstraat 76, 3553 JZ Utrecht, The Netherlands.*

"David the Dogman has provided a forum on the Internet through which thousands of dog trainers communicate with each other, learn from each other and become therefore better trainers. Every day I see him give advice and support to other trainers that is wise, safe and sound. Thanks David."

Bonnie Anthony *of "Bonnie's Canine Training", a much respected mountain and air sea rescue dog training centre.*
LUJU19A@prodigy.com

"I met David the Dogman through the Internet a few years ago and I was so amazed with his brilliance on dog behaviour. I will cherish all of his advice and enthusiasm in helping me make my dog training business a successful one. Thank you, David!"

Dick Russell, *Dog Obedience with Dick Russell, Greenwell Springs, LA, USA.* sitstay@premier.net

"David is one of the friends, councilors and confidants whom I have never met face to face, but through the electronic medium of the Internet. He's one of a small handful of dog trainers, worldwide, for whom I have the greatest respect and admiration. When it comes down to the hard questions, he has the ability to cut through the fluff, target the true problem and provide the elegant solution."

An owner.

(I am just as proud of this testimonial from an ordinary dog owner as I am of those from the preceding world-acknowledged canine expert):

"First of all I would like to thank you and your assistants for having us at your classes. Our foster dog used to be a very insecure and frightened pup. As you know he has grown into a big dog now and enjoys going to the classes at which he has improved a lot. Over the eight months that we have participated I have learned a lot myself and have seen a lot of changes in other dogs, especially problem dogs, or should I say "problem owners", because owners have to learn how to treat their dogs. Thanks again. Maybe "Bommel" will never be adopted so he will be ours for the rest of his life. But he is a well-behaved and loving dog at home and then what does it matter to have five or six dogs?" Elisa.

That sort of letter makes my job and the jobs of thousands of canine behaviourists all over the world so worthwhile for our objective is happy owners and happy dogs.

INTERNET SITES.

These sites have been researched from a number of sources, special acknowledgements being due to Cindy Tittle Moore (http://www.k9web.com/dog-faqs/) and Herbert Mullican Jr., Maryland, U.S.A.

If you have any comments about any of them, I would be grateful to receive them by E-mail for the next edition of this book – david@thedogman.net

Note: Where American sites have been featured the spelling has not been changed to the English version of the word.

SEE DAVID THE DOGMAN IN ACTION

A 45 minute video "An Introduction to Dogs", in which David the Dogman demonstrates his work, is available for £9.95 (postage included within Europe).

Visit his site:

www.david@thedogman.net.

(Note an NTSC version for American videos will be available in the near future)

BREEDS

AKC Recognized Breeds

Kept by info@akc.org.

http://www.canismajor.com/dog/topic1.html#Profiles

http://www.akc.org/bredgrp.htm

Any Breed K9 Training and Breed Information

http://www.anybreed.com/

Beagles On The Web

http://beagles-on-the-web.com/

Bernese Mountain Dog Homepage

http://www.berner.org/

Border Collies

www.bordercollies.co.uk

American Collie Site. This US site is full of Border Collie goodies and is also concerned with the herding dog. It contains ranching information and includes some excellent pictures of working dogs.

http://www.bordercollies.com

Canis Major Publications's Breed Profiles

Kept by

webmaster@canismajor.com.

http://dspace.dial.pipex.com/town/square/tac61/breeds.htm

Deerhound

http://www.deerhound.org/glossary.htm

Dogs UK Breed-Specific Pages

Kept by

willchapman@dial.pipex.com.

http://www.geocities.com/Heartland/Valley/1742/

Eastern Sighthound Breeds

Kept by Sari Mantila,

smantila@neutech.fi, http://www.webring.org/cgi-bin/webring?ring=hairlessdogs;list

German Shepherd

http://homepage.netspaceonline.com/~gened/shepherd.htm

German Shepherd Dog Homepage

http://www.gsdca.org/

German Shepherd Dog Ring

http://dbirtwis.interspeed.net/gsdring.html

German Shepherd dog training club

http://www.k9netuk.com/breed/bgsdtc.html

(Hoflin) German Shepherd Dog Homepage

http://www.hoflin.com/b/germanshepherddog.html

(Sherry's) German Shepherd and Dog Links

http://www.telusplanet.net/public/smorgan/sheplinks.htm

Golden Retriever

http://www.golden-retriever.com/orthoped.html

Golden Retrievers In Cyberspace

http://www.rahual.net/hredlus/golden.html

Hairless Dogs

http://www.cta.it/aziende/enci/razze_en.htm

International Shepherd Network

http://www.flash.net/~aero/

Italian Breeds Ente Nazionale della Cinofilia Italiana

Kept by enci@cta.it. http://www.bahnhof.se/~rapp/index/index.html

Labrador

http://www.labradorworld.com/gryphon/pano.htm

Malinut

http://www.malinut.com/home/index.shtml

Norrbottenspets

Kept by Kent Rapp, rapp@bahnhof.se. (Swedish) http://www.northernterritories.com/starhawk.htm

Northern Breeds

Kept by Chris Cooper, ccpub@thegrid.net. http://www.petnet.com.au/dogs/dogbreedindex.html

PetNet's Dog Index

Kept by Denise Humphries, petcare@interconnect.com.au. http://rarebreed.com

Rare Breeds Homepage

Kept by Laurie Wessely, lwessely@rarebreed.com http://www.webring.org/cgi-bin/webring?ring=retrievers;list

Rare Breed Network

http://www.rarebreed.com/

Retrievers

http://www.webring.org/cgi-bin/webring?ring=houndring;list

Rottweiler Homepage

http://members.tripod.com/~RottHome/

Scenthounds

http://www.webring.org/cgi-bin/webring?ring=setterring;list

Setters

http://www.webring.org/cgi-bin/webring?ring=irun;list

Sighthound

http://www.coil.com/~steve/small-dogs.html

Small Dog Breeds

Kept by Steve Conley, steve@coil.com. http://www.gae.unican.es/general/dogs/breeds/spain/espanolas.html

Spanish Breeds

Kept by Angel Camacho, camacho@esanu1.unican.es. http://www-nmbe.unibe.ch/abtwt/swiss_dogs.html

Swiss Canine Breeds

http://www-nmbe.unibe.ch/abtwt/swiss_dogs.html

Swiss Dog Breeds

ept by Marc Nussbaumer, nussbaumer@nmbe.unibe.ch. http://www.k9web.com/dog-faqs/breeds/

rec.pets.dogs. Breed-FAQ's

Kept by Cindy Tittle Moore rpd-info@netcom.com. http://www.versatiledogs.com/

Versatile Dogs Homepage

Kept by Christie Coy, versatile@email.net. http://worldclassdogs.com.bs/Breeds.html

World Class Dogs Breed List

Kept by
Webmaster@WorldClassDogs.com.

COUNTRIES

Australia

http://www.vca.org.au/

Australian Dogs Page

Kept by Shane Baker,
sbaker@pcug.org.au.
http://www.pcug.org.au/~sbaker/
dogs.htm

Canada

Canadian Dog Show. Info/Links

Kept by info@compupets.com.
http://www.compupets.com/index.html
http://www.webnet.qc.ca/chiens/

Finnish Kennel Club

http://www.kennelliitto.fi/

France

Club Français de L'Airedale Terrier et
Divers Terriers.

http://www.chez.com/cfat/

Germany

http://www.jagdspaniel.de/
homepage.htm

Holland

http://ourworld.compuserve.com/
homepages/rpoerbo/

Hong Kong

http://www.netfront.net/~greenx/

Iceland

http://www.smart.is/bhsi/

Italy

http://www.leonet.it/news/bulldogs/

Israel

Kept by
info@interclub.co.il (Hebrew)
http://www.interclub.co.il/dogs/

Japan

http://www.st.rim.or.jp/~ito/d/
dogmark.html

New Zealand

http://www.wave.co.nz/pages/cobset/

Norway

http://home.sol.no/~lmelvold/

Spain

El Mundo Canino,

Kept by Angel Camacho,

camacho@esanu1.unican.es. (Spanish,
English)

http://www.gae.unican.es/general/
dogs/dogs.html

Sweden

http://www.algonet.se/~boxer1

GENERAL

Acme Pet Canine Directory

http://www.acmepet.com/canine/
index.html

All About Dogs

http://www.ptialaska.net/~pkalbaug/
index.html

All Dogs.com

http://www.all-dogs.com/

Allpets, Alldogs

http://www.allpets.com/alldogs/doghead.html

American Kennel Club

http://www.akc.org/

Animal Pet Shop

www.animail.co

ASPADS

The Associated Sheep, Police & Army Dog Society was established during the 1920's to promote Working Trials in the U.K. It is the largest Working Trials Society in the U.K. and has many highly qualified and experienced members

http://www.aspads.org.uk/

Assistance dogs

http://www.uwsp.edu/acad/psych/dog/assist.htm

*Bad Dog Chronicles

http://www.baddogs.com/

Barnet & District Dog Training Club. One of the best clubs which I visit whenever in London. North London's premier dog training class with more than 20 years of practical and competitive experience by top dog behaviour experts. E-mail: k.mcnicholas@pmail.net

BBC Weather Centre

http://www.bbc.co.uk/weather

Behaviour courses, books

www.cats-and-dogs.freeserve.co.uk

Best Dogs

http://www.bestdogs.com/

Blue Cross (Rescue)

www.bluecross.org.uk

Bones and Raw Foods Diet List

http://www.onelist.com

British Canine Shopping Centre

http://fido.k9.co.uk/index.htm

British Police & Services Canine Association

http://www.k9netuk.com/training/bpsca/http://

Canine Circle

http://www.webring.org/cgi-bin/webring?ring=caninecircle;list

Canine Connections

http://www.cheta.net/connect/canine/default.htm

Canine Online

http://www.canineonline.com/

Canine Specialties

http://www.telepath.co/luftwolf/awards.htm

Canine Websites

http://www.dogpatch.org/dogs/dogweb.cfm

Canine World

http://www.canineworld.com/

Canineworld

Kept by David the Dogman

david@thedogman.net

www.canineworld.net

Clicker Training

Karen Pryor, the author of "Don't Shoot the Dog!", "The New Art of Teaching & Training."

http://www.karenpryor.com/

Cool Dog Site Of The Day

http://www.st.rim.or.jp/~ito/d/
dogmark.html

Cool Mutts

http://www.webring.org/cgi-bin/
webring?ring=mutts;list

Council of Docked Breeds

www.cdb.org

Cyber-Dog

http://cyberpet.com/cyberdog/

Deaf dogs

Kept by
barry.eaton@virgin.net
www.dogsworldwide.com/
deafdogtraining.htm

Dingo Homepage

Kept by Denise Humphries,
denise@wwwins.net.au
http://www.wwwins.net.au/dingofarm/

Disabled, dogs for

http://www.vois.org.uk/dftd/html/
HOME.HTM

Dog Connections

http://www.uncc.edu/lis/library/
reference/human/dogs.htm

Dog Connections Directory

http://www.geton.net/pets/dogs/
main.htm

Dogs Down Under

Kept by Denise Humphries,
wwwins@wwwins.net.au.
http://www.wwwins.net.au/dog/
downunder.html

Dog Groomers Online

http://www.groomers.com/

Doggy Info on the Web

Kept by Wilf LeBlanc,
webmaster@bulldog.org
http://www.bulldog.org/dogs/

Dog InfoMat

Kept by Sandi Dremel,
webmaster@doginfomat.com.
http://www.doginfomat.com/

Dog-Inn

Kept by bruno@dog-inn.com
(Danish, English)
http://dog-inn.com/

Dogs' Names

www.petrix.com/dognames/
allnames.html

DogNet

http://www.erols.com/ufgator/dognet/

Dog Patch

Kept by Mary Jo Sminkey,
maryjo@dogpatch.org.
http://www.dogpatch.org/dogs/

Dog Links on the Internet

http://www.thelinks.com/to/dogs.html

Dog Trainer's Forum

http://www.dogforum.com/forum2.shtml

Dog and Pet Business Index

http://www.dogbiz.com/

Dogs On The Web

http://www.hsc.usc.edu/~rnelville/
doglinks.html

Dogs U.K. Homepage

http://dspace.dial.pipex.com/town/
square/tac61/dogsuk.htm

Dogs UK

Kept by Will Chapman,

willchapman@dial.pipex.com.

http://dspace.dial.pipex.com/town/
square/tac61/dogsuk.htm

Doggy Information

http://www.bulldog.org/dogs/

Dogpatch Doghouse

http://www.dogpatch.org/dogs/

Drugs

innovative techniques used in the States
to sniff out drugs in moving vehicles:

http://www.prolegal.com/quantum/
narcomobile.htm

Electronic Zoo

Sponsored by the American Veterinary
Medical Association. Browse for animal
information by species, from cats and
dogs to cows and reptiles.

http://www.avma.org/ezoo/

Encyberpedia Dogs

http://www.encyberpedia.com/
dogs.htm

Friskey Pet

http://www.friskeypet.com/

General dog

http://www.k9web.com/dog-faqs/

Grooming courses.

E-mail: valmore.demon.co.uk

www.demon.co.uk/webbcom

How To Love Your Dog

(for kids), kept by Janet Wall,

garden1@home.com.

http://www.geocities.com/Heartland/
Estates/1210/

InfoDog.com Homepage

http://www.infodog.com/

Informational Dog-Related Web Sites

http://www.lib.ubc.ac.uk/internet/news/
faq/archive/dogs-faq.www-list.html

In The Dog House

http://www.w3-sales.com/artist/
doghouse.htm

Justice For Dogs

http://www.kc3.co.uk/profile/dogs/

K-9 Info Net

http://www.angelfire.com/ca2/k9info/
index.html

K9 National dot Net

http://www.k9nation.net/

K9 Net UK

Kept by

barrie@b-jam.demon.co.uk.

http://www.k9netuk.com/

K9-Systems

Scotland-based Terrier and GSD information,
kept by Iain Thomson,

http://www.clearlight.com/~k9sys/
k9sys@hpserv.clearlight.com.

K-9 Web Homepage

http://www.k9web.com/

K-9 Zone Dog Resources

http://www.ecst.csuchico.edu/~hheff/
DogStuff.html

Kahoos K9 Line

Kept by Shelley Ledfors,
kahoos@iceinternet.com.

http://www.iceinternet.com/kahoos/

Koehler method of dog training

http://www.geocities.com/Heartland/
Meadows/4159/koehler.html

Links to dog related sites

http://trfn.clpgh.org/animalfriends/
dog_link.html

Lost dogs, U.K. List of lost and stolen dogs

http://www.pavilion.co.uk/lostdogsuk/

Mall Of Cyberspace – Dogs

http://www.zmall.com/pet_talk/dogs/
dogs.html

Massage therapy

www.petmassage-rehab.com

Nerd World: DOGS

http://www.nerdworld.com/
NewPet.com, kept by
webmaster@newpet.com.
http://www.newpet.com/

Obedience shows

Schedules to down-load and news about
the UK Obedience scene.
http://ObedienceUK.VirtualAve.net

OzDogz

Kept by Michelle Wrighton,
wrighton@mail.dmn.com.au.
http://www.dmn.com.au/~wrighton/
ozdogz/

PAWS with a cause.

http://www.ismi.net/paws/

P.D.S.A.

www.pdsa.org.uk

Petnet's Doglover Page

Kept by Denise Humphries,
petcare@interconnect.com.au.
http://www.petnet.com.au/dogs/
introdog.html

Police site

Innovative techniques used in the States
to sniff out drugs concealed in moving
vehicles.

http://www.prolegal.com/quantum/
narcomobile.htm

Pro Dogs Network Homepage

http://www.prodogs.com/indexf.htm

Pro Dog Networks

(kennel club pages, rescue pages,
health information, services for groomers,
boarding kennels, trainers, health
organizations),

Kept by prodogs@prodogs.com.

http://www.prodogs.com/ handlers

Project K-9 Homepage

http://members.aol.com/projectk9/
dogs.htm

Purina Pet Care Center

Excellent all-round site.

http://www.purina.com/

Redek's General Dog Links

http://www.skypoint.com/~redek/gen-
dog1.html

Sled Dog Clubs/Associations

http://members.aol.com/absauk/
index.htm#sledding_mags

Super Dog Website

http://www.superdog.com/

Top Dog Endeavors

http://www.tdog.com/

TravelDog

http://www.traveldog.com/

UK Obedience shows

http://ObedienceUK.VartualAve.net

Videos and books

http://www.crosskeysbooks.com

Virtual dog

http:/www.virtualdog.com

http: //www.crapco.com/dog/
index.html

Working dogs

http://workingdogs.com/doc0177.htm

Working and Services Dogs

http://www.king.igs.net/~brica/
giveus.htm

Working Dog Web

http://www.workingdogweb.com/

Worldwide Canine

http://www.worldwidecanine.com/

WWW.Canines.Com

http://www.canines.com/iconbar.html

World Class Dogs

Kept by Karen Pryor

Webmaster@WorldClassDogs.com.

http://worldclassdogs.com.bs/

World Of Dogs

http://planetpets.simplenet.com/
worldof.htm

GUIDE DOGS.

Guide Dogs for the Blind Association

E-mail : leamington@gdba.org.net

Guide Dogs

www.assistance-dogs-intl.org
http://members.tripod.com/
~dogmaster/index.html
http://www.geocities.com/Heartland/
Meadows/6074/index.html

MEDICAL GENERAL

http://www.leos.net/articles/ocd.html

http://www.seeingeye.org/
panostei.shtml

http://www.barkbytes.com/medical/
med0041.htm

http://www.vetinfo.com/dpano.html

http://www.worldaccessnet.com/
~harldane/puppy.htm

http://www.hcis.net/heartlandvet/
panost.htm

MEDICAL SPECIFIC

An excellent site for specific diseases and
problems prefaced with the warning:
"Diagnosis cannot be made without
examination by your vet". The main
page has a list with links to the specific
problem.

http://clients.hcis.net/HeartlandVet/
acvcdogs(1).htm

Epileptic dogs

http://www.rt66.com/~dalcrazy/list.html

Seizures

http://www.vet.ohio-state.edu/docs/
seizure/index.html

PUBLICATIONS

A Dog Owner's Network

http://adognet.com/4M/obd.html

Akita World Magazine

http://www.hoflin.com/Magazines/
Akita%20World.html

All about Dogs

http://msn.co.uk/default.asp

All Ways For Dog Lovers

http://www.thuntek.net/dogtrain/

American Dog Week

http://www.dogweek.com/

Animal Universe Magazine

http://www.kat-ent.com/
animaluniverse.htm

Borzoi Quarterly Magazine

http://www.hoflin.com/Magazine/
The%20Borzoi%20Quarterly.html

Bull Terrier Quarterly

http://www.hoflin.com/Magazines/
Bull%20Terrier%20Quarterly.htm

Canine Review Magazine

http://www.wkpowerlink.com/
~caninerev/Viewer.html

Canine Times

http://www.caninetimes.com/

Canine Training Systems

http://www.caninetraining.com/

Corgi Quarterly Magazine

http://www.hoflin.com/Magazines/
The%20Corgi%20Quarterly.html

Dachshund Review Magazine

http://www.hoflin.com/Magazines/
Dachshund%20Review.html

Dalmation Quarterly Magazine

http://www.hoflin.com/Magazines/
The%20Dalmation%20Quarterly.html

Direct Book Service

http://www2.dogandcatbooks.com/
directbook/

Doberman World Magazine

http://www.hoflin.com/Magazines/
Doberman%20World.html

Dog and Kennel Magazine

http://www.dogandkennel.com/

Dog Information Newspaper

http://www.woofs.org/

Dog Journals

http://www.rapidnet.com/~cldavies/
dogs.html

Dog Lover's Bookshop

http://www.dogbooks.com/toc.htm

Dog Magazine Links

http://www.nuttart.com/online.htm

Dog Magazines

http://www.planetpets.simplenet.com/
dogzines.htm

Dog Owner's Guide

http://www.canismajor.com/dog/
guide.html

Dog World Magazine

http://www.dogworldmag.com/

Dogs Monthly Magazine

http://fido.k9.co.uk/dogs_monthly/
index.htm

Dogs on Line

http://msn.co.uk/default.asp

Elkhound Quarterly Magazine

http://www.hoflin.com/Magazines/
Elkhound%20Quarterly.htm

English Cocker Quarterly

http://www.hoflin.com/Magazines/
The%20English%20Cocker%20Artly.html

Flea News

http://www.ent.iastate.edu/FleaNews/
aboutfleanews.html

German Shepherd Quarterly Magazine

http://www.hoflin.com/Magazines/
The%20German%20Shepherd%20Qrtly.html

Golden Retriever World Magazine

http://www.hoflin.com/Magazines/
Golden%20Retriever%20World.html

Good Dog Magazine

http://www.prodogs.com/dmn/
gooddog/index.htm

Irish Wolfhound Quarterly Magazine

http://www.hoflin.com/Magazines/
The%20Irish%20Wolfhound%20Qrtly.html

Labrador Quarterly Magazine

http://www.hoflin.com/Magazines/
The%20Labrador%20Quarterly.html

Malamute Quarterly Magazine

http://www.hoflin.com/Magazines/
The%20Malamute%20Quarterly.html

Our Dogs Magazine

http://www.ourdogs.co.uk

Pets

http://www.magazinenet.co.uk/pets.htm

Pet Behavior Newsletter.

http://www.webtrail.com/petbehavior/
pbnews.html

Pet Dogs Magazine

www.petdogs.com

Pet Health News

http://www.newss.ksu.edu/WEB/News/
NewsReleases/pethealth.html

Pet Product News

http://animalnetwork.com/petindustry/
ppn/default.htm

PetView Magazine Online

http://www.petview.com/

Police K-9 Tactical Training Film

http://www.navysealteams.com/
k9Cop.htm

Poodle Review Magazine

http://www.hoflin.com/Magazines/
Poodle%20Review.html

Rhodesian Ridgeback Quarterly Magazine

http://www.hoflin.com/Magazines/
The%20Rhodesian%20Ridgeback%20Q.html

Shiba Review Magazine

http://www.hoflin.com/Magazines/
Shiba%20Journal.htlm

Siberian Quarterly Magazine

http://www.hoflin.com/Magazines/
The%20Siberian%20Quarterly.html

The Canine Times Magazine

http://www.caninetimes.com/

The Healthy Dog Newsletter

http://www.healthydog.com/
home2.html

The Samoyed Quarterly

http://hoflin.com/Magazines/
The%20Samoyed%20Quarterly.html

The Shepherd's Dog

Border Collie quarterly journal
http://www.gis.net/~shepdog

Tracking Guide

http://miraclemile.com/tracking/

WorkingDogs.com

http://www.workingdogs.com/

Working Sheepdog News, published bi-monthly with sheepdog trialling news, dates, results. Articles on training and general sheepdog information

E-mail: mail: wsn@pock.demon.co.uk

VETERINARY

Animal clinic, London

http://www.scoot.co.uk/
ark_veterinary_clinic/1.htm

Europe

Animal Care College (Canine Studies Institute) Information.

http://www-icdl.open.ac.uk/icdl/export/
europe/unitedki/animalca/

Animal Care College

General Certificate of Canine Studies.

http://fido.k9.co.uk/animalcarecollege/
course5.htm

Encylopedia of Canine Veterinary Medical Information

http://www.hcis.net/heartlandvet/
panost.htm

Heartland Veterinary Hospital

http://www.hcis.net/heartlandvet/
panost.htm

Net Vet

http://netvet.wustl.edu/vet.htm

Veterinary Links Vetweb

The FREE Information Network for the Veterinary Profession from the manufacturers of Pedigree ® and Whiskas ® Dover Veterinary...

http://www.vets.co.uk/links.html

"The Veterinary Journal"

an international journal of veterinary research which publishes original papers and reviews on all aspects of veterinary science.

http://msn.co.uk/default.asp

Veterinary Journals; Table Of Contents.

http://www.medvet.umontreal.ca/biblio/
vetjr.html

Veterinary Medicine Publishing Group.

http://www.vetmedpub.com/

Vet site.

http://www.vetweb.co.uk/